Working with Children in Need

Studies in Complexity and Challenge

of related interest

Groupwork with Children and Adolescents
A Handbook
Edited by Kedar Nath Dwivedi
ISBN 1 85302 157 1

Play Therapy
Where the Sky Meets the Underworld
Ann Cattanach
ISBN 1 85302 211 X

Play Therapy with Abused Children
Ann Cattanach
ISBN 1 85302 120 2 hb
ISBN 1 85302 193 8 pb

Child Abuse and Child Abusers
Protection and Prevention
Edited by Lorraine Waterhouse
ISBN 1 85302 133 4

Good Practice in Child Protection
A Manual for Professionals
Edited by Hilary Owen and Jacki Pritchard
ISBN 1 85302 205 5

Working with Children in Need
Studies in Complexity and Challenge

Edited by Eric Sainsbury

with a foreword by Tom White CBE

Jessica Kingsley Publishers
London and Bristol, Pennsylvania

First published in the United Kingdom in 1994 by
Jessica Kingsley Publishers Ltd
116 Pentonville Road
London N1 9JB, England
and
1900 Frost Road, Suite 101
Bristol, PA 19007, U S A

Library of Congress Cataloging in Publication Data
A CIP catalogue record for this book is available from the Library of Congress

British Library Cataloguing in Publication Data
A CIP catalogue record for this book is available from the British Library

ISBN 1-85302-275-6

Printed and Bound in Great Britain by
Cromwell Press, Melksham, Wiltshire

Contents

Acknowledgements

The inspiration for this book arose from discussions with Helen Martyn and John Simmonds, tutors on the Advanced Social Work Course at Goldsmiths' College, University of London and within the Course Advisory Committee. They and their colleagues, in collaboration with NCH and Kent County Council, have demonstrated long term commitment to the development of skilled social work practice in matters to do with child care and protection, and I owe them sincere thanks for undertaking the negotiations necessary to the production of the work. It was particularly impressive how many of their former students wished to be associated with it, and I wish to thank the following for their ideas and contributions: Jo Adams, Barbara Bittle, Isobel Bremner, Gillian Bridge, Sue Brookman, Dorthe Bucknell,Linda Charlton, Gillian Coates, Susan Cooke, Viv Davies, Sarah Donlan, Dominic Dubois, Tess Duncan, Jo Gordon, Barbara Hammerton, Eve Hopkirk, Jackie James, Ravi Kohli, Kathryn Lambourn, Robert McCandless, Trudi McCullough, Judy Marshman, Gabriel Parlour, Dianne Powell, Lesley Read, Jean Ross, Patricia Ross, Anita Singh, Bob Temple, Rita Wiseman.

My thanks are due also to Susan Wates for making available trust funds to cover the costs of preparation, and to Richard Dyster (NCH Action for Children) for administering the money.

Compiling the work, the typing of case extracts and making sense of editorial changes were the tasks of Margaret Jane, Valerie Mann and Sheila Fuller. I wish to thank them for their efficiency, patience and cheerfulness, and to thank Jessica Kingsley and her colleagues for their unfailing encouragement.

Foreword

Social Workers continue to be much in the public eye – sometimes as a result of a report of a scandal or of where things have gone seriously wrong in an individual case. Yet numerous public opinion surveys reveal that the public generally are more understanding of the complexity of the problems social workers deal with, and more supportive of the social worker they have had contact with, than newspaper reports imply.

The public, properly, have high expectations of social work practice and social workers are themselves generally very keen to improve the standard of their work.

Compared with other professions, and despite an explosion of wider publications, relatively little written material is available, based on actual case practice, which will help social workers improve their day-to-day interventions in people's lives.

For several years I chaired the Advisory Committee of the Goldsmiths' College course leading to the Diploma in Advanced Social Work (Children and Families) and was always impressed with the quality of students' written work produced from their practice.

The 'students' concerned were, of course, experienced social workers anxious to improve their practice by attending a widely respected advanced social work course and I'm very grateful that a number have agreed to share their work with a wider audience.

The intention of this book is to provide examples of sensitive and innovative practice through a collection of essays on working with children in need, edited by Professor Eric Sainsbury, from the work undertaken by students during the Goldsmiths' Course.

The writings deal exclusively with social work practice, rather than administration and legal issues, and will be helpful to social work practitioners in showing the challenges, difficulties, heartache and important achievements of their work.

Not all the work described in this book achieves an ideal standard – what work does? –but the 20-plus case illustrations are always stimulating and thought-provoking, and encourage the reader to ask 'What would I have done in this situation?'

NCH has benefited in recent years from significant numbers of staff participating on the Goldsmiths' Course and a number of their studies are included in the publication.

This will be a useful book for all engaged in social work in the child care field, and in social work training courses at all levels.

Tom White
Chief Executive, NCH Action for Children

Introduction

Most books about social work are properly concerned with the values and methods of practice. Increasingly since 1968, emphasis has been given to the experiences and feelings of those who use services and to the importance of achieving forms of help which will feel relevant to the specific needs of specific users in their personal and cultural circumstances. Relatively few studies, however, have attempted to record what it feels like to be a social worker in emotionally challenging, critical, intractable and tragic situations; or to record the interplay of feelings between worker and client when efforts are made to achieve empathy and to promote movements of attitude and emotional response in circumstances where problems seem – initially, at least – to be well nigh insoluble.

This book, made up of case studies and course-assessment projects, seeks to offer some insights into these kinds of situations. It does not set out to offer guidelines for better practice – though the practices recorded here are often remarkable for their sensitive insights into the needs of disturbed children and their families; neither is it suggested that all the work recorded here is (by whatever criteria) very good. But the book offers vivid and honest accounts of how social workers have attempted to help children, and at what costs to themselves.

The origins of the book

The case studies presented here were work undertaken by trained and experienced social workers during the course of their post-qualifying training on law and practice in working with children and families. The workers were employed in many Social Services Departments (mainly but not exclusively in London and the Home Counties) and in major voluntary organisations. Their training course aimed, amongst other things, to help them to develop imaginative and innovative skills in working with children and families, and the achievements of some of these advanced students were, indeed, remarkable.

At the outset, therefore, a decision had to be taken whether to publish only the best work, or to record the somewhat wider range of skills and insights that are present on any post-qualifying course, particularly when one compares the earlier and later work of a particular student. The latter route was followed: thus, the book offers examples of good work, but also examples of things going wrong; it records the achievements, the difficulties and the stresses of conscientious and experienced social workers who are seeking to improve their skills. Other books are readily available which provide counsels of perfection; this describes what happens in social work as currently practised.

Audiences

For this reason, it is hoped that the book will be of interest first to the general reader who wishes to know what social workers actually do when faced with the presence of abused and damaged children. The recent spate of social work scandals and enquiries, particularly as recorded in the popular press, has given rise to widespread condemnation of social workers – as inept, over-bearing, blinkered, bureaucratic, and as likely to harm the very people they are paid to help. Good work, sadly, gets no popular publicity. So, for the general reader, this publication records what really goes on in situations of neglect, injury and abuse.

Second, it is hoped that this collection of case studies will be of practical help in social work training courses at all levels. In order to give as many examples as possible of social work practice, all of the case material is edited, shortened and sometimes truncated. It is possible in every case, therefore, to raise questions of major importance in social work training:

- Are there alternative explanations of this situation and the participants' responses to it?
- What alternative routes could the social worker have followed in this case?
- How far were the achievements in this case dependent on the support of colleagues, the flexible and sympathetic response of managers, and the availability of space and resources?
- At the end of this recording, what is likely to happen to these people? What should be the worker's *and the agency's* next moves in this case?

All of the work recorded here was time-limited, partly because of professional commitment to planned, focussed and structured intervention, and partly because of the time constraints within a training course. This raises a more general question concerning the responsibilities of the agency towards children and families where the local authority has statutory duties which extend for several years after the closure of the work recorded here, and where continued support is desirable in order to sustain the somewhat dramatic and positive changes in the lives and feelings of these children.

Third, it is hoped that these essays will interest social workers and team leaders; partly because they reflect competent professional practices in being an advocate for the child, in developing sensitive and responsive ways of working, and in recognising that intervening in a current crisis may have both positive and negative longer-term effects. But in addition, these studies show the importance of constructive working between social workers, their supervisors and their managers in three aspects.

First – sensitive, responsive and constructive work with hurt children can only take place if the social worker has the time and space to think, to plan and to help. Second, because of the virtually infinite complexity of human needs, there can be no standard answers and there must always be room for professional debate and monitored experimentation. This is a constant dilemma for managers: is it possible to resolve the need, on the one hand, for standardised procedures and accounting systems, and the need, on the other hand, to permit professional independence and flexibility? Probably this cannot be satisfactorily resolved, but awareness of the problem on both sides may allow it to be mitigated. Third, these case studies (and the professional disputes to which, potentially, they give rise) illustrate the difficulties of assessing needs 'in the real world', and, by implication, the resultant temptation to seek certainty in theoretical or bureaucratic constraints. To be faced by a vulnerable and hurt child, and to face the awesome responsibilities of trying to help, is stressful and isolating for the social worker. What is needed is not more procedures or more sophisticated theories but good team supports and the right kind of supervision. Some of the present case studies show the value of supervision; some show how things can go wrong *for the worker* when the supervisor fails.

The general lessons to be drawn from the book

As all social workers know, every new case presents a challenge of new insights and new learning. But certain themes are recurrent in the studies which follow, and it may be useful to list them as a general introduction to the work.

(1) The importance of ascertaining how the child sees the current situation and how he/she perceives desirable outcomes.

(2) The importance of giving time to comprehending what relationships *mean* to the people in them, and how the social worker's relationship fits into that meaning.

(3) The importance of seeking the co-operation of child and parents in exploring what will inevitably be painful memories and experiences.

(4) The importance of being sufficiently sensitive, and of spending enough time, to be able to distinguish between immediate wishes and longer-term wishes and hopes, and between perceptions of reality and recourse to fantasy.

(5) The importance, in situations where the negatives of behaviour and feelings are all too apparent, of finding ways of translating negatives into positives, of re-channelling the strengths of feeling into constructive actions and constructive motivations. Sometimes this transformation cannot be achieved – social workers cannot perform miracles – but we have examples here of how patient, sensitive and planned work can sometimes succeed in ways which fall only a little short of the miraculous.

Besides these professional themes, there are also certain recurrent managerial issues which have already been touched upon. The contributors to the book would, it is suggested, wish to emphasise the following components of good management:

- ensuring supervision which supports experimentation while guaranteeing the safety and well-being of service-users;
- providing, and giving time for, systems of support for social workers who need to find their way through feelings of stress, inadequacy and involvement;
- not assuming that a worker's need for support necessarily means that the worker is not coping adequately with his or her duties: accepting that if social workers do not occasionally need support they are probably not performing at a professional level;

- seeking ways of alleviating – though not resolving – the dilemma of professional integrity and choice within a context of agency purpose, function and public accountability.

The shape of the book

The case studies have been arranged in chapters. The first is concerned with one-to-one work with children who have suffered neglect or physical injury; it introduces the usefulness of play and drawing as means of finding out what the injuries have meant in the experience of the child, and as means of helping the child to come to terms with earlier suffering. Second, there is a similar chapter about helping children to talk about and to come to terms with earlier experiences of sexual abuse. The third chapter provides examples of work within and across divisions of race, language and culture: white workers with black clients; black worker with white clients – and, in the following chapter there is an example of a black worker with black clients within a predominately white agency; and the use of interpreters. Unfortunately, the material available does not permit a full exploration of these various combinations, but it illustrates some of the issues which need to be addressed by agencies working within anti-racist and anti-discriminatory policies. Chapter Four glances briefly at some of the issues faced by young people who have been in local authority care and who need help in effecting a transition to the responsibilities and independence of adult life. The fifth chapter addresses specifically the stresses experienced by social workers in matters to do with child protection. The final chapter deals with a few administrative and inter-professional issues in child protection – here again, not complete because of the limited scope of the material available, but illustrative of certain problems.

This is not a text book. It does not claim to be comprehensive. But it presents some of the realities of a complex and difficult area of social work practice.

NB: These case studies span a period of ten years; some pre-date the implementation of the Children Act 1989, and allowance should be made for this when reading the accounts.

CHAPTER ONE

Direct Work with Young Children in Situations of Neglect and Injury

This chapter is centrally concerned with examples of how children can be helped to come to terms with disruptive and abusive earlier experiences. Much of the work described here illustrates the methods, skills and values of play in seeking to enter and understand the child's world; and a case is made – albeit implicitly – for training in these skills.

Play therapy can be employed to achieve a range of purposes. In Sam's case (aged eight), the social worker sets out to help him to overcome his timidity and preoccupation with being a well-behaved child; he is anxious to avoid any further emotional disruptions in his life. He is now with foster carers, and the worker has an additional concern to discover whether this placement should be made a permanent one.

For Victor (aged nine), the aim of the work is to help the child to overcome persistent nightmares and occasional stealing, both of which appear to be associated with unresolved grief following his mother's death. Here again there is an additional concern arising from his father's somewhat repressive discipline.

With John (aged nine), therapy addresses the child's difficult behaviour at home. This behaviour soon becomes apparent in contacts with the social worker; play therapy can, on occasion, get out of control, and the work with John raises an important issue of how to achieve a constructive and helpful balance between permissiveness and the setting of boundaries. It is not infrequently found that, in the course of learning how to express fear, anxiety and ambivalence as a prelude to resolving past trauma, children go through phases of exhibiting tremendous rage and defiance towards their helpers: an anxious and friendly child may suddenly appear to be demonic and destructive. As one contributor remarked,

'The difficulty for social workers is to know how to allow the expression of overwhelming pent-up rage and to channel it in constructive ways which prevent destruction or mutilation – of the self, of other people or of the environment'.

In Eric's case (aged five), the therapeutic task is preparation for long term placement, based on helping him to understand why he is in care, and to alleviate the guilt he feels that, in some way, he is responsible for his parents' rejection of him.

The chapter starts with the case of Chris (aged eight). It illustrates the complex situation in which a social worker may become involved. It sets out a rationale for undertaking play therapy as essential to Chris's future wellbeing. It also provides examples of how a child's personal emotional disturbance is reflected in the way in which he plays. Here, and in the subsequent case studies, the emotional pressures on the social worker are illustrated: no worker should embark on the techniques illustrated in this chapter without recognising the extent to which children can transmit the gravity of their unhappiness, and can unwittingly trigger our own earlier unresolved anxieties.

Chris (eight)

Chris was the second of three children. His elder brother Paul fell from a window and fractured his skull when Chris was three years of age. When his younger brother David (now aged seven) was born, the father deserted and the parents divorced when Chris was aged four. Mother has been estranged from her own family for some years.

When Chris was four years old, he set fire to the family home, and David nearly died from smoke inhalation. After a period in bed and breakfast accommodation, the family was rehoused. Shortly afterwards, there was a series of complaints from neighbours that Chris and David were neglected; in addition, Chris was involved in sexual acts with a neighbour's child.

Both children spent a short period in voluntary care. An investigation indicated that both children had been sexually abused. It seems that sexual acts had taken place between siblings. This concern was renewed following their return home: there were suspicions that Andrew (12) was engaging in homosexual acts for money; Chris threatened to kill himself. Chris and David are now in care. Their father has visited occasionally, but does not wish to have any continuing relationship with his children. Mother has re-married: her husband is fifteen years her junior. Chris and David were separately placed with different foster-carers; Chris's first placement lasted for nearly three years (from age five to age eight); he and David have been reunited in a second placement for the last six months. Chris's behaviour is described by his foster carers as overtly sexualised. The children's mother visits them every two weeks.

The social worker identifies the following needs:

(1) To devise an appropriate plan for Chris's future.

(2) To consider how far the mother can be a partner in this planning; Chris's relationship with his mother is unclear. (A psychiatric assessment of the mother strongly advises against returning Chris to her care.)

(3) To assess Chris's relationship with David, and to decide whether the children should continue to live together.

(4) To assess how far to initiate and encourage contact between the children and their father, and, possibly, members of the wider family.

Given the complexity of these issues, it is essential that the social worker is able to create an atmosphere of trust in which Chris can express his views freely. In view of his age, one cannot wholly rely on his ability to find words which adequately encapsulate his ideas and feelings – indeed, few if any adults, could find the right words. For children, play is the child's 'work' and is an important medium of self-expression: it is likely to reflect the emotions which are currently felt; it provides opportunities for sharing with, or rejecting, another human being without having to do so verbally; it is based on familiar motor activities, and thus provides a safer affective environment than struggling with language. The following extract from the social worker's record indicates how Chris was able to use play to express his complicated feelings.

> I collected him for the first session at the Family Centre and from this we established a routine where he asked me many questions on the way there, telling me about himself when I was taking him to school after the sessions. Chris went into the room, walked round, picked up the gun, pointing it at me. I remarked that it felt like he wanted to shoot me. Chris replied 'somebody'. I reflected this back, 'You are feeling you want to shoot someone'. Chris – 'Yes'. He examined the clay then went over to the sand and water, proceeding to test out the rules of the room. I tried to convey to him his right to use the hour in *his* way, which I would respect, but bringing him back to our agreement not to leave, hurt himself or me. Chris chose the *Pied Piper of Hamlin* for me to read, saying with great passion at the finish 'that cannot be the end; I know a different ending, those children should have gone back to their parents'. He

then went over to the finger paints, checking out again if he could use all of them. (Throughout this session, I was trying to establish with him that this was his time in which there would not be any pressure.) He then began to smear the paint thickly onto the paper, with little regard for colour and adding the sand until he made a sticky substance on the paper. At the end of the session, on the way to school, he told me he had been to court where it had been decided he could not live with his mum any more. He was reluctant about my accompanying him through the playground; it was playtime when we arrived so we arranged an acceptable way of my ensuring he was safe in school.

On the way to the second session Chris spoke of his first foster carer, telling me he did not believe in God any more as he asked for something four months ago (the time of his move) which did not happen. I read him three stories at his request – Billy Goats Gruff, Red Riding Hood, Jack and the Bean Stalk. I had made some coloured dough for this week's session (finger paints were expensive to replace weekly) which Chris proceeded to use in the same way as he had used the finger paints in the previous session. Kramer (1978) describes how playful activities with paint and other materials are ways of breaking taboos, getting dirty, wasting materials, engaging in primitive childish pleasures. Chris's play grew more intense with this material; I can liken his attitude and posture to a surgeon, with me as his assistant. He hardly ever allowed me just to observe; I mostly had to join in with any activity.

During this session Chris wanted to smear me with paint and dough. Chris said at the end of the session 'that was really good, I want to do this next week', but wanted the dough plain, which he could colour. Despite my attempts to protect the room, it took me two hours to clean and there was a memo from the secretary when I returned to the office about paint on the wall. By the time the third session arrived there had been a directive that we had to use a different room, despite my own and a colleague's attempts to keep the same place for our sessions. There also had been the possibility our work would have to cease. This session there were questions about the new room, with Chris splattering sand and paint everywhere and again trying to smear me. I considered that for me to be smeared would be inappropriate touching. I also knew from my assessment that Chris had never been held, or controlled in his toddler years and his 'boundaries' had been abused by sexual molestation. Dorfman (1951) writes of the problem of limit setting, commenting on how 'the therapist establishes no limits upon the child's *verbal* expression of his feeling'. Some feelings she states are not permitted to be directly expressed in actions. She also adds that 'there is now far more concern with the problem of determining just what activity restrictions are required in order to permit the therapist to remain emotionally accepting of the child'. Smearing was unacceptable to me and I was apprehensive that windows (there were many in the new room) would be damaged. I conveyed these feelings to Chris. I therefore decided to limit the activity of throwing paint and sand and I did not allow Chris to smear me. With the new room I had to re-establish the rules and our agreement. Chris accepted that I did not want to be smeared with paint and he did not attempt to do it again.

Kramer (1978) found that deprived and disturbed children are notoriously wasteful and unless waste is tolerated it is not possible to work with them at all.

In the fourth session Chris asked if I liked the room. I acknowledged that new places did feel strange for a while. He went straight to the dough, water and sand. Then for the first time he broke away from me and went and sat with his back to me playing in the sand, announcing he was making a swimming pool and proceeded to put figures into it. He came back and gave me an order to make clay balls. He then joined the balls together to make a large ball of clay and I found that in this session he began to think about colour, realising if he mixed too much black he would lose the brighter colours. He then very carefully put paint onto the clay mound. He showed pleasure, something I had been told Chris found extremely difficult to express saying 'It's wonderful!'. I then had to help him shift sand from one container to another. Chris complained when the hour was up, saying I had decided only an hour. I reflected to him about adults making the decisions he did not want and he agreed. He wanted to stay and drink out of the bottle, I reminded him that it would be there next week.

The fifth session was again with the dough, water and sand, together with the paint. The mixture spilled over the table and the analogy of playing with faeces seemed obvious. He enjoyed getting his hands thickly covered in the mixture, squeezing them together and flicking the mixture off. This I concluded was anal behaviour typical of a child in the second or third year of life. This could have been aggression, or developmental play; also I have found sexually abused children often use materials in this way. Chris did not paint during any of the sessions; he used the materials as a sensory rather than artistic experience. The important point was that Chris was not only allowed to be very young again but the 'bad' and messy side was being accepted. He did in fact say to me with great feeling how he loved getting messy. He spoke of rainbows in this session, with the dark depressed (black) angry (red) colours being left until the end when he put all the colours in the bowl with the mixture and sat in it. Over the weeks Chris's attitude and way of speaking to me in the sessions was in a manner which made me feel dominated and abused. Dorfman (1951) indicates 'to be accepted as a person despite one's glaring deficiencies seems to be an important part of therapy'. It is therefore necessary for the child to bring his real feelings, no matter how anti-social, out into the open, when he feels safe enough to do so. She goes on to say that he cannot be sure that the therapist really accepts him until the child has tested out by demonstrating the rejected aspects of his personality.

In the sixth session, Chris sang whilst he was mixing the colours; by now he had realised that he could have control over the colours he made. For a child who had many experiences over which he had no control I thought this was a notable realisation. He was very particular and thoughtful about the colours and they were in his song 'All the colours in the sea are going in the pot' which he sang repeatedly. He played sand castles, putting a flag he had made on top. The mixture in the buckets, which was beginning to smell badly, was very special to him and I was ordered by him not to throw it away. This, again, I thought linked back to a retentive anal stage. We talked about our goodbye on the way to school, which Chris knew was only two more sessions away.

The seventh session: colours were dominant, orange, yellow, blue, (now his favourite colour), mauve and green. He sang again, 'Aren't I clever', to a made up tune. He told me he was lucky to do this, to have this time. He did not use all the dough this session and talked of his first foster carer. He then purposefully did not use the black, linking this to the darkness of his earlier life. Kramer (1978) observes that often there are moments of illumination when a child can see the pattern of his growth and find his own solutions.

Chris's body posture was relaxed in this session. He was beginning to look at the dough mixture with the sand, contemplating and feeling the gritty sensation, remarking on it to me. He again made a swimming pool, throwing the figures away, saying 'I don't want people, I want the frog animal'. I said to him, 'you feel you do not want people in the pool'. Chris replied 'there was only room for animals'. I believe this was an indication of hurt at being let down by adults and feelings of rejection.

This extract raises several issues, which will be taken up in the course of the following case studies. There is some evidence to suggest that the work so far has been successful, in so far as Chris's emotional age appears to have advanced a little (from messy to constructive play), the intensity of his negative feelings has somewhat abated (he now sings when he plays), he has accepted certain limits of play without loss of spontaneity, and he is willing to share play with his social worker. He has also displayed and has had accepted negative feelings towards adults. At the same time, there remain considerable uncertainties about the answers to questions about the aims of the work, and one can envisage the social worker needing at this stage to re-think her plan of work, possibly moving from a non-directive to a more structured use of time.

These matters are exemplified in the studies which follow, and certain methods of work are explored in more detail.

John (aged nine)

In this case extract, the social worker at an early stage introduces the idea that play equals work, and John is encouraged to set out the rules governing their time together. This approach contrasts with the non-directive play used with Chris: in a sense, work with John is simpler as the issues to be addressed are more clearly defined by the circumstances of his referral.

The case study shows how the environment of play/work may affect the feelings expressed. It also demonstrates how a child can (wittingly or unwittingly) 'manipulate' certain outcomes which are contrary to the worker's intentions. In this instance, John shows a tendency to put the worker and the grandparents in opposition to each other, and it becomes clear that play activities should not take place in isolation from support and work with the family.

The work with John (and that with Victor – see below) indicates that children may sometimes express their concerns at a symbolic level of communication, and that the significance of the symbols employed may not always lie within the conscious understanding or control of the child. Thus, the worker may find herself led into a range of possible interpretations, not all of which can be checked out with the child. Bearing in mind this non-rational level of communication, and the defences which it sometimes breaches, workers need to be cautious of trying to verify their interpretations by directly asking questions about meaning; in any case, and at all ages, it is sometimes fruitless to ask people *why* they feel as they do or *what* they are actually feeling. Answers are likely to be incomplete and misleading, not least because of the problem of finding the right words to describe intense and mixed emotions.

Position at outset of the work

John had lived with his maternal grandparents, Mr and Mrs W, since he was aged five. This was at his mother's request following a non-accidental injury investigation by an inspector of the NSPCC. Later, a 15-year-old youth, a relation through marriage, was convicted of assault, causing actual bodily harm.

I started the work at a time when John's grandparents were finding his behaviour difficult to cope with. He frequently interrupted their conversations and television viewing, demanded immediate attention from them and was, sometimes, untruthful. In particular, Mr W found John's untruthfulness difficult to tolerate. He requested that John be referred to the local Child Guidance Clinic with the comment 'there must be something wrong in his head for him to be telling lies'. I was reluctant to make the referral as, it seemed to me, John's untruthfulness was fairly typical of most children of a similar age. I was also concerned that a referral to the Child Guidance Service would lead his grandparents to think of him as 'abnormal' and 'disturbed'. More important, I was concerned that John would believe himself to be 'bad'.

Having discussed my concerns with the grandparents, we agreed that I would undertake some direct work with John. It was agreed I would do eight to twelve sessions, after which we would review and assess his behaviour and his grandfather's request for referral to the Child Guidance Service.

The objective of the work was to enable John to make some sense of the reason for his placement with his grandparents, explore with him his untruthfulness about minor incidents and help him to find more acceptable and appropriate ways of getting attention.

John was, at the outset of the work, having weekly contact with his mother and younger brother. Contact with his father had ceased two years previously and his whereabouts are unknown.

The Sessions

Prior to our sessions, I explained to John the purpose of our spending time together and what the focus of our work would be. He was aware that his grandparents sometimes found his behaviour difficult and were concerned that he might not be happy living with them. (They had on occasion asked him if his naughtiness meant he did not want to live with them.) He seemed to understand the objectives of the work and became subsequently enthusiastic about our sessions.

I worked with John for seven weekly sessions of one hour, and three fortnightly sessions. The sessions took place either in his home or at the beach. During the sessions at home, we used a mixture of drawings, writing, colouring, ecomaps, life history, story-telling, happy and sad faces. At the beach, we ran, shouted, threw stones in the sea and sometimes sat quietly listening to the sound of the waves.

John entered the first session with a great deal of enthusiasm. We began by recapping what the purpose was for our having 'special times'. He was clear about why we were meeting and accepted that while we would have fun and enjoy ourselves we would also be working. John had difficulty understanding the concept of contract; we therefore drew up what John called rules. He was keen to choose the rules but reluctant to write them. At his request, I did the writing, writing exactly as he dictated. The rules read as follows:

(1) No mucking about while we are working.

(2) See how John is getting on at home and at school.

(3) One hour each week for eight weeks.

(4) To help John, we will let Grandad and Nan see some of the work.

We discussed the rules, why he had chosen these and his understanding of them. I was much enlightened by his interpretation of rules one and two. He had chosen the words 'mucking about' because he knew from our discussion that, as well as playing, the time was really meant for us to work. Rule two, he explained, was so that I could check that he was being treated all right at home and at school. I was somewhat uncomfortable with rule two as I had a hunch that he saw me in some kind of police role in relation to his grandparents. This was confirmed in a later session.

In this first session, I let him choose the direction of the work, reflecting back to him as I thought appropriate and actively participating when he requested me to. This approach was based on my reading of Axline (1947) and Oaklander (1979). He began by drawing a house. The occupants in the house were himself, his grandparents and me. I commented that I did not live with him. He knew this, he said, but he wanted me to live with him. We had some discussions about this, at the end of which he wrote the words 'I would like' by my name and by his grandparents' names he wrote 'lives with me'. I wondered why he had drawn us at windows and asked him to tell me about his drawing. He explained we were all at windows so we could see out, and people would know who lived in this house.

We then talked about why he lives with his grandparents and what he likes about living with them. He said the reason he lived with his grandparents was 'I got my mum and dad thrown out of the club'. I did not understand what he meant and he was unable to enlighten me. The manner in which he commented about getting his parents thrown out of the club perturbed me and my intuition told me it had something to do with his having power. Later, in discussions with his grandparents, I learned that it was to a member of the Working Men's Club which his mother and cohabitee frequented that he had shown the injuries which had led to the NSPCC non-accidental injury investigation. As a consequence, their membership of the club had been suspended.

In the second session we again returned to why he lived with his grandparents and why he had a social worker. To help him to understand, I used Fahlberg's (1981) three parent circles: birth parents, legal parents and parenting parents. He had difficulty with the concept of the legal parents. He had problems separating out his feelings for me and accepting that I am a representative of the Local Authority, who is his legal parent. Also, at this session I introduced the Ecomap (Fahlberg 1981). He entered this piece of work with much enthusiasm. He coloured the Court House, his grandparents' house and the school in bright colours – orange, yellow, red, purple, blue, green and pink; his parents' house he coloured in black and brown. By his grandparents' house he wrote the words 'warm and happy'. By his parents' house he wrote the words 'horrible and freezing'. This latter evoked very painful memories for him and for a time he sat curled in a ball looking sad and dejected. His posture and tone of voice portrayed a sad, unhappy child; however, he denied any such feelings. His initial enthusiasm abandoned him and he opted out, telling me he was too tired to do any more work. I acknowledged how he was feeling and said it was all right to be sad and that we could complete the Ecomap another day. After a little while, he drew a sad face and in response to my asking if he knew whose this face was he replied that it was his. I encouraged him to talk to his sad face. In a lowered tone of voice he told the face it was not special and not good at anything. He then took a piece of paper and wrote the words 'horrible, freezing and fierce' and then drew a fierce face. He laughed at the face, looked towards me and told me this was his and that sometimes he could use his fierce face to frighten people away. I asked what he would like to do with his fierce face today. He said he did not really have a fierce face and told me he only ever felt happy.

The next session was slow to begin. John told me on arrival he did not want to do any work and he did not want to talk about feelings. He did not want to complete the Ecomap. With the use of 'word feeling' cards, (Oaklander (1979), I became aware of John's difficulty in expressing feelings and of his difficulty distinguishing between sadness and anger. With some difficulty, and as he chose a card, he drew or wrote what the feeling was for him. Happy equalled a large circle which was a ball, he is happy when he plays ball; special was being with his grandparents. The next card had 'horrible' on it; he was unable to draw the feeling, but said it was when he lived with his mum and dad. I encouraged him to talk about the feeling, but he was unable to do so. I used puppets to talk about their feelings. I started them off gently, talking about where they came from and who they lived with. One of them I got to tell a story very similar to John's; John identified with them for a time. He rejected the identification when the puppet talked about feeling cross and told the puppet to stop talking. As we were nearing the end of the session I asked John how he would like to spend the remainder of the time. He chose to sit next to me and asked me to give him a hug. We sat like this for a little while and ended the session this way. I was much affected by this session and left feeling that I was carrying some of the hurt that John felt unable to express. It seemed so much had come up in this and the previous session, I did not know what to deal with and what was of most significance for John.

The next session we spent on the beach. John became very free during this session, and with increasing energy and force he threw stones into the water. He felt strong throwing stones, he said, and for a time we played a competition as to who could throw their stone the farthest out to sea. He suddenly picked up a large stone, then commented 'this one is my mum, I am going to throw her really far out into the middle of the sea'. He said that was what he wanted to do to her when she was nasty to him and he lived with her. He picked up another stone and again with great force threw this into the sea with the comment 'that one is my step-dad'. I heard the words step-dad but wondered if he meant dad. To test this, I commented 'that is your dad'. He corrected me 'no, it's my step-dad'. He then ran along the beach calling to me to follow him and shouting the word 'free' over and over. Later, when we were sitting quietly, listening to the sound of the waves, I remarked that he had been shouting out the word 'free'. He talked about feeling free now he had thrown his mum (the stone) in the sea. The feeling he had when he threw mum into the sea was anger and he wanted to hurt her.

I was pleased that he had been able to give expression to his aggression and anger. However, I was concerned that he might not understand that what he had done was a symbolic throwing of his mother and step-father into the sea. I spent some time talking to him about the difference between doing something symbolically and in reality, and I almost ended by making him feel guilty.

On the return journey to his home he talked at length about his grandad, conveying the impression that grandad was/is his hero. Not for the first time he commented on my appearance telling me I always looked nice. He asked if I would always visit him, which led again to us having a discussion of my role as a social worker. His wish was that I could be his mum and live with him; but he also saw me in the role of Authority and as someone who kept a watch to make sure he was cared for and not being ill treated. Further discussion led to my realising that he attempted to use me as a threat with his grandparents. It emerged that when he did not want to carry out a command or a request, he would tell them that it was me who was in charge and not them. I spent a considerable time during our next session pointing out that this notion was wrong.

The next session we also spent on the beach and, as on the previous occasion, John was again more free. He was less inhibited in expressing his feelings, especially those of anger, hurt and being scared. In this and the following session which took place in his home, I became aware of his low self-esteem. This was a surprise to me as, for the most part, he presented as a self-confident and assured child. With this realisation, I was able to recognise some of the cause for his demands on his grandparents and, as they expressed it, his constant interruption of their conversations and television viewing.

General comments

Throughout the sessions my thinking was often focused on John's feelings and how he was affected by the work we were doing. Several different things would emerge during a session. Mostly, I was able to take a lead from John and it would be clear which area of work we should concentrate on. However, there were occasions when this was not obvious and I would wonder if I had given John the correct lead. A major issue was what I believed were his grandparents' expectations of the sessions. I was confident John had the ability to learn from the work we were doing; I was not so confident that his behaviour would change as positively as his grandparents hoped.

Evaluation

The work helped John to look at the reason for his placement, and at the end he was clearer about this. He learned to accept and keep to boundaries and by the end of the sessions was showing signs of being more appreciative of his grandparents' need for time and space for themselves. The work was successful in enabling John to express his underlying anger towards his mother and her husband.

The most successful piece of the work was that which disabused him of the idea that being subject of a Care Order gave him licence to disregard his grandparents' day-to-day care of him and their authority to set limits and boundaries.

John's evaluation of the work was 'it was good, going to the beach was great, Bruce's story was silly, I liked the colouring and drawing but not the writing, the feeling cards were hard.'

His grandparents reported an improvement in his behaviour. They stated that he is less intrusive, is prepared to wait for a natural break in their conversation before jumping in with what he wants to say. Grandfather said he was glad that a referral to the Child Guidance

Service was not made. On reflection he did not think John was/is all that bad.

The work was at times painful for John and me; it was also a lot of fun and certainly rewarding and worthwhile.

Learning

The two main learning points for me in this work were:

(1) The need for and realisation that if I am going to help a child come to terms with his life situation and enable him to confront his hurt and pain, I need to have time immediately before sessions to clear my mind of other concerns.

(2) The other important learning experience was the value of working with the child's carers and of giving them (with the child's permission) some feedback on the child's perception of things.

Victor (aged nine)

The following account shows how a boy was helped to deal with hitherto unexpressed feelings about the death of his mother. Victor's father (Edward) has had similar difficulties in permitting the expression of his own feelings as well as his son's. Thus, father and son are offered help; and an example is provided of the importance of working with a parent as an essential partner in helping the child. Here, as in the case of John, the use of symbolism is explored, notably in the connections between death, nightmares and ghosts.

Stepfather	Edward, aged 60 years, whom Victor believes is his natural father
Mother	died aged 42 years, when Victor was aged three
Sister	Sarah, aged 24 years, living away from home
Brother	David, aged 27 years, living away from home

At age nine years, Victor is a small thin wiry boy with a sharp oval face, dark eyes and brown hair. He is intelligent and highly articulate, co-operative and well mannered. Outwardly he appears a well-adjusted, happy child. At the beginning of my work with him I had only small indications of his inner world. For example, I did not know how he had dealt with his mother's death. He appeared untroubled, yet his behaviour when with a woman who might replace her indicated this was not so. As well, I learnt from Sarah and Edward that he had been having frequent nightmares and a few months previously had been stealing.

For this account of my work with him, I will trace and discuss the development of my relationship with him and then analyse in more detail the themes which emerged.

Development of the relationship between Victor and myself

I have had nine meetings with Victor.

The first session was a surprisingly open one in which Victor spoke easily of painful matters. We walked near his home talking of his feelings about his mother and her death, his loyalty to her and his wish not to have a replacement for her. He told me that he had nightmares. We discussed ways of helping. We agreed to ask his father for a photograph of his mother that he could keep and this was later promised. Victor was agreeable to my suggestion of regular meetings. In retrospect it was perhaps too easy.

The next was equally surprising but in a different way. Victor showed me his garden but effectively kept me at a distance by climbing a tree and staying there. He implied that he did not want the closeness of our last meeting and the risk of pain arising from the subjects discussed. He further excluded me by telling me the problems we had discussed were now solved. In retrospect I think this may have reflected his feelings of exclusion by his father from information and help concerning his mother's death and from his mother herself.

In *Psychotherapy with Severely Deprived Children* (1983, p.108) Hoxter says 'an examination of the manner in which the child inflicts pain and the nature of the feelings of the recipient of the pain can reveal much concerning the child's particular internal experience of suffering'.

For some weeks I doubted the use of my visits to Victor but there was a quality of strength and courage about him which encouraged me to continue to offer myself as someone with whom he could share his feelings. He was always welcoming and there were small signs that my visits mattered to him. In one meeting he enjoyed pounding some clay I had brought, and made a number of objects including a clock. He asked for the initial of my first name and wrote on the back of his clock 'To EH from VD'. However, he still firmly excluded me from his feelings: I asked if he had the photograph of his mother which had been promised and he said 'I've forgotten all about that now'. I did not know whether he meant the photograph of his mother or his feelings about her, so I asked him. He said 'Both' very firmly. I did not pursue this, knowing that he would lead me at an appropriate time and recognising his defences.

Perhaps Victor thought he had tested me sufficiently for when we next met our relationship took a different turn. After playing a variation of the Squiggle game (Winnicott)[1] together, Victor led me into his feelings by telling me of his fears when he had had an operation the previous year and how he thought he was going to die as his mother had done.

On my sixth visit to him Victor was waiting for me in his bedroom and invited me in. I brought him some pages of a colouring book. He was very pleased, looked through them and worked on one. It seemed important to him that I thought of him when I was away from him. I reminded him of matters which we had talked of before so that he knew that I remembered and valued what he told me. At the end, he gave me three small cloth toys which he had made: I had given him a present and he reciprocated.

I was leaving when Victor once again led the way, talking of fears when in hospital, his feelings about his mother's death and how impossible it is for him so much as to mention his mother to his father; it distresses the latter so much. It seemed Victor felt safe enough with me to let tears come to his eyes. I too felt sad and touched. I comforted him but he would not allow himself to give way to his feelings and cry at length.

Victor may have felt that I had given him what Truckle (1983) describes as 'mental space' and 'the experience of being attended to, remembered and valued'. Truckle says 'the child may then feel safe enough to bring his own worries and concerns to the worker in both verbal and non-verbal ways'.

With Victor's permission, I told his father of his distress, news which he received impassively. However, I think this did not reflect his true feelings as, on my next visit, he opened the door to me, stony faced. He had 'forgotten' I was coming. Victor was playing with a friend. Edward phoned him and summoned him home in tones that sounded like a punishment.

---

1   This is called 'Take your pencil for a walk' which I learned in an experiential session at Goldsmiths. Oaklander refers to Winnicott's use of a similar technique using doodles (Winnicott 1984).

When Victor arrived, having had his visit to his friend interrupted, I did not know what his attitude to me would be. I commented on this to him but he said he didn't mind. I asked how he had been after my last visit when he had been upset. He said hesitantly that I had upset him and that he hadn't been going to tell me as he was afraid I would tell him off. I asked why I should tell him off but he didn't know. I said 'You were upset. Some things are very upsetting. Isn't it all right to be upset?' Victor indicated that it was if he was in the mood but he wasn't in the mood that day. We agreed feelings were again not to be discussed.

As I prepared to leave, I intended to telephone his father later to make a further appointment to see Victor. I thought he was angry with me as I had broken unwritten family rules on feelings and had touched on a painful area which Victor and his father colluded to ignore. I was concerned he might stop my visits but wanted to avoid a disagreement in Victor's presence if the matter was discussed then. To my amazement, Victor himself negotiated the next meeting, tugging at his father's arm asking when I could go again.

I felt very concerned about the future of my work with Victor and thought that, if not handled sensitively, his father might sabotage it. I was influenced by my reading of *The Piggle* by Winnicott (1978) and in particular by the after-word written by the parents of the child nicknamed 'The Piggle'. They say 'It has been of great value to the parents to be allowed to participate in a process of growth and reparation. This has prevented what can often be observed, the parents feeling left out in the cold and so perhaps prey to feelings of rivalry and competition with the therapist.'

I thought that Edward could have similar feelings and be worried and even envious of my relationship with Victor. I decided to offer Edward an opportunity to talk in general about my relationship with Victor. I also thought it essential that Edward be offered time for himself, as Victor had, to talk of his grief. It seemed crucial too, to remove my work with Victor to a place outside his home where he would be free to communicate with me on issues too dangerous to raise there.

In a meeting which followed between my line manager, myself and Edward, he denied any worries about my relationship with Victor but readily accepted the offer of time for himself with my supervisor. He also agreed to my taking Victor to the playroom at the local Child Guidance Clinic for our sessions together.

I had already prepared Victor for the proposed meeting with his father, telling him its purpose and emphasising to him the continuing confidentiality of our sessions. He seemed glad I had told him. At the beginning of that session I brought the toys he had given me at a previous meeting to visit him. He greeted them like old friends. Afterwards he gave them back, adding a picture of a submarine for me to keep.

Meeting away from home, Victor seemed released from its constraints and our relationship took a new turn. He enjoyed the novelty of the car journey to the clinic and played with vigour and enthusiasm in the sand tray there. Returning home he told me more of his feelings about his mother's death, the importance to him of his father, his loneliness, his father's distress at the mention of his mother and the dilemma this poses for him. He told me that he liked the playroom and wanted to return there. I promised we would go there regularly. The next time we met, he ran towards me, face lit up as he saw me. When we reached the Child Guidance Clinic he walked straight into the playroom, without waiting for me to announce our arrival at the office. In a way, I felt we had arrived.

Within the matrix of this relationship several themes have emerged which I will now examine in detail.

Food A theme which has occurred noticeably but not predominantly is food and eating. Once Victor described with great relish the best meal he ever had. On another occasion I had taken some pages of the colouring book with me to give him. One consisted of a telephone with the inscription 'If you could call anyone in the world who would it be' and another page inviting a child to write or draw a wish. Victor looked through them all with interest and pleasure and chose one on which a plain dinner plate features and the instruction 'design your own dinner plate'. Victor interpreted this as an invitation to draw the meal itself. He spent a long time drawing a plate of meatballs, fried potatoes, peas and carrots. He did this with such absorption that I felt he could have eaten the meal.

Loneliness Victor has told me frequently both directly and indirectly of his great loneliness. In an early session he drew a man. In talking about the man together I asked what would make him happy. Victor replied 'having lots of friends'. I enquired what would make him sad and he said 'being lonely'. Victor agreed that the man was like him. In a later session Victor showed me his collection of soft toys. I encouraged him to give them voices as Oaklander (1979) describes in *Windows to our Children*. The badger told us he was 'gentle and loving but sometimes lonely'. I reminded Victor that he had told me he too was often lonely and he acknowledged this, telling me of a specific instance when he had been so. He raised the subject again when we were returning from our first session at the Child Guidance Clinic. I had commented on the traffic and people going home from work. Victor said he was glad he had his Dad at home, that he didn't go out to work, otherwise he'd be even more lonely. In talking about his loneliness I think Victor has been telling me how much he misses his mother.

Nightmares Victor has repeatedly told me he suffers from nightmares. In the early days of our relationship he declared these had stopped. As he has grown to trust me, he has told me they do continue. They feature monsters and vampires which bite and frighten him. I do not yet understand precisely what these mean except that they are some manifestation of his fears and worries. It may be that in future work with him I can encourage him to draw the monsters and get them to speak to him as Violet Oaklander describes.

Ghosts feature regularly, sometimes in a light hearted way and at others in a way which frightens Victor. The record 'Ghostbusters' is his favourite and is played frequently. However, on three occasions he has told me that he sometimes sees a ghost. He said that sometimes in the night a shape comes to him which he told me in a frightened way was 'a ghost' which was his Mummy. Although sounding frightened, he described it as a 'nice ghost'. He spoke more fully about it in the car returning from our first session at the Clinic. He referred to it as more frightening than nightmares. He said he'd seen the outline in the hall and thought it was his mother. I asked him why he thought she came to him and he spoke of knowing that she was watching him and he felt that in a way this was quite nice as he felt looked after.

I think that Victor's concern with ghosts, especially that of his mother, suggests that he is struggling to understand what has happened to her and what death means. In an early session with him he gave some indication of his perception of this. Victor was at the time occupied drawing a man and I asked him if he wondered why I came to see him. He said 'to talk to me'. I said something to the effect that some boys and girls got very worried after the death of their Mummy and I didn't know if this was how it was for him. He told me of his Headmistress breaking the news to him that his Mummy had died. I asked what he thought that meant. He said that she was in heaven with God, that she was happy and that she was watching him. This explanation given to him by either the Headmistress or Edward may be one which presents Victor with difficulties and confusion.

Bowlby, in Volume 3 of his trilogy *Attachment and Loss* (1980) points out that children in Western cultures 'are unlikely to be present at the time of death; not infrequently information about it reaches them only much later and then in a misleading form'. He says, 'the surviving parent is extremely likely to tell the child that the father [or mother as with Victor] has gone to heaven or been taken to heaven. For those who are devout, this information accords with the parents' own belief. For many others, however, it does not, so that from the start a discrepancy exists between what the child is told and what the parent believes. This creates difficulties.'

Edward is not, to my knowledge, a devout man, so the concept of his mother being in heaven may be puzzling to Victor. Even more disturbing may be the idea that she is watching him. I am sure that Victor needs further help in understanding the nature of death and having the opportunity to correct any misperceptions.

When I first met Victor I did not know how he had dealt with his mother's death. Edward told me he never asked about his mother and did not seem interested. I did not know if it was possible that Victor had mourned his mother without his father being aware. Victor, however, told me clearly that he had been trying to cope with the knowledge and feelings of his loss by forgetting about them. In my third meeting with him, as I described earlier, in talking about the photograph of his mother which had been promised him, he said he had forgotten about that now. When I asked whether he meant the photograph or his mother, he said 'Both'. At the time he told me of his perception of what had happened to his mother he seemed anxious and uncomfortable. When I commented on this he said he didn't like to talk about his Mum, he tried to forget all about it.

I knew Edward had difficulty in dealing with painful emotional issues. Then, in my second meeting with him, Victor told me he hadn't liked to ask his Dad about the photograph of his Mum, because he didn't want to upset him, commenting that he did not like to see him cry. In a later session, when he had been telling me of his fears at having an operation he told me that he never mentioned that word 'Mummy' to his Dad unless he absolutely had to because if he did, his Dad's face would go red and he'd do this – he gestured passing a hand over his eyes as though brushing away tears. I commented that I thought this had been very difficult for him because he hadn't been able to show his feelings at all, he'd had to bear all the sadness by himself. I said that I thought it must be like carrying a great weight. It was then that tears came into his eyes, which I described earlier.

Again, free from the emotional restraints of home and in the safety of my car returning from the Clinic he spoke of his mother and his great sadness at her dying, saying he felt the mother was the most important member of the family. He said he never liked to talk to his Dad about this because it would upset him and he didn't like that so he just said he'd forgotten all about her and so he told his Dad a lie. It became clear to me that Victor had had to repress his feelings about his mother because his father could not cope with them.

When I realised that Victor had repressed his feelings about his loss or at least contained them all within himself, I felt very concerned. 'Those who have worked in the field and especially the clinicians are clear that nothing but confusion and pathology results when news of a parent's death is withheld from children or glossed over and when expression of feeling is discouraged either implicitly or explicitly' (Bowlby 1980).

Bravery Victor has talked admiringly of strength and bravery and sees himself as having these qualities. In an early session we played 'Take your pencil for a Walk'. In his squiggle he found a canoe which led to our discussing rowing. He spoke of enjoying this, commenting that he was very strong. He told me of his admission to hospital the previous year for an appendectomy and how frightened he was then, saying 'You see I'm very brave'. In a later session he spent an absorbing hour in drawing a picture of a boy whom he named Andrew Brown. I encouraged him to him to tell me of Andrew Brown's family, his likes, dislikes, fears, worries etc. Victor said Andrew 'was very brave – nothing frightened him – even if he saw the Loch Ness monster he'd be brave and wouldn't be frightened'. I commented that being brave wasn't just a matter of not being frightened but about being able to talk about fears and worries. Victor said 'Like I do with you'. I agreed. Victor's bravery and strength is encapsulated in the way he has tried to care for his father and to save his father distress. This quality in Victor shines through and is touching in one so young.

Fear of death Underneath bravery lies fear and there is evidence that Victor is frightened that he too may die. While playing the Squiggle game and talking about his enjoyment of rowing he told me of his fear of swimming, his hatred of swimming pools and how he can't manage to take his foot off the bottom. I think he was indicating his fear of drowning and dying. He enlarged on this later in the session when he told me very graphically of the admission to hospital with a bad pain. No one told him what was happening except that he was to have an operation. Victor told me 'I was terrified. I thought I was going to die'. He told me of the operation, going to sleep, and of his surprise and relief on waking. He thought to himself 'I've survived'. I commented that I could understand how frightened he must have been at having an operation when his mother had had one and he agreed this was why he had felt so scared. When Victor showed me his soft toy animals, the badger said he'd be unhappy 'if he had a bad headache' while Teddy said he'd be sad 'if shut up in a box all alone'. I thought this referred to Victor's mother's illness and the excruciatingly painful headaches which were its symptoms and how she ended 'shut up in a box all alone'. I thought this indicated not only his worries about her and what had happened to her but what might happen to him.

Separation There is evidence that Victor is grappling with understanding and coming to terms with the wider issue of separation of which his mother's death is a part. The two games which he has brought to play with me are Kim's Game and Trumps. The former consists of having a number of objects available which the opponent sees and later has to list. It features the objects leaving and returning, being remembered or forgotten, that is, held in the mind or lost. Trumps has a similar theme in that cards are given away and then recalled. In my relationship with Victor he assumes that I will not remember matters which he has previously told me or discussed together. Recognising this, I have taken care to show him that I do not forget him when I am not with him. With that in mind, I brought back the toy animals which he gave me. On my last visit to him, he told me about his toy car Garfield which he said he has had since he was little and will be keeping for his own children. He fetched Garfield to show me. I thought that Victor was being more hopeful and was telling me that, though some things leave and disappear, some things stay.

Defences I have already described how Victor has used denial and repression as defences and has gradually been able to drop the former as he has grown to trust me. I have also noted that Victor spends a great deal of time playing out with friends. Before I started work with Victor, Edward told me that he never seems to be at home and is always wanting to be out and about. I think that as Jewett (1954) describes, in '*Helping children cope with separation and loss*', he may be using activity as a defence. Jewett says 'Children who are working at denial in this way may also have difficulty in being alone. They need constant playmates, company or diversion to help keep their minds off what has happened' (p.31). I was extremely surprised to learn that Edward very recently told my colleague that Victor is very much an indoor child, prefers to be inside playing on his own. It may be therefore that Victor has stopped using activity to help him in denial.

Edward My colleague and supervisor has met Edward on two occasions and will be meeting with him regularly. It is clear from this that in spite of past efforts he has not been able to grieve for his wife and presents as someone very recently bereaved. As he has kept secrets from Victor, so he kept secrets from his wife and was not able to tell her that she was dying. He has been able to see this connection. The theme of loneliness continues as Edward describes himself as a loner, his wish for a companion for himself and one for Victor also. He has talked of the problems of Victor being an only child and he an only parent and how they rely on each other for companionship. I have noticed that, although it is no longer necessary, they share a bedroom and this illustrates their reliance on each other. As indicated earlier, I think that there is some role reversal, with Victor having to take care of his father, repressing his grief and subjugating his needs to those of Edward because he perceives him as not strong enough to cope with them. As a parent sometimes represses grief in order to keep going and care for a child, so Victor has shut out his feelings to avoid distressing his father.

As our work continues with Victor and Edward, we hope to be able to reach a point when we can bring them together to acknowledge each other's grief and help them to mourn together.

Sam (eight years, eleven months)

Like Victor, Sam is a diffident and timid child, and the work undertaken is in part concerned with disinhibition, rather than the control of behaviour. The work again involves partnership with a parent (in this case, a foster-mother) in order to ascertain whether the foster placement should be made permanent.

In the course of the work, Sam discloses a degree of earlier parental abuse which distresses both the foster mother and the social worker, and which may lie behind his present (excessive) willingness to please the adults in his life. The problem for social workers when faced with disclosures of this kind is how far and in what detail to discuss them. Here, the social worker appropriately recognises that, for Sam, the mere fact of sharing these experiences is emotionally helpful; that no additional therapeutic purpose would be served by dwelling on them at length; and that to do so might get in the way of the essential tasks of the intervention. Professionals sometimes do a great deal of harm to children by exploring abusive situations in minute detail: one cynically sometimes wonders who is getting a thrill out of the investigations. This presentation offers an appropriately balanced approach.

Here again, we can observe the child's use of symbols and the intense feelings which work of this kind may produce in the worker herself.

History

Sam is the only child of his unmarried parents. Mrs T (who changed her name by deed poll) has been married previously and was divorced. She then lived with Mr T until Sam was four and a half. At the time of their separation, a Matrimonial Supervision Order was made in respect of Samuel. Mrs T started living with Mr L very shortly afterwards. They both had bed-sits on the same floor of a boarding house, sharing with others cooking and toilet facilities. They also had two large dogs. Mr T moved to London (60 miles away). He had drinking problems and a criminal record.

During those first four and a half years, from reports from health visitors and neighbours, Mrs T seemed to have left Sam alone a great deal, caring for the dogs more than for him. She has a job as a kennel maid. There were also allegations of ill treatment, with the health visitor noting that Sam appeared over-friendly to her and frightened of his mother when she asked him to tidy up. The NSPCC were involved at this time.

At the age of three, Sam was seen by an Educational Psychologist and referred to a local special school for children with language difficulties. He was seen as having minimal language skills and no ability to play, as hyperactive and with difficult behaviour problems. He was also excessively clean and neat. He attended the special school and progressed well, enjoying school and his peers.

After his parents' separation, Sam's life at home with his mother and cohabitee, Mr L, did not improve. Again, there were allegations that the two adults went out drinking every night, leaving him alone. Mr L, like Sam's father, had a drink problem and, as was later discovered, convictions for grievous bodily harm and burglary. He also had an approach to child care that demanded subservience, good behaviour and high achievement. He told the social worker that he had taught Sam for six hours one day when keeping him off school to hide bruises. Mrs T was also heard to utter threats of throwing Sam out of the window with his arms and legs bound. Mr T also alleged she hit him.

In March 1984, Sam was removed from the care of his mother and Mr L by the Police, under a Place of Safety Order. Mr L had beaten him and his mother when she tried to intervene. He was placed in a foster home with three young children and a dog. A Care Order was made in June 1984. Mrs T had visited him, though not regularly, and showed no understanding that Sam was upset if she failed to do so. Mr L also visited. With both of them, Sam was cheerful and pleasant and did not appear to miss them when they left. Mrs T expected to marry Mr L, but he, when questioned by the social workers, said he would give no guarantee to social services that he would not hit Sam again. Mrs T's visits dropped off and no rehabilitation was tried. Sam's behaviour in the foster home became too much for his foster carers. Outbursts of anger, destructive behaviour and some violence to the younger children and dog were observed. He was then removed to different foster carers Mr and Mrs F in September 1984 where he was the youngest child in a family of three grown up children. Two of these still lived at home, though were starting their own careers. This family structure provided him with much more security.

Sam settled with the F's, though there had been problems with bad behaviour and aggression at school, and the F's applied to adopt Sam. They were assessed and approved as prospective adoptive parents for Sam, Sam was accepted for adoption and approval given for the match. After this, things appeared to stagnate for three months. The social services appeared to have concerns that were not disclosed nor, apparently, resolved

Sam

Sam is a thin, blond boy with an anxious look. His eye contact was poor and he tended 'to check things out by means of sidelong glances rather than direct eye contact.' (Fahlberg 1981)

He showed little bad behaviour at home but was worrying at school – so much so that he had again been referred for special schooling. He needed to be the centre of attention, needed a deal of supervision and could be aggressive. He was also extremely anxious and could not be left one minute to wait after the end of school before his foster mother picked him up. She also reported that he had difficulty in distinguishing between irritating and really bad behaviour, expecting and, indeed, asking for punishment, either corporal, or being sent to his room for very minor misdemeanours. He was not now so obsessively neat or really very destructive but still looked to his foster mother to ask for permission in many areas of behaviour. Mrs F had clearly put great importance on tidiness and sees this as a virtue but she was ambivalent about power issues. She wanted Sam to ask for permission but was irritated by his asking.

My task

The social worker had three main areas of concern. Despite Sam's timidity and willingness to please, the Social Services were not sure of his emotional commitment to his foster parents. Second, they felt there was a deep uncertainty in Mrs F's commitment to Sam, which was rooted in her own history. Mrs F never knew her own natural parents and had had six foster placements before being successfully adopted at the age of ten. She did not want to talk about this and had a defensive and somewhat hostile relationship with the social worker. Third, because of her temperament and manner, which approached being childishly jealous and possessive at times, they were not sure about her suitability as a permanent mother for Sam.

My task, therefore, was to assess these three areas. With much help and information from the social worker, I decided (1) to visit and negotiate with Mrs F about the work that needed doing; (2) to negotiate weekly meetings with her, Mr F and Sam; (3) these would be on a timed basis to complete a particular piece of practical work.

Method

Guided by Fahlberg's (1981) *Attachment and Separation*, I decided to do a Life Book. Apart from helping Sam to be clearer about his past, it would also, if done with Mrs F, show not only the nature of the attachment between the two of them but would encourage a healthy one if that needed doing. This last should be encouraged 'even if the plan for the child in foster care is to move him. By so encouraging attachment it will help him cope with his ambivalent feelings about his birth family...and help him learn more about his past.'

This is a very sensitive task and, with Mrs F's background and personality, would seem to need extra care. I felt that a straight approach using photographs and information may not give enough opportunity to Sam and Mrs F to sort out their own feelings; thus, following advice about using an indirect approach, I thought that a freer kind of communication technique was needed and decided to use play methods. From the description of Sam and his history it was probable that he was very frightened of expressing openly his fears and hopes. I doubted if he could say what his needs were and this was paramount if I was to investigate the tasks set above. As Winnicott said, what I hoped to offer was a 'warm, friendly, personal help aimed at enabling (Sam) to come to terms with himself and his situation, and to provide opportunities for him to establish relationships and build loyalties for himself which can last a lifetime' (Winnicott 1984).

With this rather daunting task in mind, I bought a range of play materials, hoping that one at least would enable Sam to express himself, share some of the painful experiences of the past and so lead to the creation of a Life Book. I did not have an office that would provide a relaxing environment and as I did not want to put any more strain on Mrs F than was necessary, I decided to hold the sessions at their own home. Further, I decided to use Mrs F as a co-worker, having 'special' knowledge of Sam, thereby giving her status apart from that of foster mother. I would present myself as an 'expert' in working with play materials with children in order to give them a chance to come to terms with the past. I was setting myself up as a role model and I expected her, as an 'expert' like myself, to be able to give space and value to Sam as someone separate from herself. By doing this, I felt she would be able to distance herself and to see a difference between her needs and Sam's. I hoped that both of us would be able to encourage Sam to express his view of the world and to make his needs clearer to me and Mrs F and to himself.

The issues raised for me at the time were:

(1) Whether I could both allow Sam space *and* engage the powerful figure of his foster mother. I had real fears that this might not be possible. I did not know whether her hostile relationship with the social worker would be transferred to me.

(2) Whether this was the right time for Sam to engage in such work. Timing is crucial in such an exercise and I would have to be sensitive to any resistance that Sam showed.

> 'It's not a simple matter to judge the proper moment for bringing a child into therapy.' (Oaklander 1969)

However, I would not find this out until I started.

(3) Whether, if I succeeded in engaging Sam and his foster mother, I could deal with what came out. While this feeling is one that commonly occurs when starting such work, I knew from past experience that the journey we took together may be dangerous in that it may touch on important, and possibly dormant, emotions in myself. I needed to be aware of this and of the need to set up some kind of support/supervision. The danger area I especially realised would come if Sam could not remain with the Fs.

(4) Whether, if all this happened, I would be able to complete the task properly in the time allocated without raising undue expectations of long term intervention with Sam or his foster mother. When thinking about this, really the problem was whether I would complete the task to my own satisfaction and be able to leave it. Endings and parting are important and often difficult issues. I am not sure that I always deal with them well.

The sessions

In all, ten sessions were held spanning three months. I also had a prior one negotiating with Mrs F. I spent sometime buying an assortment of materials for Sam's use, settling on wax crayons, fibre tip pens and paper, Playdo, two sets of pipe cleaner doll families (with three generations) and a Life Book folder.

I took these to show Mrs F and to discuss my role and the task I had. Mrs F was initially somewhat suspicious and prickly, but enjoyed looking at the materials. The sessions ended up positively and I left her some papers to read on direct work with children. She accepted that Sam needed to be more relaxed and that an exploration of the past may help, but she also said that he was already better than he had been. She further accepted her role as an expert in having special information about Sam and wanted to work with me. I further discussed with her the basis of the work, in other words, allowing Sam to set the pace and to choose the materials. While she accepted this, I was not sure whether she would be able to allow it to happen.

In our first joint session with Sam, I brought the bag with the materials and asked him to unpack it. My aim in doing this from the very start was to show Mrs F and Sam that he had a choice and control in what he did and how he did it. The bag of materials was to be for his use only during the duration of the work together. I also wanted to see *who* Sam was, not what I thought he was like.

> 'I must begin with the child from where she is *with me*...without an overlay of preconceived biases and judgements about her.' (Oaklander 1979)

Sam unpacked the bag very carefully. He presented as quiet, well mannered, anxious to please and very careful to let his mother have her say in this session. He showed very little impatience and she almost took over the centre of the stage. In this session I felt my job was not to challenge this overtly but to show by my manner that I valued what Sam said and supported his choices. His first was to look at the photographs. He identified everyone in them except his father and then wrongly identified somebody else as Mr L. All this was done very quietly. He then chose the Playdo and became much less withdrawn, creating a scarecrow and then smashing it up. He also wanted to keep marks of his own fingerprints in the Playdo so that they could harden and become permanent. From this session alone I could see that Playdo would prove to be very important to him, engaging his emotions and providing a channel through which they could be explored and expressed.

He then drew a picture of a five bedroomed house/flat in very 'unhappy' rain with a sun and a rainbow. It also had a car slipping off a very muddy road into a river. He asked me to write down what he said as he drew and then we would put that piece of paper on the picture. When he had finished the picture he sighed heavily, looking at it. I asked him whether the picture told us anything about his life. He looked frightened and said, 'No', then said, 'I can tell you that the house is very pleased that there is a sun and a rainbow.' After a pause, I asked him if he was the house. He grinned broadly at me and said, 'Yes.' He asked me not to write this down. Sam had been physically abused in a flat and now lived in a five bedroomed house.

He asked Mrs F to hang the picture in the living room which she agreed to do. My understanding, though tentative, was that while he could not say it in words, he was telling me that the past was very bad, the present much better and that he wanted to make a statement about this now, that is, the fingerprints and the drawing.

These three themes of photographs, rough physical work with the Playdo and depicting his present family in rainbow colours repeated themselves over the next few sessions. However, he added a new theme in the second session. He unpacked and used the dolls. He enacted a scene whereby an older man beat up two parent figures and rescued the children in the family. The mother and father figures were sent to prison. Sam got very angry doing this, trying to tear off the figures' clothes. During this session also, he talked, while he beat up some Playdo, of a giant as big as a house who attacked an elephant. He added that the elephant won, 'Of course'. He repeated again his fingermarks, saying this time that they were elephant marks. Towards the end of this session he became somewhat frantic but relaxed when I told him I could continue to visit him as long as he wanted us to play together.

The emotion in this session, especially with the Playdo, was considerable and Sam displayed an anxiety which I felt was roused by the depth of feeling he displayed. At one time, when Mrs F had left the room momentarily, he threw the Playdo around, doing Karate chops on it. He expressed anxiety at the end of the session and begged for reassurance that I would keep coming. By the end of the session I felt that my feeling that the time was right for Sam to work had been confirmed.

I had tried to introduce the idea of a Life Book. Sam was politely interested and wanted to put a big photo of himself on the first page but did not show the same enthusiasm for this as for his unstructured play. The construction of the family tree of his present family was enjoyed by him with his foster mother. While doing this he used rainbow colours again for his present family, but was not interested in doing his 'birth' family. I felt I had to stand back in this instance and let him lead the pace. Mrs F was also listening a little bit more in this session and not pushing Sam to say particular things. However, the family tree only covered her side of the family. Mr F was dismissed as being unimportant.

As the sessions progressed, Sam let out more about the past. With the dolls he talked about parents going off to the pub and getting drunk and again of being rescued by an older man (the social worker). With crayons he drew a monster with delight and anger. There were common features between this monster and the social worker's description of Mr L. Most important, he introduced the concept of magic. A boy elephant became a magic elephant with a magic horn, trunk and wings to fly away with and to beat the giant with. Again, anxiety was roused by the work and Sam released it by punching and kneading the Playdo. At this point, it was only obvious that magic was very important but I was not sure what it meant. Most simply, it appeared to be necessary in order to triumph over bad and therefore, by reflection, to be a statement of how powerless Sam felt either now, or in the past, or both.

What appeared to be happening, although in the thick of it it was difficult to see this clearly, was that Sam was getting in touch with his feelings, especially his anger and fear. He also appeared to be gaining more real and relaxed control over himself and his world. For instance, in session five he set out to control his foster mother. He rolled out some Playdo and made them into handcuffs and handcuffed her, telling her that she was his prisoner. Both of them enjoyed this and laughed a great deal, but the message not to interfere or to be powerful was there and I felt was received by Mrs F.

Their interactions during sessions by now had relaxed and Mrs F was able to let Sam dictate to her how to be involved. However, at the beginning of sessions she often would try to tell me of the problems of the preceding week and when Sam had been naughty. I felt this was inappropriate and in order to challenge this I arranged to see Mrs F alone between sessions as I felt her underlying message was that she needed 'special' time. During this arranged session, I asked Mrs F how she saw things going in the sessions. She started by saying that she felt that Sam was more relaxed and was significantly more open about his family and his past to her. She, however, somewhat triumphantly said that he was talking more to her than to me. When I pointed out that this was success as Sam needed to share his history with her more than with me, she started to open out to me about her own possessiveness towards her children. This led to a useful sharing of her own experiences as a child, her anger at not being protected by those in authority. She talked about her need to be a good mother and in charge of the children. She also saw anger as very important and felt that Sam had not been able to express it easily. While this was clearly correct, I felt she identified her own need to express anger so strongly that she could not actually be sensitive to when it was appropriate for Sam. I mentioned her sensitivity to suppressed anger in others, saying that it would be a very useful support for Sam and this allowed her again to talk of her own history and the loss of her adoptive father and how angry she had been at her adoptive sisters. She went on to talk about herself at times as being very worthless and her need to prove that she is not. After this session I was worried that she would be concerned and possibly hostile because she had been so open to me, but this proved not to be so and I feel it allowed her to listen more sensitively to Sam.

Before the next session (the sixth), I began to think that Sam needed an overt statement from those in authority about his future. My reasons were that whenever we talked about his present family he gave almost too clear an idea that they were good (i.e., the rainbow colours) and that they were his family. It seemed as if he was ramming his message home and again I felt reflected an anxiety that he is not sure whether he will be allowed to stay. I talked about this with my supervisor and Sam's social worker and they agreed that this should be checked out with Mrs F. I therefore talked to her, asking whether she agreed with my assessment and giving my reasons. Not surprisingly, Mrs F agreed wholeheartedly with my assessment and said she and her husband were very clear that they wanted to go ahead with the adoption. Typically, she also wondered why social services had not done anything about it beforehand. I arranged with her and the social worker that he should visit during the week to talk to Sam about what was meant by adoption and to say that his home was to be with the F's if that is what he wanted. It seemed to me that the social worker was the person to do this as from Sam's play he had played an important authority role. The social worker visited and also during the week, Mr and Mrs F of their own volition visited the solicitor to start proceedings.

It appeared to me, then, that in the six sessions an assessment had already been made and acted upon. Sam clearly was saying that he needed this family and Mrs F was saying that she was the right person for Sam. The very process of assessment had brought them closer together and their commitment was public. Yet I also felt that the work was not finished. Sam had not completed his own journey through the past. This was now his focus. He had convinced us of his prime need for stability and could not open up the more vulnerable aspects of his experience. This he did in the next two sessions. It also was clear to me that Mrs F had not finished her journey. While she was separating herself and her needs from Sam in a much more sensitive way, she was also only beginning to talk to me about her past and how aspects of it differed from Sam's and yet also were similar to his. I therefore felt that the focus should change from the assessment about whether they stayed together to an exploration of what they needed to share.

In the seventh session Sam started with Playdo, giving me some and saying that we would both make snakes. He told me that his would be bigger and he would win. As the competition commenced he became more anxious as we rolled out the Playdo, telling me again that he *had* to win. He then said his snake needed magic to win. He added a different colour Playdo in the form of coloured balls and made his snake longer. Because I did not really understand his 'magic' I commented to him that magic was important, and he then looked directly at me, saying, 'Yes, without it I would die'. He had won the competition by making his snake longer, but then paused, looked at my snake and said 'You need some magic too' and proceeded to share out his magic Playdo, putting some into my snake. He then removed the magic from both snakes and said we should roll up the snakes, leaving this extra Playdo out. He said 'I don't need the magic any more. We must put it away quick.' He asked me to make a bowl with a lid for the magic and, using a female doll, come to collect it and take it away. All this was done with the utmost concentration and involvement. The magic was never needed again.

On reflection, I felt that Sam's ability to discard his magic came from his clear certainty that he now had a safe home which had given him the security to feel that he did not need anything extra to make sure that things would go well for him. He also showed from his new strength a touching concern for my snake, the loser. This gentle concern came up later in another context.

In the eighth session, Sam again was playing with the Playdo, this time rolling it into little balls and was able at last to talk about the abuse he had suffered on the night that he had been taken into care under a Place of Safety Order. He was not overtly frightened but spoke quietly and with deep feeling. He told his foster mother and me about that night. He described how naughty he had been while his mother and her cohabitee were at the pub. He had mixed his mother's make-up and Mr L's tools all together in a big mess on the carpet. He then related how when Mr L returned he had been very angry and started beating him with a belt. His mother had tried to intervene but had not succeeded in stopping Mr L, so had run down the stairs to ring for the police. He had been very frightened at the thought that the police would come as he thought they would beat him also for being naughty. This was because when he had been naughty previously his mother and Mr L told him that the police would take him away and lock him up. He had been very surprised that when the police came they had actually been cross with Mr L and nice to his mum and him. Then he related how he had ended up in the hospital where he met the social worker who had taken him to his first foster parents. I asked him at this point if he thought Mr L would kill him when he was beating him and he said, again with direct eye contact, that he thought he would die. He was also able to say how scared and lonely he had always felt when left alone as had often happened. He went on to talk about his first foster parents and how naughty he had been there. With Mrs F's help, at this point he said this was partly because his mother didn't visit a lot, also because he felt they had stopped her visiting and were cross with her. He also said that once or twice they left him alone when he had been naughty and he had got very scared as it reminded him of when he had been with his mum, and of Mr L.

It was difficult enough for me to hear Sam talking about this, but Mrs F became very angry, breathing hard and grasping the chair with tense hands. I saw Sam looking at her a bit askance and asked him if he knew why she was angry and he said, 'No', so she told him herself that she was very angry for him as she felt that no child should have been treated like that. He accepted that quietly. After he had finished talking I asked him if there were any more secrets and he said yes, but he didn't want to speak about them now. Mrs F said she had secrets too and would tell him one day and that it was best to share secrets but only when you felt ready. Mrs F gave me a very speaking look at this time. Later, privately, she told me of the sexual abuse she had suffered in one of her foster homes and how she had been unable to talk about it until the night before her wedding when she told her mother. She described her anger and helplessness and said again that she felt no child should have to suffer in that way or in the way that Sam had. By holding on to this information during the session and allowing Sam to set the pace she demonstrated to me that she was now more clearly distinguishing her own emotional need from Sam's and was dealing with those needs in a more appropriate fashion.

Sam's quiet disclosure of the abuse built a great deal of tension in him, Mrs F and myself. It was difficult to know how best to deal with this but Sam himself knew and began throwing Playdo at Mrs F and this activity quickly developed into a play fight with Mrs F pretending to kill him and throw him on the floor and he rolling around and laughing, gasping and almost crying. They ended up after ten minutes with Sam sitting on her lap like a small child, being cuddled. It was clearly an enormously important emotional release for them both and completed the experience for them and for me. It was totally right but the exclusiveness of their relationship isolated and saddened me for it showed that, while I had an important part to play, I was only transitory in their relationship.

In the next session, Sam seemed to lack an immediate focus or, indeed, to know where he wanted to go and during the time told me quite clearly that he did not want to do his life story book. He felt he was not ready but might be ready later. I and Mrs F had by that time accepted that this was probably so and agreed that we did not need to go on as we had originally planned. Instead, we all agreed that I would at this time only visit once more to say goodbye but that if, in future, they wanted me to visit I would do so. Mrs F and I talked over the last two sessions and she asked for more reading and to be included in any training courses on such practice. I agreed I would mention it to the principal social worker, which I did.

The last session was short and taken up by Sam handing over photographs and other memorabilia and art work we had done together in a special envelope. We also talked over the whole process and said our thank yous and goodbyes. At the end of the session it was possible for Sam to say to me that he would like me to visit when I felt sad. Mrs F and I parted with a feeling of mutual respect.

Conclusion

In terms of the task, it was clear to me, first, that Mrs F was now fully committed to Sam and had come to terms, at least partially, with her own past. Second that, given her own personality quirks, she also gave love, stability and an understanding of difference to Sam. Third, and this was by far the easiest, that Sam saw himself as part of the F family. He now accepted his past, did not need to deny it and was clearly bonded well with all of the members of his family.

As Winnicott (1984) writes:

> 'The immediate purpose of communication…is to get in touch with the children's real selves, what they are feeling about themselves and their lives at the time of meeting.'

Finally…Eric (aged five)

This is a very brief extract: Eric's personal history is disturbed and neglectful, and with constant movements both geographically and in relationships with a bewildering number of adults. The extract is included because it demonstrates the resilience of a child in appalling circumstances, and his ability to care for others.

> One day we went for a walk and passed the cemetery. Eric asked all about cemeteries and wanted to go in. Whilst in there a man was putting flowers round a grave. I explained about that. We then went on to the park and Eric stopped and picked a flower and gave it to me. 'That's for you,' he said. I was not sure of the significance of this but I have kept it in his life story book; maybe one day he may wish to pick a flower for his mum, maybe I was the keeper of his flower for his Mother. Later in the session Eric said, 'You play with me cause my mum left me'. I asked him if he knew why she had left him; he replied, 'because of Nick'. I asked him if that made him feel sad: in a soft voice and moving to sit on my lap he said 'yes'

and then aggressively 'I'm a foster boy'. With that he ran back to the nursery.

This had been a moving session for us both. On other occasions Eric drew himself as a monster and two books became important to him: *The Missing Monkey*, where a small boy loses his toy, but eventually finds it, and *Bruce's Story*, where a dog leaves home to be placed with a new family. Eric has ended most sessions with both stories.

At one session, another boy asked why it was always Eric who came to play with me. Eric replied before I could "Cause my mother left me'. 'So has mine' replied Steven. At this Eric put his arm round Steven, saying 'You can come too then'. I saw this as a major step in Eric's ability to share and acknowledge common ground.

Postscript

All the cases presented here concerned boys; this was not a deliberate choice, but reflected the material available. It merits discussion whether families (and possibly social workers) encounter special problems in the care of boys, and whether boys show higher levels of vulnerability.

In editing the material, the phrase 'play therapy' has been avoided wherever possible, although it is frequently used by social workers. It is necessary to clarify that the focus is on working with young children; that 'play' is often the most effective means of communication; and that, in this context, 'play' is often hard work for both the children and their social workers. Indeed, 'play' often requires expressing and sharing very painful feelings and experiences: it is not 'fun' and is therefore, perhaps, an unfortunate word.

Implicit in this chapter is the matter of the problems encountered by some families when help from grandparents is not available for some reason, or when the potential contribution of grandparents is overlooked by social workers. In this context, promotion of the view that grandparents may be effective carers (Children Act 1989) is timely.

Finally, this chapter indicates the importance to workers and children alike of suitable space for their work together. Direct work with young children needs privacy, the regular availability of the same room, and access to materials (some of them messy) which do not have to be 'tidied up' after every session.

CHAPTER TWO

The Experience of Sexual Abuse

In the course of a small-scale study carried out among 33 field social workers in one London Borough (a project in 1991), it was found that 68 children and 55 adults amongst their current cases had experienced sexual abuse during childhood. Approximately two-thirds of the victims were female: 40 males (including three adults) were among the victims. Although it would be unwise to make generalisations from these figures, it seems to be true for this Borough that every field social worker has three or four victims of sexual abuse on his/her caseload: that is, about 10 per cent of current cases.

From another perspective, Wolf (1989) found that, from a sample of 5000 male sex offenders, 27 per cent had themselves been victims of sexual abuse, and a further 17 per cent had witnessed abuse during childhood.

The project found that, of 123 victims in the study, only 59 were receiving or had received professional help in coming to terms with their experiences: the older the former victim, the less likely it is that he or she has received supportive help in coming to terms with the experience.

While it would be naive to assume that help is needed in every case, two hypotheses can be formulated: first, that there is continuing unhappiness or disturbance among a substantial number of service-users (and many others not known to the services) as a result of unhelped and unresolved earlier experiences of sexual abuse; and second, failure to resolve these difficulties contributes to abusive behaviour among former victims. (Wolf found also that, among male sex offenders, about one-third had been victims of physical violence, or had witnessed it, or both: this may indicate a link between violence and sexual abuse, but this cannot be ascertained with any certainty.)

The response of social workers to the possible scale of this human need is mixed. The project found that, among the 33 workers in the study, the perceived presence of victims of abuse in their caseloads varied from nought to 75 per cent. Only 14 expressed confidence in dealing with the issue. Six workers openly expressed lack of confidence/competence as a reason for their lack of interest in it; two were frankly uninterested in it; 15 cited lack of training as a factor in their not dealing with the issues that were, perhaps, latent among their clients.

The following three case studies show ways in which young children and their families may be helped in various ways. In the case of Emma, the child is helped to disclose that abuse has taken place and to resolve her complex feelings of loyalty and fear towards her mother and her mother's cohabitee. In the case of Marie, we are helped to understand the planning of the work, the therapeutic use of play, and the means whereby parents may be helped to engage positively in the resolution of the child's difficulties. Jane's and Lizzie's case provides an account of the complexity of the family's development, feelings and responses to the disclosure of abuse, in which parental denial and lost hopes need to be overcome.

Emma (aged seven)

Emma's mother, Cathy, has lived with a succession of men, and has found difficulty (according to the maternal grandmother) in feeling consistent affection towards any of her three children. The day nursery, in Emma's pre-school years, reported that Emma's physical condition seemed poor, her behaviour was aggressive, and that she was sometimes sent to the nursery unattended by her mother. The police received reports from passers-by of Cathy's chastisement of Emma in the street.

Social work has been complicated by divergent opinions of Cathy's parental attitudes and abilities. A psychologist, to whom the family was referred by Emma's school, reported, 'For a young single parent coping with her children's demands, she is doing remarkably well. I hope that any help she is given does not undermine her confidence in her practical abilities.' On the other hand, the school has reported to the local authority that Emma displays unexplained burns, cuts and bruises, and will not say how they have happened.

The case was referred to a Family Centre, where the social worker recorded the following:

Assessment/Intervention

The purpose of my intervention, negotiated with the local authority social worker and ratified by a planning meeting, was to assist Emma's mother's parenting skills. Other people involved have expressed disquiet; the head of a specialist day care facility speaks of her clingy, crying, difficult behaviour, especially after times with her father, a former cohabitee; a worrying report from the medical officer about her physical development; neighbours' fears. But nothing tangible has arisen which would prompt any resolute action to take place. Psychological and psychiatric reports state that her mother's parenting abilities are at an acceptable level.

From reading the files and discussion with the social worker, questions concerning the relationship between Emma and Cathy have to be raised; Emma was 'shaken like a rag doll' when only a few days old by her father; where was the mother protecting her small child? There are other instances of possible lack of protection; scalds, burns, running off, and violence by a subsequent cohabitee.

Given these concerns, and given that Emma's behaviour has led to her admission to specialist day care, the local authority social worker and I felt that individual work with Emma for a prescribed number of sessions might be beneficial to her and give her the freedom to express some of the unexpressed and unreleased feelings she must be carrying around with her. Should she have any incidents locked up inside which she wishes to speak of, it is hoped that a safe environment will offer her the chance to do that. My own role, as well as providing that environment, will be to observe and facilitate her on her journey.

Part of the intervention must include Emma's mother and grandmother and I accordingly visited them to inform them of our concerns, the decision to work with Emma and to gain their co-operation. This visit also gave me a chance to observe the family, particularly the relationship between Emma and Cathy. What I observed was a family with no clear boundaries, enmeshed behaviours and a mother who appeared disassociated from her daughter, that is, showing no interest in her play or our discussion, and with no eye contact except with her own mother. The one contact she made with Emma was to grab her roughly and shake her for some trivial happening: she seemed to reach a point where she was on the verge of losing control till her own mother intervened.

Theoretical influences

Before offering direct work to children we should be clear about why we are offering it and the implications inherent in the work. I think it safe to say most children coming to our notice would be under some stress. Accepting that this is the case, then there is a need to alleviate it:

> 'by channelling the children's energies towards gaining more control over their environment, facilitating expression and communication of fears and worries; and helping them find support and muster courage, that will turn them from passive victims into active modifiers of their own lives.' (Ayalon 1987, p7)

Stress causes distress and has to be dealt with (the sooner the better); but stress, through play, can be transformed into the challenge of discovering inner strengths.

The activity of play involves the whole child, integrating feelings, thoughts and behaviour, thus helping to promote a positive self-image, something few disturbed children have. It helps the 'discharge of accumulated tensions...helps reduce helplessness and increases the opportunities of gaining mastery over self and the environment, thus reducing the threat'.

However, we as workers must ask ourselves what we can responsibly undertake, bearing in mind that we may stir up powerful feelings within ourselves as well as in the child.

To go into sessions with children with a set agenda and set ways of working would, in my opinion, be wrong and I would agree with many of the things Oaklander (1979) says about our approach to work with children:

> '...the creative process is open-ended. I don't always know *why* I'm doing what I do at the moment. Sometimes we do things because I'm experimenting, or because it seems that it might be fun, or because the child wants to do it. Some of my best therapy sessions have happened this way'. (p 194)

This is not permission to be ill-prepared; merely encouragement to be flexible yet confident that we have the knowledge and sensitivity to respond to the child's needs as they become expressed.

Process of intervention

The first two sessions with Emma were full of expressive play and, ultimately, led in a direction I had not anticipated. She had no trouble settling in my room (bright, large and full of toys) and immediately began asking me questions about my room and my personal life. Because of her questions about me I showed her a book I have made which encompasses several issues – sharing (picture of myself, home and son), clarification (of my role and work), feelings of isolation (the child sees other children come to see me), permission giving (other children cry, talk or don't talk).

She liked this book and asked if she also could make a story, although she could not write it. She then changed her mind and said she would do it next time. I asked her if she would like to draw her family, which she did. She first drew herself in brown, then her mother, father and Nanny, all in black with large heads. She offered some information:

> 'No one in the family was nice'

and that policemen

> 'take some kids away.'

> 'I didn't run away.'

She added spontaneously

> 'My dad doesn't hit me.'

Q. 'Does anyone?'

A. 'My mum sometimes.'

This exchange illustrates how a child can give the worker information in a testing-out fashion. Whilst she was saying she didn't run away and her father didn't hit her she was looking at me closely to gauge my reaction. It was too soon for me to press her on these points but they could be recorded and returned to.

She then drew a picture of her mother and herself, scribbling angrily in red on those parts of herself where (she said) her mother had hit her.

Q. 'What does it feel like when your mother hits you?'

A. 'Nothing.'

Q. 'I wouldn't like it if I was hit.'

A. 'Sometimes I'd like to cry', looking sad.

She then went off to the sand and buried all the people she could find and our first session finished.

In the next session, after burying dinosaurs in the sand and experimenting with daubing paint on paper for some time, all the while asking questions and generally conducting herself in a way which suggested she had other business on her mind, she finally made the statement which had been hovering unspoken in the air between us. She wanted to write the story she'd mentioned last week. Would I write it for her. She dictated the following:

'About Daddy'

'Daddy keeps playing with me. We play toys. We play toys when we go to bed. We play with toys in my bedroom on the bed. He plays bricks in the box. Sometimes sleep in the same bed. Daddy's a nice Daddy. His name is Richard. Some games I like. Some games I don't like. Those are puzzles.'

She stopped and looked at me for a few moments. I thanked her for her story and asked if she had finished. She said 'Yes' and went off to play in the sand. Again, it was important to hold back and respect her pace. Perhaps she had something to tell me, perhaps she didn't. It was not my place to make interpretations but it was correct for me to check out her information later.

In her next session she had a wonderful time using finger paints, eventually almost washing her hands in an array of colours. She took much the same pleasure when playing in the sand (when not burying everything in sight), again almost washing her hands in the sand, feeling it run through her fingers or smoothing it. My guess would be she hadn't had the opportunity to revel in the normal sensory experiences a young child could expect and was now taking that opportunity.

She went to the blackboard and scribbled. She asked me to join her and I copied; I then suggested we make pictures from our scribbles and Emma found a happy fish and a naughty fish. I asked her to be each fish and say what that felt like. Her description of the happy fish was short and limited; about the naughty fish she was able to be more verbal and became animated. She drew another fish and said the fish were watching her. She then went back to the sand and buried several male toys. I asked who the men or boys were and she replied one was 'horrid' and another 'hurts someone'.

Q. 'Who does he hurt?'

A. (*Taking another figure*) 'That little girl. He shouldn't do that...not hurt little boys or little girls in real life.'

The atmosphere in the room had become tense. Her body language had changed from the pleasure of the paint and the fun of the scribbles; she was alert, eyes looking at me ready to pick up any reactions that weren't to her liking. She showed extreme vigilance and I knew the next few moments were vital if, indeed, she did have something to tell me.

I did not want to influence her in any way but let her know I was listening totally.

Q. 'Last time you said you played a game with dad you didn't like.'

A. 'Yes in the bedroom.'

This led to Emma fetching the anatomically correct dolls (kept on a ledge at the side of the room) and saying

'Daddy touched me.'

This was a bad moment for me. I didn't want to hear what Emma seemed likely to say, yet I could not leave Emma in the dilemma of perhaps being silenced.

Q. 'Where did Daddy touch you?'

A. 'There.' (*She pointed to the bottom of the Emma doll and giggled.*) 'The bum.'

Q. 'How did he touch you on the bum?'

Emma stuck her finger into the anus of the doll then put the Emma doll back on top of the daddy's lap.

Q. What touched you there?'

She undressed the Peter doll and told me he had a big willy. Then she undressed the Daddy doll and she put her finger in the bottom of the Emma doll again.

Q. 'Did anything touch you there?'

A. 'Yes.'

Q. 'What?'

A. 'Daddy's willy. No he didn't.'

Q. 'Did Daddy touch you or didn't he touch you, Emma?'

A. 'Yes he did. It hurt. No he didn't.'

She went away and was beginning to look upset.

Q. 'Is it true Daddy's touched you in the bum?'

A. 'No.'

Q. 'Why did you say he had? Can you tell me?'

A. 'It's true.'

In an effort to clarify this situation I asked her a hypothetical question.

Q. 'If Dad did that with his willy how would it be? Would it be soft, hard, little or big? Can you tell me?'

A. 'Hard.'

Q. 'What would Daddy be doing?'

A. 'He'd be moving about.'

She laid the Emma doll on her back and looked at me. I said I didn't understand what Daddy might be doing and could she show me. She took down the trousers of the Daddy doll and said:

'First of all he'd take down his trousers.'

(She held onto the penis of the Daddy doll.)

'Then he'd go on his knees and he put his penis in here.'

(She put her finger in the anus of the Emma doll again.)

I said I didn't see how he could do that and she lifted the legs of the Emma doll over her shoulders and put the daddy doll on his knees putting his penis right inside the hole of the anus. She looked at me and said it happened a few times. She then became very upset and cried. She was by now a very different child from the one who had played. I comforted her and read her 'Kanakulu', then left her free to play for at least ten minutes before taking her upstairs to her mother. The session had run over by about 20 minutes.

Given Emma's ambiguity at different points I felt it more appropriate to discuss this with her social worker before saying anything to her mother. I immediately phoned JN and discussed this with her and she will now take appropriate action.

Next week: ascertain when, anywhere else, anyone else, daddy who?

Emma was very happy to see me and literally sprang happily into the room. She wanted to use the banging toy which she did for at least ten minutes.

Q. 'You've been at Steven's house with Mummy over the weekend, haven't you?' (*This information given to me by grandma on the phone.*)

A. 'Yes.'

Q. 'What's that like?'

A. 'He painted the walls.'

Q. 'What's Steven like?'

A. 'He's horrible.'

Q. 'Why?'

A. 'He hits Mummy. He hits me sometimes. He's horrible.'

She went back to the banging toy and concentrated on that for a while.

Q. 'Do you remember what you told me last week about Daddy?'

A. 'Yes.'

Q. 'Which Daddy did you mean?'

A. 'Daddy Richard.'

Emma went on to say she was with her daddy last week on her own and that her mummy went out (this was after our session last week).

Q. 'Where did you go to bed that night?'

A. 'I went into Daddy's bed.'

She said she had slept all night with her father, that she had gone up to bed first and gone to sleep and he'd woken her up later by cuddling her. She went and got four dolls – Peter, Mummy, Daddy and herself – and put the Emma doll and the Daddy doll on a cushion for the bed, Emma on her side and the Daddy getting into bed, lying down facing her. She said she said to Daddy: 'Get downstairs'. She had the Daddy doll and Emma doll facing one other on their sides and she put her own finger in the vagina of the Emma doll and said 'He put his willy in there'.

She went away from the dolls looking upset and went to the sand.

Q. 'Is it difficult to tell me?'

A. 'Yes.'

Q. 'Why?'

A. 'I don't like it.'

Q. 'Do you like seeing Daddy?'

A. 'Yes.'

Q. 'Do you want him to carry on doing this or do you want him to stop?'

A. 'Stop.'

Q. 'Has anybody else given you those sort of touches?'

A. 'No. Sometimes I run away when Daddy tries to do that. I go downstairs and get a drink.'

Q. 'What does Daddy do?'

A. 'Goes downstairs and puts me back to bed again.'

Q. 'Have you ever cried when Daddy's done that?'

A. 'No.'

Q. 'Has Mummy ever been there when Daddy's done that?'

A. 'No.'

Q. 'Has Peter?'

A. 'No.'

Q. 'Did you ever try to tell anyone what Daddy does?'

A. 'Yes. Mummy.'

Q. 'What did she say?'

A. 'Go away.'

At this point Emma started sobbing, and I held her till her sobs ceased. Then we sat side by side in an armchair and made up a fairy story between us.

At the beginning of the next session Emma told me of a current dream. She said she doesn't like it and wants it to go away. It was a not uncommon dream; many disturbed children seem to dream of monsters coming to eat them up.

I asked her what she wanted to do with the monster.

She wanted to bury it. How would she bury it? Under tons and tons and tons of sand which would then change into mud and it couldn't breathe and it would die. So with her eyes closed, still on the bean bag, I asked her to do that in her mind and to let me know when it was done.

After some minutes she said it was done. 'Is it finished then?' I asked. She considered. 'No, it wasn't.' The sand and mud were all piled up like a mountain and she wanted it squashed down flat so the monster was right under the ground. 'How could she do that?' After some consideration she said with a giant steamroller. She went ahead and finished off as she had described and gradually came back from her experiences into the room. She had not been frightened or embarrassed and had had a good time, judging by her participation and pleasure at the finish.

She has not spoken again of this dream. (I am not suggesting that this one exercise will rid Emma of her fears and anxieties *vis à vis* her abuse or parenting; we can only deal with specific fears/anxieties as they are presented.)

We now seemed to move into a different stage. In the background, Cathy had been cautioned and told not to leave Emma alone with any man, and although she agreed to this we were unsure of her ability to adhere to it, and she showed that it was an inconvenience (she liked to leave Emma while she went off to see other boyfriends, for example). I think it likely that Emma was somehow made to feel, at the very least, a nuisance for her disclosure.

She spent long periods of time just messing paint on paper and feeling the paint on her hands. Her behaviour had regressed and she clearly felt safe to be even 'littler'. She painted a big block of white then surrounded it with thick black paint and said 'Mummy said I've got to cover it all over'. She fetched the musical bells and asked me to sing to her while she shook them.

On our next session she came into the room, went straight to the bean bag, curled into a foetal position and lay there. She said once or twice 'I'm so tired, I'm so tired' but nothing more. I reflected back that she was tired and said I'd leave her quietly until she was ready to talk or play. She remained like that for twelve minutes, checking occasionally that I was still in my chair and still there for her. The rest of the session was spent distractedly going from one thing to another, jumping at the noises outside and continuously asking if Mummy was coming back and when Mummy was coming back.

Above all she projected a profound sadness into the room, and showed a marked reluctance to speak or show her feelings. I decided to acknowledge the feeling openly by saying I could feel the sadness and that it made me sad too. I asked her if she'd like to find a sad face (amongst the different facial expression pictures I keep) and we could look at it. She found one.

'Yes', I said, 'I feel just like that right now. How about you?'

Then she started crying. (The work continues.)

Evaluation

This piece of work was a reinforcement for me of several important issues:

> 'Direct work cannot be successfully done in a vacuum. It is something that needs to be planned and co-ordinated in relation to the overall plan for the child and in co-operation with other significant adults in the child's life.' (Aldgate and Simmonds 1988, p.8)

Throughout, the local authority social worker and I had worked closely together with mother and maternal grandmother on the planned intervention, preparations for the diagnostic interview which she undertook and the ensuing plan for Emma to work jointly with her mother in another setting.

The second important element was that of a child's uniqueness; this should never be lost sight of in our efforts to find effective ways of working with children. Because Emma and I managed to create an environment which was safe and free from criticism or competition, Emma was able to release traumatic information and so allow us to plan an informed course of action. If her mother subsequently refuses to co-operate in work with Emma (though co-operation is, ideally, the result we would like to see from this intervention), then that is a vital piece of information, telling us a great deal about her commitment to her. Should that happen we anticipate Emma continuing with me as we have now established her needs more clearly. Although five sessions were originally planned, flexibility must always be possible.

Since informing Cathy of Emma's allegations, we have found that she has been more open with us and occasionally makes eye contact, which she never had done before. Communication is slightly easier.

Emma and I established a good rapport, although she has experienced much pain in the room with me. Perhaps the rewards of such work are best illustrated by Emma herself when she turned to me, hands covered with paint and smiling delightedly:

'I'm allowed to do that here, aren't I?'

In the following case, we are informed of the context within which work with a very young child is undertaken, and which requires the social worker to adopt several roles: as child therapist, as family social worker, as assessor of abuse, and as a report writer for a court. Part of the skill of child protection work lies in the clarifying of these diverse roles and in the flexibility adopted within each. The contribution of foster parents as partners in the helping process is also indicated.

Like Emma, Marie is troubled by 'monsters'. Bearing in mind the disturbed and sometimes chaotic lives of these children – Marie has had fifteen changes of address in three years – the children's resilience is remarkable; but one is left with anxious uncertainties about who the monsters are. The social worker writes the following description of her work.

Marie (aged six)

This is an account of direct work with a young girl who experienced many moves and family disruptions during her first three years and, since being in care, has had a further change of home to deal with. Superficially Marie has seemed quite resilient to all these changes and she has not been a difficult child for foster parents to manage. However, my knowledge of Marie's troubled family history and the capacity of children in such situations to suppress their confusion and fears led me to undertake some individual work with her. My hope was that by addressing these fears she would be better able to understand them and her past and to move on to a more hopeful future.

This outline starts with a summary of Marie's history, which I have explained in some detail so that the influences and events that have shaped her development so far can be understood. I have then moved on to my assessment of her situation and the planning I undertook before starting the work. The actual process of the work, and my own and Marie's reaction to it, forms the main part of the commentary and I have concluded with an evaluation of my intervention and some thoughts for the future.

Family history

Marie was made a ward of court at birth following an application to the High Court by the local authority who had many concerns about her mother's ability to care for her. Rachel had neglected her first child, Ken, who despite intensive support to maintain him with his mother, had eventually been placed for adoption.

Contrary to all expectations Rachel cared well for Marie for the first two years of her life, during which time her progress was monitored by means of a supervision order to the local authority and through child protection procedures. However, after the birth of her second daughter, Esther, Rachel's standards began to fall; she frequently left the children with friends and did not see to their physical needs adequately. When they were with their mother they would be constantly moving from place to place, usually following violent rows between Rachel and whoever was her current partner.

Both were admitted to care after Rachel had left them for two weeks with an acquaintance who could no longer cope. The local authority obtained interim care of the children in wardship proceedings and they were placed locally with short-term foster parents.

Rachel showed little commitment to the plans to 'rehabilitate' the children to her care; her contact with them was erratic and she was abusive to and unco-operative with her social worker. She and Marie's father, Mark, abducted a friend's child and, following this incident, Marie and Esther were moved to another foster home ten miles away, the address of which has been withheld from Rachel. This move was the fifteenth change of home Marie had experienced in just over three years.

The children are still in this foster home where they will remain until more permanent plans are made for their future. Rachel has supervised contact with the children twice a week for an hour and a half at our Family Centre, and Mark has supervised contact with Marie once a month at our district office. A colleague and I are currently in the process of undertaking a full assessment, according to the Department of Heath Guide 'Protecting Children', as to whether restoration to their mother is still a viable plan for the children or whether a permanent separation should be recommended to the court. A two day hearing at the High Court has been listed.

Marie is a very attractive, well built child with dark hair and eyes. Her foster mother dresses her in pretty skirts and dresses, with slides and bows in her hair. She seems to be aware of and enjoys her physical attractiveness. She has consistently reached all her physical developmental milestones but at the time she was admitted to care she showed a slight delay in her speech.

I began my work with Marie when she had been with the foster family for four months. She had settled there very well and was extremely attached to her foster mother, although initially she had been rather indiscriminate in her affection towards adults, particularly men.

She occasionally exhibited sexualised play in this and the previous foster home, for example inserting small objects into her vagina, asking other children to lie on top of her. The possibility of sexual abuse had been raised when a tampon was found in her knickers whilst she was still in her mother's care. This was investigated at the time and no physical evidence of abuse was found.

Her foster mother described her as a generally happy child, although prone to sudden mood swings. She would also have bad tantrums over issues of discipline and control.

She was reluctant to talk about her mother and to a lesser extent her father, or her life before coming into care; and occasionally this reluctance was transmitted into action when she would refuse to get dressed and ready for contact visits.

Assessment and planning

My assessment and planning have been an ongoing process as new details have emerged in the course of my work. I outline here the assessment I made at the beginning of my work and the intervention I planned based on this.

Although there were clear indicators that Marie's past parenting had been poor in some respects, her ability to form new attachments and her minimal developmental delay were evidence that she had also had some good experience of parenting before care. Her tantrums and testing out behaviour were, however, indicators of the impact that an unsettled life had had upon her.

The 'loss' of her mother when she was admitted to care was obviously very confusing and painful to her and she seemed to be blocking this experience in order to cope with it. The second 'loss' of her first foster mother added to her insecurity and she was obviously troubled by the uncertainty of her current situation and the knowledge that this could not be a permanent home. She was particularly confused about the roles of different 'mummies' and 'daddies' in her life.

She was also presenting some possible behavioural indicators of sexual abuse through her play with peers and her provocative approaches to adult men.

This initial assessment helped me to identify the need for direct work with Marie around the following areas:

(1) Her personal history

(2) Her current situation 'in care'

(3) The roles of different mummies and daddies

(4) Exploring further the possibility of sexual abuse

In negotiating my intervention I was aware of my wider statutory role in relation to my assessment of the family. It was inevitable that I would gain information from Marie both about what her experiences in her own family had been before care and what her future needs might be. I also had to constantly bear in mind that Marie was a ward of court and that I would be obtaining evidence for the wardship proceedings. Also I might need the court's permission if a formal interview regarding sexual abuse was indicated.

Ideally I would have organised weekly sessions with Marie at our Family Centre which is familiar to her through her contact visits and where there are good play facilities. However, because of the distance from there to the foster home and the pressures already placed on the foster mother's time through twice weekly contact visits, I arranged fortnightly sessions in the foster home. The foster mother guaranteed that I would have sole use of the front room for these sessions. I also prepared a bag of toys and play material which I take with me for each session. This includes paper and crayons, pots of Playdoh, necklaces, bangles, shawls (for dressing up), a happy/sad doll, a complete family of little dolls and dolls furniture, a bag of plastic animals, cars, cups and saucers and a cuddly teddy. I planned to speak to the foster mother at the end of each session about particular themes she might be able to pick up on in the time between sessions and also to give me the opportunity to discover how Marie had reacted to our sessions.

I told Rachel of my planned work and have since kept her informed of themes that have emerged, particularly Marie's continuing sexual play. She has been involved with me in one session focused on

Marie's Life Story Book which was very successful and I plan to involve her in further sessions.

Process

I decided to organise each session into structured and unstructured parts. The main purpose of the structured time was to work on Marie's Life Story Book and to look at issues around her being in care. The unstructured time was for her to explore and get in touch with what she was feeling about her situation and to help me gain access to her internal world of needs and wishes in order to better understand and help her. I planned to be non-directive in my intervention during this time, allowing Marie to set the pace and agenda, an opportunity which she is not offered in any other setting. For the purposes of this commentary I have examined the development of each part separately although in practice they invariably overlapped.

The structured areas of my work were much more prominent in the earlier sessions when they provided both me and Marie with something concrete to share and communicate through. Marie was also more contained in these early sessions than the latter ones and more easily able to apply herself to a particular task. Her ability to trust me as our relationship has developed has enabled her to let go of this more co-operative helpful side of herself and to expose her more chaotic, angry feelings.

The making of a Life Story Book has been the main focus of my structured work. I have had no difficulty in obtaining photographs of Marie at different stages in her life from her mother, her previous and her current foster parents. We have spent time talking about the people in these pictures and what was happening to Marie when they were taken. Marie has responded to these pictures with great enthusiasm and has invariably wanted to refer to some if not all of them during each of my sessions with her. It was as if she needed to confirm that there is some order to her life and that she is important. I have also felt it important for me to acknowledge that there have been some good times in her life of which she has happy memories. She particularly enjoyed a session which I arranged jointly with her mother (Rachel) to look at pictures of when she lived with her own family. During this session Marie started by sharing each photograph with both me and Rachel, but as she became more engrossed in her memories of the time she spent with her mum she began to physically exclude me and cuddled up very close to her. This session felt warm and positive, and, by excluding me, Marie ensured that the painful memories she had of these times, which I am associated with, did not intrude.

She has occasionally excluded me from her play or made me feel not wanted during our sessions by telling me I'm not invited to her party or that her friends will hurt me. This may be her way of letting me experience some of the painful feelings she is defended against.

Another structured way of working has been to help Marie draw a map of her week. She has quite a hectic time with contact visits to her mum and to her dad and sessions with me, as well as attending playgroup and Sunday School. This map-making was an attempt to provide her with a visual plan of what happens each day. As with the Life Story Book she would frequently refer to this map at the beginning of sessions although her need for it has now diminished significantly.

I have found several of the techniques outlined in Ryan and Walker's book *Making Life Story Books* (1985) helpful, particularly the games of likes and dislikes, happy and sad faces and for work around Marie's birth certificate. We spent two sessions exploring the concept of the three parents (Fahlberg 1981) in a simple form, mainly relating to the difference between her own mum 'Birth Parent' and her foster mum 'Parenting Parent'. Marie became quite obsessed with the idea of new babies after I had shown her pictures of a baby developing in a woman's tummy and of herself as a newborn baby. This is a theme which has run fairly consistently through her unstructured play and which I will discuss in more depth later.

I found it useful whilst undertaking the unstructured work to analyse it in terms of:

(1) The themes which ran through the sessions

(2) Marie's reaction to the work and

(3) My own reactions and intervention.

I have therefore chosen this way to discuss the work here.

As I had expected, family relationships, particularly the roles of different mummies and daddies, have formed a significant part of the sessions. Interestingly, daddies have been referred to more often than mummies and Marie has often chosen to draw pictures of daddies. She always seemed quite relaxed and willing to talk about daddies, who perhaps felt less emotionally loaded than the subject of mummies. The only times she has become anxious or upset has been when we have discussed her sister Esther's dad, Phillip, who had lived with the family for some time. Marie found it difficult to hear that he was 'like a daddy' to her but was Esther's 'real' daddy and became angry when I talked of sending some photographs to 'Esther's dad'.

The subject of mummies has been more painful to Marie and she has been very reluctant to talk about her own mother. She has frequently explored the possibility of whether I might be a mummy for her, asking me about myself, where I live and who I live with. At other times she has used me to express some of both her angry and loving feelings towards her own mum, telling me of the awful things she will do to me or of all the things she wants to give me. This has obviously felt safer than expressing them directly about her own mum, although she has occasionally been able to do this saying she is cross with her or that she still loves her. Her strong attachment to her foster mother Betty and her fear of losing her has also been evident in her play. Most of her drawings have been drawn for Betty and she has regularly needed to leave the room to check that Betty has still been in the house, particularly during sessions that have been difficult for her. She has expressed her fear of losing Betty by projecting this anxiety on to her, in one session very poignantly stating 'My mummy Betty would be upset and cry if I went away.'

The theme of babies has been prominent since I started the work. Marie's obsession with babies seems to be a reflection of her wish to have all the love and continual contact with a mother that babies have. It is likely that she does have memories of her own babyhood which are good and that she is trying to recapture these good feelings. In several sessions she has cuddled up on my lap and asked me to rock her and sing to her and has then imitated sleep. It also seems linked to her struggle to work out who she is and where she belongs. She has often expressed amazement and disbelief that the pictures of her as a baby are actually herself.

From our early sessions together it became evident that Marie had had some experience of sexual matters. In four consecutive sessions she would go through the following ritual with the toy dolls, of placing the doll she labelled mummy on a toy bed, placing the doll labelled daddy on top of her, and then placing the bed on top of the television in the room. Initially she elaborated no further but later talked of daddy putting his willy in mummy. She has also drawn figures, who she has referred to as mummy, with large penises between their legs and in our most recent session made what she called a 'sausage' with the Playdoh but subsequently called a willy which she proceeded to lick.

Another theme has been that of monsters and fierce animals. Marie has either drawn monsters or chosen to play with a toy lion or bear, and has then referred to them as a good, nice monster who she would stroke herself and then ask me to stroke. This may be a reflection of her wish to control or deny the wild and angry parts of herself.

Marie quickly realised that our sessions were special times for the two of us to talk together. According to the foster mother she eagerly anticipates the sessions beforehand and she usually rushes into the room when I arrive. She has become quite angry if other children have been around in the foster home, pointing out to them that it is only she who comes into the room with me.

After a few sessions I began to try to establish which topics make her defensive. Talk of her own mother, being in care, and to a lesser extent mention of Phillip have invariably led to some form of avoidance. She has regularly left the room to show something to Betty, but has always made it clear to me before she left that she would be back and that I should not leave. Often, in order to drown out something painful that she thinks I might be about to say, she has started talking or even singing in a very loud voice. She has frequently resorted to quite bossy behaviour, telling me what to do so that she can control the subject matter. When this has failed she has physically stopped me from talking by climbing all over me and becoming aggressive. In one session she became so anxious that she started to throw all the toys and drawings I had with me around the room and was unable to hear my attempts to calm her.

Some of these sessions have been very difficult and upsetting for me and on leaving them I have questioned their value or have wondered if I have handled them badly. I have been helped through supervision to realise that the chaos and confusion I am feeling may be all part of Marie letting down her defences and exposing me to the pain and chaos she is feeling. I have had to guard against my own defences preventing me from hearing and feeling what Marie has been communicating to me.

I have endeavoured in my work with Marie to allow her to go at her own pace and have used the technique of reflecting back to her what she is saying in order to help her see things for herself. I have also been helped through supervision to identify the feelings Marie is expressing and to feed these back to her so that she is aware I am hearing and feeling what she is communicating. I have not always found this easy and at times have realised that I am hurrying her through things in order to fulfil my own agenda, or that I have intervened too quickly, thus stopping her train of thought.

Evaluation

My work with Marie is ongoing and I plan to see her until she is either settled back with her mother or in a permanent placement. This is therefore a midway evaluation which I am likely to modify and expand over time.

One thing of which I am confident is that my work has provided a regular 'space' however brief just for Marie. She usually has to fight for individual attention and time in the large, busy foster home; and during contact visits the demands which Esther, now a lively 21-month-old, places upon her mother, prevent her giving Marie much quiet time to herself. Marie has made it clear through her eagerness to get involved in our sessions, and by her statements to other children in the foster home about them, how important this time is to her.

I also think it has been important for her to know that there is someone who knows about all aspects of her life; in some ways I feel I am providing a 'bridge' between her foster home and her natural family. The scope of all these different people and their relationships to her must be difficult for her (at such a young age) to grasp. It is therefore important that I act as the container of all this information, to which Marie can have access when she needs it.

She is still reluctant to discuss her own mother and her past with her foster mother, perhaps through fear of upsetting the relationship she has with her. She does however increasingly share information from her Life Story Book with her in between our sessions, and I plan to involve the foster mother in some of our future sessions.

In terms of my overall intervention in the case and my planning for Marie's future, I feel the knowledge I have about her development and needs is invaluable. Whether she returns home or moves to an adoptive placement this knowledge will enable me to work with her future carers to ensure that her needs can be met.

The following issues have been important in my own learning.

(1) I am aware that many children in care, particularly if (like Marie) they are not currently presenting particular behavioural or management difficulties, are not offered help in their own right. This is partly due to pressures on social workers' time, and partly due to lack of confidence or fear of doing more harm than good. This help needs to be considered as a matter of course for all children who are in care for any length of time, and training and support should be available to those who do the work.

(2) I have become aware of the dilemma of balancing my role as Marie's worker against my wider role as key worker for the case. I have mentioned earlier the advantages of gaining information about Marie in terms of planning for her future. However, I am also aware that my role in decision making and planning for the whole case has occasionally made me anxious and less able to single out Marie's needs from all the other pressing concerns of the case.

(3) The length of time the legal process has taken has been a continual concern. Whilst the wardship proceedings have provided a flexible legal framework within which to manage the case, the length of time we have waited for a full hearing has certainly not been in either of the children's interests.

(4) I believe that having a clear theoretical framework within which to make sense of the work has been of great benefit to me. The insights I gained from supervision have helped me to make sense of what occasionally felt like total chaos! I very much hope I will have the time and opportunity to continue my learning in this area.

(5) Marie has been offered stability and love in her foster home which has enabled her to feel sufficiently secure and contained to address some of the upsetting things we have covered in our work. Without this the work would have been much more difficult, if not impossible.

The following case study presents a different situation from those of Emma and Marie. Where they have experienced constantly reconstituted family structures and frequent changes in the setting of their lives, Jane and Elizabeth were born to law abiding and – at first glance, at least – loyal and united parents. For this family, the tragic allegation of child abuse must be exceptionally stigmatising.

The case study, as recorded here, does not deal with the therapeutic work undertaken. Its purpose is, rather, to show how disturbance and unhappiness seem to be transmitted between the generations, and how unresolved difficulties in the past reverberate in the present. One feels great sorrow for the parents whose lives together steadily crumble into hopelessness and helplessness.

It was apparent in the cases of Emma and Marie that the social workers' own emotional stability was put at risk by the pain in the children's situation. What, one wonders, is the future of the Sheldon family? And have social workers the skills and resources available to them to rescue this family from hopelessness?

Jane (aged thirteen) and Lizzie (aged ten)

Family Composition

Father:	Christopher Sheldon
Mother:	Jacqueline Sheldon
Children:	Jane
	Elizabeth (known as Lizzie)

Family background

Mrs Sheldon is the eldest of seven children; her memories of childhood are in the main rejecting and unhappy. She had a strict mother who showed her little affection and she was expected to look after the home and her younger sisters and brothers all of whom were academically much more able than she was. Her general recollection is of a background with little warmth and of oppression from her mother, and frequent rows between her parents. She has been left with feelings of inadequacy, jealousy and with difficulties in expressing her real feelings.

Mr Sheldon, the elder of two sons, suffered because of his younger brother being very clever. He is slow and has difficulty in expressing himself. He also finds it difficult to socialise. He managed to complete mainstream education, but not easily. His mother, a highly strung and anxious woman, although kind and caring, was undemonstrative and may have found it hard to accept her son's shortcomings. Mr Sheldon's father is reported by a relative to be quiet and reserved and also undemonstrative. Mr Sheldon's influence with his daughters has been minimal and he took little part in their upbringing.

Mr and Mrs Sheldon and their parents are members of the Christadelphian Church and the couple met through the Christadelphian community. Mrs Sheldon until recently held strongly to the teachings of the church, one of which is that divorce and separation are unacceptable.

The family live in a three bedroomed terraced house.

Background since Jane's birth

After Jane's birth Mrs Sheldon suffered from post natal depression and was an in-patient in a psychiatric unit. Concern was expressed by the hospital social worker about her inappropriate handling of Jane during the first year. There were long term feeding difficulties and Mrs Sheldon told the social worker that she had been smacking Jane. Jane was made the subject of a care order on the grounds that her proper development was being impaired. She was removed from home and placed in a residential nursery. With regular visiting and social work support it was felt that Jane could return to her parents. She continued to remain the subject of a care order which is still in force. She lived at home for three months and then was temporarily placed in a foster home by the Social Services Department. This came about because of serious concern about her disturbed, distressed behaviour and because of suspicion that she had been sexually abused. One month later Mrs Sheldon miscarried but although depressed she was able, with family and professional support, to avoid hospital admission. When Lizzie was born, Mrs Sheldon again suffered from post natal depression for which she was treated on an out-patient basis. With this and family support she managed to cope and both daughters remained at home.

As the girls grew older and the family problems lessened, the Social Services Department reduced their contact. However, four years ago Mrs Sheldon was reported by her health visitor as not coping and there were marital difficulties. Mr and Mrs Sheldon, from the outset of their marriage, had frequent rows in which Mr Sheldon resorted to violence. Mrs Sheldon left her husband for a short time and took the girls to a Women's Refuge. This is the only time she has left the marital home.

Three years ago, with Mr and Mrs Sheldon's agreement, the Social Services Department applied for Jane's Care Order to be revoked; but on investigation during the next few months new grounds for concern arose regarding Jane. Her behaviour was by now becoming uncontrollable, she was touching people inappropriately, her eating habits were described as repulsive, she was pulling her hair out. She presented as a very unhappy child, who showed an increasing preoccupation with sex.

Mr and Mrs Sheldon and the paternal grandparents blamed the school for her problems.

The problems continued and eventually Mr and Mrs Sheldon were persuaded that it would be in Jane's interests to spend a period in a foster home; but the paternal grandparents were very opposed to this idea.

Within two weeks of being in a foster family Jane began to disclose details of experiences of being sexually abused and stated that her sister Elizabeth had also been sexually abused by their father.

Elizabeth

Two years ago, following a strategy meeting which involved the mother and the local authority, it was decided that a Place of Safety Order (Sect 1 CYPA 1969) should be taken to protect Lizzie. A medical examination revealed no evidence of sexual abuse, neither did discussion with Lizzie, who completely denied that any abuse had taken place.

Lizzie was placed with foster parents and was made the subject of a Care Order CYPA 1969 Section 1(a) last year.

Lizzie is an attractive, frequently smiling ten-year-old who chats away in a friendly manner, but who also finds it difficult to communicate feelings about herself and her family. She seems a happy outgoing child whose behaviour is more like a six or seven year old.

Lizzie's mother has always admitted to a closer relationship with Lizzie than with Jane, but still found her management hard to cope with. At home Lizzie was stubborn, had tantrums, 'anything to get her own way' which she usually did and often to the exclusion of Jane.

Lizzie received mainstream education until she was aged seven, when she was admitted to a special school, because of emotional and behavioural problems. Her behaviour was described as attention-seeking, unable to settle or concentrate. On admission to the special school her behaviour deteriorated and she displayed tantrums, kicking, scratching, tearing things off the walls, turning tables over and screaming.

Her language skills were poor and she was functioning at about three years behind her chronological age. Her progress was very slow indeed.

Lizzie settled in her foster home apparently easily and her foster mother experienced the usual kinds of difficulties with a child of this age, but nothing like the school had experienced, until she took Lizzie on holiday last year. From that time Lizzie produced tantrums, fighting, screaming, stubbornness, jealousy and unpredictability. The foster mother has managed Lizzie with patience and understanding, control, kindness and a lot of talk and explanation to which Lizzie has responded.

Lizzie has had regular supervised visits from her mother apart from a period last summer when her mother was staying with her parents. The relationship is friendly, but Mrs Sheldon finds it hard to concentrate on Lizzie and constantly wants to talk about her own problems.

I visit Mrs Sheldon fortnightly to work with her on her relationships with the children, as well as supporting her through this difficult time – of losing her children and both she and Mr Sheldon being charged with offences against the girls.

Family

Mr and Mrs Sheldon's marital relationship is dysfunctional and the boundaries between the family members are unclear. Mrs Sheldon relates to both her children more as a sister than a mother and when she tried to take on the 'mother' role found herself ineffectual. She was also jealous if any attention was given to the girls by their father. Minuchin (1974) describes intergenerational boundary confusion where a passive, dependent mother is replaced in child rearing activities by the oldest daughter, who is being molested by the father. Practitioners not infrequently report incest victims taking on a maternal role in the family.

Mrs Sheldon talks about having escaped from her own family where she describes herself as being a 'skivvy' only to find herself in the same situation in her marriage, with a dominating, uncommunicative husband – a relationship with no freedom for outside friends and activities. Mrs Sheldon found the sexual demands that her husband made of her embarrassing and unwelcome, lacking in warmth and intimacy and she consequently rejected him.

Victims

As previously stated, Mrs Sheldon was unable to relate to her daughters as a 'mother' and both girls took on a kind of parenting role, particularly Lizzie, who was the brighter and less disturbed of the two girls. Mrs Sheldon was not close to her daughters and was unable to express any emotion towards them. Neither was Mr Sheldon able to show affection for his daughters.

Jane and Lizzie therefore felt unsupported; their mother was a passive partner in an abusive situation.

Mother

From my conversations with Mrs Sheldon and the girls it seems that she was to some extent a participant in the abuse although she actually denies this. She is a dependent woman who tolerated abuse, sexual and physical, from her husband, and was unable to protect her children, because her own needs were so great that she could not threaten to leave him.

Mrs Sheldon was unable to give either her husband or daughters a nurturing relationship and this may have caused husband and daughters to turn to each other.

The damage

Child sexual abuse violates the dependent relationship with parents, causing confusion of roles and boundaries.

It also reflects an abuse of power – how can children give informed 'consent' when they are not knowledgeable about sexual relationships? Child victims of sexual abuse show considerable anxiety – they may sexualise all their relationships, as Jane did. They may have difficulties in giving and receiving love, and lack confidence. The consequences of disclosure can be also very damaging, when, as a result of telling what has happened to them, they are removed

> from their families, their security is lost, they feel responsible for what has happened, and they feel responsible for the prosecution of their parents.
>
> Mrs Sheldon is likely to remain with her husband, who is currently awaiting trial, first because her needs for dependency are great, and because of pressure from both sides of the family to preserve the marriage.

This section ends sadly – perhaps not inappropriately, as it deals with problems and needs for which our therapeutic skills are insufficiently developed and for which the resources of our services remain inadequate.

Yet, as the cases of Emma and Marie demonstrate, helpful work *is* possible, if the interest, empathy and imaginative activities of social workers can be developed and fostered.

The need for supportive and clear-headed supervision is an essential part of this development. So also are the opportunities for training and reflection. So also is the time allocation which these children and parents certainly require. In these cases, the social workers have demonstrated that, with careful planning, short-term intervention of an intensive kind has a valuable contribution to make. But if social work is simply reduced to dealing with *immediate* crises, and if task-centred work and assessment procedures are divorced from imaginative empathy, then our services for abused children will get worse rather than better. Sadly, the current climate of (assumed) economic rationalism is a world apart from the feelings and needs of the people we meet in this chapter.

This chapter ends with a fourth case study which illustrates some of the difficulties involved in the investigation of alleged abuse. In this case, the children involved as 'victim' and 'abuser' and their investigating social worker are of Asian origins. Certain dilemmas of professional practice become apparent as the case unfolds: in particular, the problem of combining an investigative role with a helping role – work with the girl successfully manages this tension, but the difficulties become acute with the boy and, as the social worker would be the first to acknowledge, it was not possible to fulfil either role to her satisfaction because of the underlying conflict of purpose. Second, the case illustrates the difficulties of working even-handedly with two children whose accounts of events are radically in disagreement. Third, in view of the age of the boy, how rigorously should he be investigated and prosecuted? (Significantly, the police preferred not to pursue the case, and the dilemma was therefore left wholly with the social worker.) The case raises fundamental issues about defining 'seriousness' if social workers are to avoid automatic/bureaucratic responses to referrals. Finally, given that the boy was making excellent progress at school and was highly resistant to the social worker's intervention, the case raises the question whether social workers should pursue hidden family matters, or professional judgements of a child's underlying unhappiness, when either course may lead to increased stress for both child and family. When, in matters of sexual abuse or misbehaviour, should social workers let sleeping dogs lie?

The following case material sets out the process of work in the social worker's own words, but, for editorial reasons and the interests of ensuring confidentiality, the work with the boy has been greatly shortened.

Vijaya (aged five) and Mohammed (aged thirteen)

Introduction

Vijaya is a five-year-old Asian girl. She has stated to her mother (Mrs Chopra) that, whilst being cared for by her childminder, Mrs Akram, she has been playing a 'dick game' with Mrs Akram's son Mohammed who is thirteen years old.

Mrs Akram referred the matter to Social Services Department because she was concerned about how this incident could affect her childminding. Mrs Akram does not believe her child could have done this. Mrs Chopra is firm that Vijaya is telling the truth. Mrs Akram was then suspended from childminding until further notice. Vijaya was now at school: she had been given a school place earlier than had been planned.

Initial negotiation of work

There was a delay of a month before this case was allocated due to a lack of resources in terms of social workers available. A multi-disciplinary planning meeting had already been held, before I became the allocated worker. It had been decided that Vijaya should be interviewed regarding her statement to her mother. It was felt that, because Vijaya is a very young child, she should be interviewed in the presence of an appropriate adult with whom she would feel safe. It was decided that she should be interviewed by a social worker with her mother. The police would observe the session and take notes for statement purposes. The interview would be video taped and could also be used for evidential purposes.

In attempting to negotiate a multi-disciplinary approach, I found the police were unwilling to become involved. I had telephoned to discuss the case with the officer involved and to arrange an appointment to introduce ourselves jointly to the family. However, the manager of the Police Child Protection Team at that time decided that they would not be observing the session or making separate enquiries themselves.

My feelings were that the police did not wish to be involved, because they did not agree with Vijaya's mother being present during the interview. I have found, in carrying out joint interviews with the police, that they have invariably refused to allow the non-abusing carer, who is being supportive to their child, to be present. I do not think they were happy with not being directly involved with interviewing Vijaya. However, this was never actually stated by them as a problem and I did not suggest this was the case.

I endeavoured to negotiate these issues further via the Child Protection Centre and my Line Manager. Negotiations produced no response from the police. Another four weeks of negotiations passed without results. I therefore decided to go ahead and begin the work, advising my manager of this, who agreed.

We also agreed that a second social worker would be made available to observe and take notes.

Purpose of work

To investigate Vijaya's statement to her mother and suspicions that she could have been sexually abused. To assess what, if any, further social work intervention is required. To engage Vijaya in direct work in order to explore her experiences. To offer assistance, advice and support to Vijaya and her mother in meeting their needs.

Methods used

In negotiating the work with Vijaya's mother, I felt a number of issues would need to be addressed before this work could begin. I therefore planned initially to clarify issues of confidentiality, video recording, Mrs Chopra's involvement in the work and the methods to be used.

Mrs Chopra was reluctant to have her daughter videoed and refused consent. She was concerned because she did not wish a video to be used in legal proceedings against Mohammed, whom she saw as only a child himself. She was concerned about the possibility of the police becoming involved, given that a referral had already been made to them.

Mrs Chopra was reluctant to be a part of the interview, as Vijaya had become very distressed whenever she had tried to question her about the 'dick game'. Mrs Chopra did not feel that her presence in the interview room would help to reassure Vijaya and make her feel safe. Vijaya had been unwilling to talk further about what had happened and worried that she had been 'naughty'.

Whilst I accepted that Mrs Chopra's anxiety could affect Vijaya's ability to talk openly, I felt the planning meeting had already decided how the interview should be conducted. This did not take into account that Vijaya may or may not want her mother to be present. I decided to ask Vijaya who she wanted with her when she came to see me. I felt she should be given some degree of control over how our sessions would be conducted and should not be put in a position of having to fit in with our agenda.

Mrs Chopra and I then planned to carry out a series of sessions with Vijaya. The initial session would be to introduce myself and get to know her. This would be followed by a series of sessions to engage her in direct work to carry out the assessment as outlined earlier. Mrs Chopra agreed to my doing whatever work was necessary, with her present in the office. She agreed to be present during the interview if Vijaya decided she wanted this. She also agreed that if she were present, she would avoid asking Vijaya questions about the abuse, and leave these questions to me.

Direct work

On introducing myself to Vijaya, I found her to be an outgoing, talkative and lively little girl. She was excited about seeing my playroom and agreed to seeing me a few times to talk about how things had been in general. She told me she enjoyed playing with her dolls, skipping, painting (favourite activity), drawing, reading books and making things. I suggested I get some paints so that we could do some painting when she came to see me.

Vijaya confirmed that she wanted her mum to come with her but decided she would see me on her own. I therefore agreed to this, with her mum near to the playroom, in case she wanted her for anything.

On the day of the interview, Vijaya's father arrived to observe with her mother. He told me that he would be taking notes of the interview. This had not been planned when I had introduced myself to Vijaya.

In this situation, it is harder to address the issue of how the child feels about their parents being able to see them. There are issues of whether I can be regarded as an appropriate adult during an interview, whilst at the same time investigating allegations of sexual abuse. Non-abusing parents often and quite rightly demand that they be involved in what is happening to their child. I felt Mr Chopra had a right as a parent to request that he too was involved. Quite often involving the parent in the work helps them to believe what has happened. I therefore asked Mr Chopra to take notes on my behalf. He was pleased to be able to help.

I think it is better to set clear boundaries of confidentiality to the child, whilst wherever possible affording the child as much privacy as possible. However, Vijaya raised this issue herself during the process of the interview.

Before beginning the session I showed Vijaya the room where her mother and father would be observing our play session and explained they would be able to see and hear us. I later pointed to the cameras in the playroom and briefly explained their use. In my experience I have found many children ask what the cameras in the playroom are for, so it is simpler to address this before the session begins.

Vijaya began the session by painting a house and we began exploring whose houses she goes to. We moved on to talking about 'Aunty Shenaz's' house where Mohammed lives. Vijaya blocked my attempts to find out the reasons why she should not visit Aunty Shenaz again, why Mohammed was a 'bad' boy and what Mohammed did. She moved on to other activities, such as my reading Spot the Dog book to her and singing ABCDEF, when she was feeling unsafe and blocking me.

She decided she wanted to play with the dolls and pulled the anatomically correct dolls out of a box. This proved to be very threatening to Vijaya: she requested me not to undress the boy doll. During this part of play she told me that the little girl doll wanted her mummy. I asked if I should get her mummy. She agreed and so I left the room to get Mrs Chopra to join the session. Soon after her mother arrived, Vijaya described how Mohammed had sexually abused her over a protracted period of time. The following is a verbatim account of the interview. (These notes were taken by Mr Chopra.)

V: (*Draws a house.*)

SW: Whose houses do you go to?

V: We go to Aunty A's,

SW: What about Aunty B? Do you go there?

V: She likes me; Aunty B was my childminder.

SW: Is she still?

V: No.

SW: Why?

V: Because he might do it again.

SW: Who might?

V: Mohammed.

SW: Are you going to tell me what he did?

V: I'll tell you later.

SW: Who looks after you now?

V: Aunty C.

SW: So you used to go to Aunty B a lot?

V: Shall I draw Aunty B's house?

SW: Yes, what colour is her door?

V: Brown. (*She mixes the paints and then paints the colour brown onto her door.*)

SW: Where is Aunty B's house?

V: It's near our house.

SW: Is it hard to talk about Mohammed?

V: Yes.

SW: Why is it hard?

V: Because it is very bad.

SW: What's bad?

V: (*Talks about painting again.*)

SW: Don't you go and see them?

V: Can my dad see me?

SW: Does it matter if he sees you? What would he say about it?

V: He would say don't go back there, he might do it again.

SW: Where do you normally stay?

V: What? Where I sleep?

SW: Where do you sleep?

V: In her bed. Shall we draw someone in the living room?

SW: Yes, who?

V: Aunty B.

SW: What happened when you told Aunty B or mummy about Mohammed?

V: Mummy told her.

SW: Why didn't you tell her?

V: Because I was scared. (*She decided to draw Aunty B wearing a green and red sari.*)

SW: Who else does Aunty B live with?

V: Her husband.

SW: What is his name?

V: S – I just made it up.

SW: Where shall I draw S?

V: In his bedroom.

SW: Where is his bedroom?

V: There (*points to top room*). This is Mohammed and Mohammed's bedroom.

SW: Who shall we draw next?

V: Mohammed and Tariq.

SW: Who first?

V: Mohammed. (*She paints Mohammed into the picture.*)

SW: What did you tell your mummy about Mohammed?

V: (*Begins singing ABCDE.*)

SW: Are you scared?

V: Is mummy and daddy looking?

SW: Does it matter?

V: I want them to look.

SW: When mummy told Aunty B, what happened?

V: I cried and my mummy rang me up. I want to start school in June not September.

SW: So you were crying when your mummy told B? Do you know why you came here today?

V: Yes, to talk about Mohammed. My mum told me to say everything about the truth.

SW: Do you know the difference between a good secret and a bad secret? I think it is important to know. Let me explain a good secret – if you were going to get a nice present for mum, would you tell her?

V: No.

SW: What's a bad secret?

V: If J was fighting and I didn't tell someone.

SW: Yes, so you know the difference between a good and a bad secret. What did your mum want you to talk to me about?

V: I want to do a puzzle game.

        (*I then did an ABC puzzle with her.*)

V: What's that? (*pointing to Spot the Dog book.*)

SW: Shall I read it to you?

V: Yes.

        (*We read Spot the Dog book.*)

SW: Shall we play houses now?

        (*V pulls anatomically correct dolls from the big basket.*)

SW: Who is that?

V: Aunty B, L, Granddad, Mohammed.

SW: Shall we play houses?

V: You are my daughter and I am the mum, what shall I do? It's to do with Mohammed.

SW: *(SW play acting at being V.)* Guess what Mohammed did.

V: *(No response.)*

SW: What do you think I want to tell you, mum?

V: Did Mohammed hit you?

SW: Something else has upset me.

V: Can you tell me what it is?

SW: I am unhappy.

V: I can make you better. What's the matter?

SW: Mohammed.

V: Have you been fighting? What has he done?

SW: I am not sure, I don't know how to explain it. He definitely upset me in his house, what do you think he did?

V: Did he hit you? Did he throw a drink on you?

SW: I think you know what happened, can you tell me?

V: You be the little girl, I'll be the doctor. The little girl is not well, so the little girl is at hospital.

SW: Can you tell the nurse what is wrong?

V: I want to go to my mummy.

SW: I am going to get mummy. *(I then went downstairs to get V's mum.)* Here's the little girl's mum. You were a bit scared.

Mum: When was the first time Mohammed upset you?

V: When we were on holiday. First he was trying to put it in my mouth and trying to kiss me on the lips.

SW: What was he trying to put in your mouth?

V: His dick.

SW: Who was that?

V: Mohammed.

SW: What does a dick look like?

V: I don't remember.

SW: Shall I show you a doll? (*I then showed V an anatomically correct doll, and asked her to name the parts of the body.*)

V: Nose, hand, the head, is that the dick?

SW: Did Mohammed put his dick in your mouth?

V: Yes.

SW: When was this?

V: No response

SW: Where did he put his dick in your mouth?

V: In the living room and in the bedroom.

SW: Where was Aunty B?

V: In the garden.

SW: How often did he do it?

V: Millions of times.

SW: When you say millions, what do you mean?

V: Monday, Tuesday, Wednesday, Friday.

SW: What about Thursday?

V: Everyday.

SW: What Mohammed did was naughty.

V: He thought he could do it and no-one would say anything. I told him when he kept doing it, if you do it I will tell my mum. He said he would put poo on my hair, and I said no you won't.

SW: Did he try to do anything else?

V: In the toilet, he tried to come in the toilet when I was in there.

SW: Did anything happen in the toilet?

V: No.

SW: What about when mum told Aunty B?

V: I did not want her to tell Aunty B.

SW: We can stop him from doing it again.

Mum: How long did it go on for? Was it since you began school?

V: Mohammed came into the bedroom when I was in bed. (*She then stated the word penis.*)

Mum: Where did you learn penis from?

V: No response.

SW: Did he put his penis into your mouth?

V: He wanted me to suck it.

SW: How old were you?

V: I was four.

Mum: Was it before you started school?

V: It was in the holidays. It was only when I was going to school. He kissed me on my lips. He did not like me.

SW: You've been a very good and brave girl.

V: I thought I would get told off, I thought I was naughty.

SW: I told V that she has not been naughty and would not be told off. (*Reassures that she has been a brave girl to tell what happened to her.*) We then talked of how good she is to talk about these things, especially as Mohammed had threatened to put poo in her hair. I told her that it was a bad secret because if she had kept this a secret he would have carried on doing what he was doing. V said she was glad she had told her mum, because now it has stopped and 'he won't be able to do it to anybody else'.

It was important at this stage to contain Mrs Chopra's reaction, whose facial expressions clearly showed she was shocked. She began asking a number of questions in succession. The questions were also leading in attempting to establish when, where and how often this had happened, I gave non-verbal cues, for example shaking my head to indicate to stop and she backed off and reduced the pressure Vijaya was under.

It was important to see Mr and Mrs Chopra separately from Vijaya after the interview. Mr Chopra was shocked by Vijaya's disclosures and Mrs Chopra was distressed and in tears. They had not realised the extent of what had happened to their child and the seriousness of what Mohammed had done. It was essential to offer support to help them contain their feelings about Vijaya's experiences in front of her, especially as she had been concerned about being naughty. I arranged to meet them again to discuss further work with Vijaya, to help her work through her experiences.

Negotiation of further work

I planned to carry out further work with Vijaya to make sense of what had happened to her. It was important within this framework to address issues of secrets, her body and how to say no to uncomfortable or inappropriate touching.

All this work was done with the involvement of Vijaya's mother. I used as open ended an approach as possible. Within this framework, I utilised a mixture of stories from books, what was happening in the room at the time, drama and drawings. All of this work was carried out in Vijaya's own home.

The initial session was to reinforce Vijaya's understanding of the difference between a good and a bad secret. She established that keeping secrets such as surprise birthday presents, surprise parties, magic tricks and so on was OK. She was clear that keeping secrets such as someone hurting someone else, for example bullying at school, cruelty to animals, or stealing, fighting and what Mohammed did was not OK. We also established that some things are never kept secret, for example hugs, kisses, holding someone's hand, sitting on someone's knee, being washed, dressed.

We moved on to reinforce again that keeping what Mohammed was doing to her a secret was bad because it enabled him to continue to do what he did to her. She was able to realise how he was not able to carry out his threats of putting poo in her hair because she had broken the secret by telling her mum. She realised that by telling someone she likes and trusts, her mum could now make sure that Mohammed was kept away from her. Vijaya imagined that the policeman would tell Mohammed off and stop him from doing it to anyone else.

The second session was concerned with appropriate and inappropriate touching. During this session Vijaya's younger brother Rajan was present. When I arrived, he was climbing on her back and trying to sit on her and she was telling him to get off. I used this to discuss what she could do if Rajan ignored her and carried on climbing all over her. Vijaya was clear that she would tell her mum and get away from him.

We then explored different forms of touch that occur at different times of the day and on different occasions, for example washing/bathing, dressing/undressing, holding hands, hugs, kisses, tickling, being smacked, fighting with other children. We talked about these forms of touch never being kept a secret.

We explored situations such as when anyone has asked for a kiss and she did not want to give them a kiss or someone was tickling her too hard and she wants them to stop. We practised saying no in different ways, for example by saying NO clearly, or shouting NO or GET OFF/AWAY, running away, shouting, screaming, getting angry and making a big fuss if necessary. She was clear that she would tell her mother immediately.

We moved on to discuss the possibility of threatening situations with people she knows and with strangers. Vijaya thought of people she could tell when her mum is not there. We listed adults that she likes and trusts amongst her aunties, uncles, grandparents and friends' mums and dads. We also explored how she could tell her dad if she was not happy about something her mum had done or said and vice versa.

Dealing with strangers was quite a tricky subject as, whilst it is important to encourage her to be wary of strangers, there could be occasions when she may well need the help of a stranger. We thought of safe strangers she could seek help from, such as a policeman, supermarket cashier, a shopkeeper, a lollipop lady/man, traffic warden. We reinforced that in this situation as well as normally she should never allow strangers to take her away in their car, or a walk to the park. We reinforced that it would be safe to go into a big shop or supermarket or talk to an official person in uniform, whom she sees in the street. We also talked about finding a phone box and ringing 999 for emergency help in a serious or urgent situation.

I ended this session by reinforcing her learning that no-one can get away with threats to force her to do anything that upsets/hurts her if she tells someone she trusts. Vijaya was clear about who she could get immediate help from at the end of this session.

The final session was aimed at saying goodbye to Vijaya and her mother. I gave some photocopies of literature for parents to Mrs Chopra to promote her knowledge and awareness of sexual abuse and protecting her children.

Vijaya was a little upset because she could not understand that I would not see her again. She wanted me to come to her birthday party and it was difficult to say I would not be able to come. I suggested that, as her birthday was still a few months away, she should invite me nearer to the date. I pointed out if she remembered to invite me then I would get permission to come. She agreed.

Evaluation

In attempting to incorporate a non-directive approach to this work, I found myself limited in how non-directive I could be with Vijaya. It was difficult to approach the work without having my own agenda, given the nature of the referral and my obligation to meet agency requirements. It is better to be honest from the start with children as to why we are here.

The direct work with Vijaya and her mother was in itself relatively straightforward. The opportunity to include parents from the very beginning, at the point of referral, is not usual. This is because of the conflict between the roles of different agencies in investigation. Quite often investigation becomes aimed at getting sufficient evidence for criminal proceedings and this in itself creates pressure on the child to 'disclose' to strangers. I do not think that Vijaya would have told me of her experiences so early without the reassurance of her mother's presence. This was evident in how quickly, after her mother had arrived in the interview room, she was able to share her secrets. However, for the purposes of criminal evidence, Mrs Chopra's presence could be construed as instrumental in Vijaya disclosing abuse, because she could have been 'primed' by her mother.

I believe that, if we are to be concerned with helping children to be as safe as possible to share their secrets, we must be able to give them the choice of whom they want with them, before we can expect them to share painful and difficult experiences.

The involvement of Vijaya's mother was important, as is the case for many young children. Mrs Chopra's involvement helped her child to feel safe enough to give details of her assault. Mrs Chopra was able to become more fully aware of the extent of her child's experiences. She was able to think about how to protect and advise her child. Mrs Chopra told me that she had learnt a lot from the sessions about advising her children of the facts of life and how to get help in abusive/ dangerous situations. She decided to purchase the books I used, so that she could teach Rajan when he is old enough to understand. He is only three years old at present. She was also grateful for other literature I gave to her.

This was a very important stage, in terms of Vijaya's development, as most five-year-olds are beginning to be more self reliant and independent. Her feelings that Mohammed did not like her came directly from her experiences of being abused by him. Her experiences have undoubtedly had a major impact on her feelings of security whilst being cared for by someone outside her family. This may delay her ability to put her trust and faith in others and could deter her from wanting to explore new people and places as a result of her experiences of sexual abuse. My work helped her to understand a little more about what had happened to her. She is lucky to have a supportive and nurturing home environment and protective parents, who have contributed significantly to her wellbeing. I believe that my work was effective because of Mrs Chopra's involvement and commitment. In working with both mother and child, I was able to equip Vijaya with the information she needed to be able to protect herself and, it is hoped, to enable her to be as safely independent as possible. There is now less chance of her tolerating abuse for a protracted period of time.

Work with Mohammed

Introduction

Mohammed is a 13-year-old Bangladeshi Muslim boy.

Mr and Mrs Akram met Vijaya's parents to discuss Vijaya's allegations that Mohammed had forced her to play a 'dick game'. Mrs Akram was distressed about the meeting, which had resulted in an argument. Mohammed had been confronted in front of Mr and Mrs Chopra. He had begun speaking in Bengali to his parents and denied playing this game. He refused to have eye contact with Mr and Mrs Chopra.

Mrs Akram did not believe that Mohammed could have initiated such a game with Vijaya. She was angry that her son is being accused of this. She was concerned how this could affect her position as a childminder.

Mrs Akram was suspended from childminding, pending further investigation into the allegations.

Negotiation of multidisciplinary work

Following Vijaya's disclosure that she had been abused by Mohammed, I attempted to contact the Police to negotiate further joint intervention. They were of the view that Mohammed should be interviewed in a taped interview setting, at the Police station, and that the most appropriate adult to represent him at the interview would be one of his parents. I was of the opinion that, if Mohammed was interviewed in such a setting, he would be more concerned with not getting into trouble with the Police than with telling the truth. I did not think that the interview rooms in the local Police station were an appropriate venue. I did not think it was appropriate that Mohammed should be processed as any suspected juvenile offender would be.

I pointed out my concerns of the possibility that Mohammed could also have been a victim of sexual abuse. Whilst the Police were clearly aware of this possibility, they thought any abuse he could have suffered as a victim could be addressed whilst he was being interviewed about his offences. I suggested that it would be unlikely for Mohammed to disclose abuse he could have suffered in such a threatening atmosphere.

I suggested that if the Police wished to treat Mohammed as an offender then they afford him the same rights in terms of proper legal counsel. I suggested that Mr and Mrs Akram may not be fully aware of his legal rights and that he be afforded a solicitor. They were emphatic that they did not think it necessary for Mohammed to have a solicitor and that one of his parents would suffice, despite possible language difficulties. They insisted that Mr and Mrs Akram should decide whether or not one of them would be part of the interview.

I suggested that I would advise Mr and Mrs Akram that it could be in their son's best interest to have a solicitor present. The Police officer did not agree with my intended action and it was clear that our negotiations were getting nowhere. So I suggested the convening of another management meeting to iron out these issues before any interviews were carried out by either agency. It took almost another four weeks to arrange this meeting, thus causing further delay.

In the meantime the under-eights worker responsible for dealing with Mrs Akram's childminding registration repeatedly brought these delays to my attention and her anxieties for the investigation to be expedited so that issues around registration could also be dealt with.

It was agreed that the best way forward would be for Mohammed to be jointly interviewed by a Police officer and myself. We agreed that the interview could take place at a special suite especially designed for children and families, in a different Police station, outside the borough. It was agreed that a joint home visit to Mr and Mrs Akram would be made by myself and a Police officer. Following this a joint videotaped interview would be held. It was agreed that Mohammed would be afforded access to a solicitor. A Bengali-speaking interpreter would be provided in case Mohammed was to revert to speaking in Bengali when confronted about the allegation.

Subsequently, the police withdrew from the case before any interviews were undertaken.

Purpose of work

I planned to gather as much information as possible about Mohammed. This work was in part an investigation into the allegations made against him. I intended also to carry out a series of sessions with him to get more specific details of his sexual development, within a general framework of exploring his life experiences. Clearly there was a possibility of his having learnt this behaviour from his own life experiences.

Negotiation of work with Mr and Mrs Akram

It was important to achieve Mr and Mrs Akram's agreement and support to carrying out further work with Mohammed. To aid communication I used a Bengali-speaking interpreter whom I met beforehand to discuss the intended visit.

My negotiation with Mr and Mrs Akram was initially problematic. It was clear that issues about how the work should be done with Mohammed had to be sorted out before this could begin. Mr and Mrs Akram were relieved that the police had subsequently taken a decision not to be involved.

Mr and Mrs Akram were concerned about my contacting his school as this could affect Mohammed's school record. He was an extremely bright student and had won a government-assisted place to attend a private fee-paying school. As I felt it was important to get the cooperation and involvement of Mohammed's parents, if the work I had planned could be carried out, I agreed to hold back from contacting his school, on the basis that they showed me Mohammed's school reports. Mohammed's reports showed he was a well-behaved, quiet boy. His educational achievement was good for his age and the class he was in.

Initially, Mr and Mrs Akram did not believe the allegations made against their son. They thought that Mohammed was a good Muslim boy who would never lie. One of the most important Muslim values is to tell the truth, which they believed he had told. They emphasised that they had confronted Mohammed repeatedly about what Vijaya had alleged and told him he would not get into trouble, provided he told the truth. Mohammed has repeatedly denied that he ever did what was alleged. They thought that Vijaya had made it up and had got the idea from the TV, family relatives, other children or her parents.

I commented that I had experienced working with other teenagers who had committed such offences and how common denial is. I challenged their views that this behaviour was impossible within a Muslim culture. After a lengthy discussion, they were prepared to consider the possibility that young teenagers, whatever their culture, could be capable of initiating such activities. They then became very concerned that, if Mohammed had done this, they did not want him to have a criminal record. On the other hand, they felt he should be confronted and told off and would need 'help to sort out his brain'.

They agreed that I carry out a series of individual sessions with Mohammed. This would include an initial session to introduce myself and get to know him. Then I could clarify why we are here and challenge/confront him about the allegations. Depending on the outcome of this, the following sessions would be aimed at examining his life experiences and general development. Within this framework, I intended to get more specific details of his sexual development.

Mohammed was described as a hardworking, studious boy who has never been in trouble at school for anything. He was a quiet boy who had had a stutter as a young child, for which he had received speech therapy. This had improved. Mrs Akram said that this was hereditary, as her brother had similar problems as a child, which he grew out of.

Direct work

During the first introductory session Mohammed was extremely wary when I introduced myself. He stated he did not know who I was or why I had come to visit, despite his mother having informed him of the purpose of my intended visit before my arrival. He seemed anxious and I noticed a slight stutter in his voice. However, he later seemed more relaxed and stuttered less.

After explaining that my visit was so that we could arrange an appointment to discuss the incident with Vijaya, he immediately defended himself, repeatedly stating 'she's telling lies'. I reassured him that he would get an opportunity to discuss this at a proper time and place and I did not want to begin talking about it on our first meeting.

I then outlined our work together and he agreed that I visit him once more at home when we could get to know each other and then we would see each other at my office for a series of sessions to discuss Vijaya and how things have been in general.

I clarified issues of confidentiality: that, whilst our work was private and would not be shared with other people, if anything of concern came up about his safety or wellbeing, I would be sharing this with either of his parents, depending on which parent he was happy for me to tell. I reassured him that if there was anything that had to be shared, then I would discuss this with him first, before we both discussed this with the adult of his choice. Mohammed confirmed he was happy with this arrangement.

During my second session we explored what he liked doing and his friends. I found him to be isolated. He told me he had no friends who lived locally, with whom he mixed socially. His only pastimes were playing on his computer, watching Star Trek videos and doing his homework. He showed me some of his favourite computer games. He shared these activities with his brother Tariq. Mohammed felt he did not 'care anymore' about not having friends. Anyway, if he did have friends he would not want them to use his computer in case it should get broken. He felt he had got used to being on his own.

I asked Mohammed if he enjoyed drawing; he only enjoyed isometric drawings. It was difficult to find a creative channel through which he could communicate, since I am limited in my knowledge of how to use the office computers to facilitate his communication. On offering him a blank piece of paper and a large range of felt tips to draw his family and where he fits in, he preferred to write things down with a pencil. I therefore used this as the main medium of direct work.

The third and fourth sessions were aimed at dealing with the allegations. I asked him to clarify why we were here and he responded 'That's obvious' and it was for showing his private parts to Vijaya. He immediately stated 'She's telling lies' and that he had never done this. Using explicit language, I told him that he had been accused of putting his dick in Vijaya's mouth, that he had done this to her everyday and lots of times, and that I wanted to know of any reasons for doing this.

He very calmly and clearly told me 'How can I have reasons when I didn't do it?' He told me that he had come to see me to convince me that he had not done it, but now realised this was pointless. He stated 'Social Services isn't neutral' and 'You've already made your mind up that I've done it.' When I asked why Vijaya should tell lies, he felt it was because she was jealous over him having more sweets than her.

We talked about what the consequences of abusing Vijaya would be. He evaded answering this by saying 'How do I know when I didn't do it?' When I suggested that he think about the consequences of such behaviour whatever the case, he then wrote down what the consequences were without any difficulty.

I endeavoured to look at how a person might feel, if she/he experienced what Vijaya says she has. Mohammed responded without hesitation, 'If I've not been sexually abused how can I know how Vijaya would feel?' This almost came across as if he had been well prepared before coming to see me.

I asked him to imagine what it could feel like and he responded they could feel 'hurt, sad and might want revenge', although he only wrote down the word 'hurt'.

I found Mohammed to be a highly intelligent and somewhat precocious boy who was always ready with an answer for every question I presented him with. He communicated in adult terms such as talking about what his 'hypothesis' was and in terms of 'neutrality'.

At other times he tried to evade giving answers. I was surprised at how relatively calm and relaxed his behaviour was, given the seriousness of the allegations that he was being presented with. He did not stutter once during this session or when I was confronting him.

When booking the fourth session, Mohammed questioned what the purpose was in him coming to see me again. He felt he had nothing to gain from coming to see me. I explained that I wanted to see him for his sake as well and the work was not aimed solely at proving whether he was guilty of an offence or not.

We talked about looking at his own life experiences and perhaps doing a story about his life. I told Mohammed that I thought he was sad and lonely and if he wanted we could look at this issue. For the first time he did not try to deny or dismiss what I was saying and miserably looked down, remaining very quiet. I let the silence go on as I felt it helped to expose his feelings.

> Mohammed's isolation and denial concerned me considerably as this linked into my work in another context with his brother. I had asked Tariq what his likes and dislikes were and, without exception, these were directly connected to Mohammed. He had liked having his own bedroom because he had disliked sharing a room with Mohammed as their beds had stood next to each other. He did not like Mohammed's bed because it was 'dirty' and 'stinks of the toilet'. Tariq liked having his own room because there was a big bolt on the door, which prevented Mohammed from getting to him when they were fighting. Tariq did not like Mohammed asking him to sleep in his bed with him. Mohammed asks this 'because he feels lonely'.

> In asking Tariq to draw the things he hated the most, he had drawn a cartoon strip telling a story. The story was entitled in capital letters THE BOSS. He told me the boss was Mohammed. The story was about him being bossed about by Mohammed, but Tariq winning in the end. In a further session with Tariq, he blocked discussing Mohammed. He retracted most of the above statements about him and said he had not meant to draw the cartoon strip about Mohammed.

The life story work with Mohammed has been begun in my fourth session. Mohammed said he cannot remember anything about his early years between three and seven years. The only thing he could recall was going to school on his first day with his uncle. He could not remember much else about that day, other than his uncle had taken him. When I asked where he lived, he recalled that when they lived in a block of flats, his uncle was not living with them. He recalled that his uncle only ever lived with them for a short period of time about a year ago and before that he used to visit regularly. He told me his uncle took him to the Mosque regularly when he was younger but they do not go so often now as his uncle has heart problems. I thought that it was interesting that whenever we were talking about his general memory of his earlier childhood, Mohammed mentioned his uncle.

I moved on to discussing what he liked and did not like about his uncle. Mohammed began stuttering noticeably and avoided eye contact with me when I focused on his uncle. Giving side glances towards me, he stated that his uncle was a very nice person and he liked him as he bought him sweets. There was nothing he disliked about him. He then stated 'I don't think it was my uncle who took me to school actually, it might have been my mum'. He then wrote this down.

I thought his reactions were strange. On the one hand he had brought his uncle to my attention and on the other he seemed to be blocking discussion about him. I was not sure of Mohammed's reasons for highlighting his uncle's presence in his life. It was either because he was feeling safe enough to draw my attention to his uncle but not safe enough to discuss him in detail. Or he was not consciously aware of having drawn my attention to his uncle and I had moved too quickly in focusing solely on him.

Evaluation and theoretical base

The work with this child has been difficult and I have mixed feelings about it.

The lack of police involvement in investigation minimised the seriousness of the allegations and suggested to Mohammed that it was not serious enough to warrant police action.

In addition, if Mohammed were to disclose experiences of having been abused himself, then he would have to be subjected to separate additional interviews by the police and a different social worker. Clearly, one should avoid subjecting a child/young person to repeated interviews.

CHAPTER THREE

Social Work Across Racial, Cultural and Language Differences

This chapter and Chapter Five offer a series of illustrations of social work practice where there are differences of race, language and culture. In situations where the worker is white and English–speaking, work with a black client who may have no English or for whom English is a second (possibly recently acquired) language presents special challenges. One obvious answer would seem to be the use of interpreters; but, as one contributor to this book has shown, this in turn presents further issues which need to be resolved. For example, should the interpreter be asked to provide a literal or a paraphrased translation? How should the interpreter respond when certain concepts or acts are not readily translatable, or when the matters to be discussed are not culturally acceptable to the client?

She concludes as follows, in speaking of interpreters, with particular reference to the needs of the Bangladeshi clients with whom she worked:

> Their task is to give an accurate and undistorted rendering from one language to another in a wholly impersonal manner. This poses the question, however, whether language can be divorced from culture and whether, when words are literally interpreted, the meaning of them is mutually understood. In Western industrialised societies this may be the case as, although languages are different, cultural values, societies and religion are far more similar to each other than to those of a Third World country. Consequently, heads of state who are interviewed on television are able to use a linguistic computer model, as they share a common culture. It is from this model that we base our assumptions about the process of interpreting.

However, the social worker with minority ethnic families is having to grapple not only with the problems of language but with those of differences between cultures and values. Rack (1982) argues this point in his book *Race, Culture and Mental Disorder*. He suggests that people from Western societies are comparatively introspective and preoccupied with the internal world. In English there is a plethora of words to describe various internal experiences of sadness, depression, misery and anxiety. Rack argues that some Asian and African cultures have fewer words to describe these feelings and will often describe them in terms of physical symptoms or somatisation. Phrases such as 'Are you well?' or 'Do you feel depressed?' cannot be interpreted exactly. Therefore it would be very difficult for a social worker to explore and assess these feelings in a family via a neutral and impersonal interpreter.

These issues of language and culture in relation to the Western practitioner are explored most fully in the field of transcultural sociology. In social work literature there seem to be far fewer examples of this kind of discussion. For example, the British Association of Social Workers (BASW) report on ethnically sensitive social work devotes two sentences to the language barrier. There seems to be a greater concentration on the use of switchboard interpreters and telephone links, which are based on the linguistic computer model.

However, my own local studies attempt to address these issues. The project I investigated was set up to facilitate investigative work with 23 boys who had alleged sexual abuse by a local man. A significant number of these boys were Bangladeshis, and the account of the Bangladeshi worker highlights the problem of talking about and engaging families when sexual abuse is involved. She says: 'A language will not be developed and refined on a subject that is rarely openly discussed'. Since there are only crude or medical terms to describe sex, it poses great problems:

> 'There seems to be no middle ground, which makes the task of discussion and disclosure far tougher than it is in any case. The fact that sexual abuse has happened has to be implied and then crude descriptive details of the abuse have to be given. When the most appropriate language is missing, one is acutely aware of feelings of shame, guilt and complete loss of honour.'

There are also other pressures that the Bengali speaking worker has to contend with, as by raising these intimate issues she is seen as breaking many taboos. The Bengali worker in the Project was the recipient of much hostile reaction. A professional interpreter would find it very hard to maintain a neutral stance in these circumstances and remain unaffected by the powerful feelings that are evoked. One Bengali speaking worker whom I interviewed was required to interpret at the Old Bailey during the course of the trial of the abuser referred to above. She said that the process 'made me feel like the victim'. On another level, she felt like the abuser when she had to interpret for the defence lawyer, who had said: 'I put it to you that you have enjoyed this experience of sex'.

The Medical Foundation, which works with victims of torture, recognises the problems that interpreters face when they are dealing with painful and traumatic events. They provide specialised training and have regular groups where interpreters can be helped to deal with these feelings.

Therefore the evidence suggests that the professional neutral interpreter is not a model that is easily translated into social work practice with Asian ethnic minorities. In order to understand what is happening and to effect change, the worker needs to know not only what is being said but also how to work with profound cultural differences which affect all levels of communication.

In one Social Services Department the 'ethnic minority' team are defined not as interpreters but as liaison workers who have a specialist knowledge of Asian culture and an understanding of agency function. Although there are many positive features to this model it has led to confusion amongst social workers, particularly with regard to their interpretative function. Some local authorities have addressed these difficulties, making this function explicit by describing these workers as interpreters while providing them with additional training in the social work tasks of the agency.

Recommendations

(1) Training

The uncertainties that social workers expressed about the role and function of workers within the ethnic minority team indicates a need for joint training on how to work together. This could provide a forum for social workers and Bengali speaking workers to clarify their expectations of each other and address sensitive issues in a safe environment. It would be helpful if they focused particularly on initial investigations.

(2)Joint supervision

Joint supervision would make a significant contribution to helping workers to evaluate their work jointly and to clarify their roles and expectations.

(3)Training focused on the culture of communities

Although most social workers have been involved in some level of antiracist training, this does not encompass learning about other cultures. In fact, some proponents of antiracist social work believe that 'cultural knowledge becomes a further avenue through which black people become pathologised'. An added obstacle to social workers' ability to discuss openly and express a need to learn about other cultures is a fear of appearing to be looking for stereotypes.

Clearly, social workers need to learn about the societal norms and values of the client group with whom they are working. A basic example of the difficulties that are caused by such ignorance is the way Asian names are misrecorded under title instead of family name. On another level, training on these issues would give the worker more confidence in dealing with the cultural issues. It is neither fair nor helpful to expect a Bengali speaking worker to deal with all the cultural aspects of the case on behalf of a white colleague.

In addition, as my study shows, there are occasions when a Bengali speaking worker can be less sensitive and sympathetic to the family than his white colleague, particularly in respect of gender and class. On occasions, black professionals may wish to distance themselves or even deny those aspects of a family's culture which might be seen as superstitious or primitive. For example, one case concerns a 14-year-old Bangladeshi girl who was referred by her school. Apart from family problems, she also said that she was haunted by a tree spirit and wore an amulet for protection. When I spoke to a member of the ethnic minority team, I was told that this was not in any sense cultural and the girl must be very disturbed. I subsequently discovered that this was not the case and that this superstition was not uncommon in rural societies. In fact her parents had taken her to a mullah who had prescribed the amulet. Given that these situations are bound to arise from time to time, white social

workers need to feel confident enough to question their colleagues'
views and to propose an alternative approach. This will only
happen if they have built up a knowledge base of their own.

(4)A role for interpreters with social services departments

I believe it may be necessary to consider the employment of interpreters to perform particular functions. At the moment parents are
not included in case conferences, but this will soon be instigated.
In this situation the role of the Bengali–speaking worker would be
mainly an interpretative one. It may be very difficult for the Bengali–speaking worker in a child protection case to be both interpreter and worker, especially if there is conflict between the worker
and the family.

There seems to be a fear that the employment of interpreters
reduces the impetus for training social workers. However, I would
argue that their roles are complementary rather than conflictual as
they address different needs and require different skills.

(5)The future

Clearly, the best solution to the problem of working with Bangladeshi families is the employment of more trained Bangladeshi
social workers. However, as this aim is achieved other dilemmas
will present themselves. Few would argue that we should practise
a social work apartheid, with Asians dealing with Asians and
whites with whites. But if we are to practise transculturally then
white social workers will be constantly dependent on their Bangladeshi colleagues for help in working with Asian families. There
is no easy solution to this problem. However, at least the additional
skills of the Bengali workers should be recognised by the department. In one London Borough this is recognised and bilingual
social workers are given extra increments.

(6)Measuring need

My survey did not address itself to the problems of obtaining a
Bengali–speaking worker or interpreter to work on a case. Since all
the cases discussed were considered to be fairly high priority, it was
possible to obtain assistance quite readily. However, many of the
cases referred to Duty workers would not fall into this category,
and in some SSDs there is no system of recording the ethnic origin
or the special linguistic needs of the families referred; it is often only
when children are placed on the Child Protection Register or come

into care that these factors are recorded. Therefore I would recommend that ethnic monitoring is instituted at the point of referral rather than on allocation.

Mr and Mrs M and their four daughters

Mr and Mrs M are immigrants from Pakistan. In the following case-extract, the (white) social worker finds herself confronted by several of the issues raised above. Mrs M has suffered with post-natal depression following the birth of her third and fourth daughters. There is a degree of urgency about various matters: the care of the children following the birth of the fourth child, and the future of the marriage. The social worker writes as follows. It will be noted that, even with the support of a Pakistani psychiatrist and GP, and despite the worker's considerable experience of work with mentally ill people, cultural factors make it difficult for the worker to understand Mrs M's needs and behaviour.

> This case study addresses the period February–September 1992 when Mrs M's mental health had again deteriorated significantly following the recent birth of her fourth child. She had requested to be a voluntary patient on a mother and baby ward in the local psychiatric hospital whilst the three older girls were cared for by their father.

> In May 1992, Mrs M was rehoused with her children in a Family Resource Centre for a three month assessment placement. For the last month of placement Mr M joined the family as he and his wife were re-united following a period of separation. The family returned home in August 1992.

Mental health issues

During my involvement with the case, I have had to grapple with defining the mental health component; the cultural component; how the two inter-relate and how these relate to child care concerns. I have had extensive discussions with the Community Psychiatrist who is himself from Pakistan and who has guided me. The family GP, who is also from Pakistan, is presently responsible for monitoring Mrs M's mental health.

Diagnosis Mrs M has been diagnosed as having post-natal paranoid psychosis. The condition appears to have started following the birth of her third child. Her mother could only comment that she was a 'loner' when younger. Paranoid psychosis is depression

of a psychotic intensity where there are delusions and/or halluci-
nations and a loss of sense of reality. Not only is the mood affected
but also there is a more generalised disruption of mental processes
including loss of concentration and initiative, loss of enjoyment,
feelings of guilt and self-reproach often leading to suicidal
thoughts.

Since the birth of her fourth child, Mrs M has not recovered to a
'coping' state, remaining emotionally very flat and tired on better
days. Most noticeable were her rapid mood swings and consequent
change in decisions; her unpredictable, non-communicative and
distant behaviour; and delusions based on paranoid thoughts. She
has learnt to mask her symptoms when she is able, perhaps because
of earlier violence from her husband, who thought her an inadequate wife rather than being mentally ill. He has also coached her
in concealing symptoms so as to minimise social services' intervention. When interpreters are used, the family have changed language to avoid being understood.

Assessment There remains a difficulty in assessing her needs,
partly because of her ability to mask symptoms, and partly because
her delusions are based on facts that have or could have happened
and then are distorted. Whilst separated from her husband recently,
she was convinced that her brother was ringing him to tell him to
separate from her; and that her parents were putting forward her
younger sister as an alternative bride for Mr M. These situations
could arise, and could only be discounted when the couple reunited and Mr M denied knowledge of these allegations. Mrs M
also has a tendency to manipulate the system whenever she can,
often to the embarrassment of her husband. I do not blame for her
for this, but it remains an unnecessary stress factor that she imposes
upon herself. For example, she has often had to visit the Department of Social Security (DSS) to verify the changes that occur with
the marital situation. Books and giro often go missing. One week,
having been apparently mugged outside the Post Office, she returned to my office for yet another weekly Section 17 payment. She
left angry and distressed, having refused a day payment, because
she did not get the £200 she requested. Even when separated, Mr
M ensures the family have enough finances.

Prognosis for post natal depression/psychosis is usually good. To alleviate the condition the patient should have a relatively stress-free lifestyle and medication is prescribed to assist this. However, following discussion with the psychiatrist, the prognosis for Mrs M remains poor. This is because she does not understand her condition and varies or stops her medication frequently. She has returned only twice to see the psychiatrist for assessment in the past six months and this was to request an end to the medication. Given her refusal to accept injected medication it has been a constant problem monitoring what she does take, having only repeat prescription information to rely on. Her prognosis remains bleak also because of her husband's attitude to her condition. Mrs M had her fourth child before recovering from having her third. It is likely she will take longer to recover after each additional pregnancy (even with a stress-free life). The chances of full recovery also diminish with each additional pregnancy. (The importance of having a son is discussed later.)

To understand why the family may be reacting as they do, the issue of mental health and race needs to be considered.

Mental Health and Race

There has been difficulty addressing the psychiatric component because of the family's hope that it would resolve itself, which is, I understand, a common reaction in the Pakistani community. This is because of the importance of maintaining family honour and because of the stigmatization of mental health problems; and also because of the need to maintain a closed family unit. An additional difficulty for an immigrant family is the difference between cultures in conceptualising what are perceived as relevant issues. Initially, I would use terms such as 'depressed', 'anxious' or 'irritable' when asking Mrs M about her condition. Not only would she deny such symptoms, she didn't appear to know what I was talking about. She would refer instead to having a pressure in her head; or agree she felt terrible or lonely and later admitted to wanting to cry frequently, and/or needing a rest. As quoted in *Alien and Alienists* (Littlewood and Lipsedge 1989), it appeared that 'Mental illness is defined by the majority culture'. I realized that the concepts we consider important may be totally foreign in other cultures. There is little value in considering the psychological approach when the predominant issue is survival, either practically or politically. I was interested to find articles relating to this. Currer's (1984) study of Asian women found that:

> 'These women saw *both* health *and* illness, happiness *and* unhappiness as inevitable in life. They did not expect or want total happiness or health. Both were given of God. It was correct behaviour *in face* of these states that was important. They did not therefore seek endlessly for the causes of their unhappiness or ill health or assume personal responsibility for them. Indeed as women in a very strictly sex segregated sub culture they saw themselves as being responsible for very little.'

It is significant that when Mrs M called an ambulance for herself both in January 1992 and August 1992 she did not differentiate which hospital she requested admission to. On both occasions she was admitted to the general hospital. After liaison between myself and the casualty doctor on the first occasion, she was transferred to the psychiatric hospital. However, on the second occasion, she was discharged home after three hours and her complaint was put down to being intoxicated. By the time I visited two days later, when I received the referral, she was angry and defiant and no longer wanted hospital admission.

Little importance appeared to be given to analysing the emotional content of life within this family. Mr M has failed to understand the impact of stress factors on his wife's health and, as a consequence, has been unable to address these himself or within the family's own network. As quoted in *Unearthing Hidden Illness* (Sone 1992), 'In Asian life there is little room for the individual, the family is the most important unit... They see illness more as something in the society not in the individual.' Mr M has not attempted to find solutions to help his wife either practically or emotionally in the long term. Presently he is at home caring for the children because he has lost his job and otherwise the children would be removed, but he has already said that this will be for only one or two months. By doing this, however, and by, for example, helping prepare the children for school when the family were within the Resource Centre, he has done considerably more than would be traditionally expected of a man of his culture; there are limits to his flexibility. The financial reasons for this are, of course, understandable, but he has possibly until recently not wished his extended family to know of the situation or for nearer friends and relatives to assist or support his wife with the care of the children.

Roles and decision making within the family

The Asian Muslim family is traditionally patriarchal, where the husband is expected to provide for his family, often by working the long hours necessary. As an immigrant family, there is also the expectation that finances will be sent home to the extended family when possible. Mrs M has voiced her own distress about this, particularly when their finances are insufficient, for example when the phone bill comes in (as many calls are made to Pakistan).

As head of the household, Mr M would be responsible for making decisions, turning to his older brothers for help and advice if necessary. Given his own father's age and ill health the brothers have adjusted their roles accordingly. I initially requested the family to consider support from other women from the extended family to help with the care of the children. This has been resisted for various reasons, partly because this is not their process for solving problems. Mr M has now written to his brother in Pakistan requesting him to visit since care proceedings began.

Mr M has spoken to the psychiatrist about his regret for the earlier violence towards his wife; now, as a counter-reaction, he is trying to keep the peace with his wife and maintain his marriage by allowing his wife more power within the decision making process within the home. As a result he has colluded with her, albeit reluctantly, and fails to point out the effect her actions will have on the family. For example, there is evidence to suggest that some separations have occurred for the purposes of claiming Income Support; actively denying past events which led to her past hospitalisations, and denying the points of concern related to child care which at the time he was also concerned about. He has written to his brother secretly, knowing that he cannot refuse him accommodation if he should arrive on the doorstep. He has been happy for his wife to represent the family at social services meetings so that he does not have to take time off from work to discuss the children. Although he has been sent a copy of the minutes, I am sure Mrs M has found it helpful to screen our concerns from him. It was interesting to note that, when she attended a case conference, he cared for the baby upstairs, although workers offered to do this. When I confronted them on this, it transpired that she did not want him at the meeting. When he attended further meetings, it proved helpful to have other men within the meeting as it appeared to help him participate within the discussion.

The woman's role

In Pakistani culture, the woman is not regarded as 'economic' other than as a 'son bearer'. Mrs M usually accepts this role, although in the past she sought employment in the local supermarket. It may have helped to relieve her isolation but was vetoed by her husband as being unnecessary because of the implications for family honour (his role). It was understandable, therefore, that Mrs M felt unable to sign the contract of work with me which she saw as undermining both her role and her husband's. She cannot recognise her inability to care for the children and is presently not happy to involve others. Although the family may be concerned about the loss of family honour, I am assured that, given the gravity of the situation, friends and relatives would normally be sympathetic and supportive.

Isolation

Asian women in England are often isolated because of the location of their communities; lack of personal networks and having young children at home may prevent them from making contact with others. This has been a difficult issue to address with this family, who say they have friends and relatives in the area but refuse to give any details of them and deny the support that could be offered. Mr M said at one point that they had stopped visiting other friends because his wife kept talking to herself; they have tended to isolate themselves further when perhaps in most need of help.

Isolation is significant for Mrs M who agrees that, were she at home, her female friends and relatives would help with the children. Traditionally, women congregate with each other during the day, often leaving the older female children to do the more menial tasks around the home. The women would all offer support with younger children, especially those below five years, as well as emotional support and companionship to each other. There is a local Asian women's group which Mrs M joined in the past. I have encouraged her to join again and have asked the group to make contact, which they did. Mrs M assured them she would attend with her new baby and that she did not need a lift, but never did.

During this period, when using a British-born interpreter, I discovered the family belong to an obscure Muslim sect called the 'Ahmedites' who are often ostracized within Pakistan as Ahmed claims to be the true leader and above Mohammed. It was interesting that other interpreters could not tell me about the significance of this, and I wonder if this was because they would have also ostracized the family. Although the family observe special feast days, generally they say that they are not particularly religious. Their local Mosque is four miles away but they have not wanted me to make contact with anyone there to see if assistance could be offered.

Sons

The woman's role is to produce sons. Sons are regarded as an economic necessity. This is reinforced by beliefs within the Muslim culture, and should a woman be unlucky enough not to produce sons then she would not be regarded as a good wife. Given Mrs M's four daughters, the pressure on her now to have a son will be enormous. Both parents come from large families so, although both parents say this is not an issue and deny wanting any more children, I would be surprised if there were no further additions to the family, especially if there was a slight improvement in Mrs M's mental state. It is already known from the GP that they use unsatisfactory birth control and have refused alternative methods.

Other stress factors for the family

Stress levels within immigrant families should not be under-acknowledged. As Littlewood and Lipsedge (1989) point out: 'Prejudice is not merely experienced as an external constraint; it becomes part of the self image which is defined by others'. It becomes part of daily life and the family needs its own strengths and supports to continue to live with it. There has been harassment in the past and it appeared that these incidents became distorted within Mrs M's delusional state. Although there have been no further reports of harassment over the past six months, it probably contributes to stress levels and, for example, prevents Mrs M from allowing the two older girls to play on the balcony of their flat.

In February 1992, the family decided not to pursue a housing transfer on the grounds of earlier incidents relating to racial harassment.

Marital problems

As for many arranged marriages, the couple met briefly before they married without a period of courtship. Although a somewhat alien concept to the Western idea of free choice in relationships, and indeed becoming an increasingly controversial issue within the immigrant Asian community, I have had to consider the strengths and weaknesses of such a contract for this family who, after all, have been together for seven years (albeit with difficulty over the past two).

Mr and Mrs M appear emotionally distant from each other in daily life but it is obviously important to them to maintain the family unit; and as the family moves into different crises this becomes more evident. Traditionally, it would be expected that the man would seek stimulation and socialization from his work or friends, whilst the woman would seek it from other married women. As this is not available to Mrs M, it has meant she has had to rely on her husband more, which has put pressure on their marriage. A considerable cause for her anger has been his long working hours and time away from the flat. She has accused him of infidelities, which he denies. The long-standing accusation that her earlier social worker was having an affair with him was a significant part of her assessment of the situation when I first met the family. Over the past months, he has shortened his working day and spent his day off with the family in order to placate his wife. It has taken two years and several separations, however, for him to agree to this. Since knowing the family, their relationship has waxed and waned. Should they be in opposition to Social Services (e.g. over child care issues) then they will unite. Following this there is usually a deterioration in their relationship as Mrs M's demands on her husband, using traditional values, become unreasonably excessive. Her relationship with Social Services then improves. Mrs M will either leave with the children to go into Bed and Breakfast accommodation or Mr M will move into the third bedroom and co-exist with the family until the next crisis occurs. Presently there are signs that he is sleeping on the settee downstairs.

Assessment of the strength of their relationship has been further complicated by the fact that they say they have been separated when this may not be true. Other Asian families in the Bed and Breakfast accommodation indicated this was said for DSS reasons, although both denied it. When insisting they were separated, Mr M would still arrive for his dinner and be expected by his wife. There was little difference in their relationship, whether they declared themselves united or separated.

Should Mrs M want to leave her husband for good, her future would be bleak. Returning to Pakistan as a single parent would be unacceptable on either cultural or practical grounds. Remaining within this country would be difficult, as for any single Asian mother with four young children; she would need emotional strength and a good support network, neither of which she has.

The stigma of mental health and the importance of family honour

Serious psychotic illness is stigmatized equally among all ethnic groups in Britain, black and white. This is especially true when the effect is uninhibited behaviour that may seriously put the family honour at risk.

Alcohol is forbidden to Muslims. Mr M keeps alcohol in the flat and probably drinks secretly. For this family who still hold many traditional beliefs, the family honour would be at serious risk when Mrs M was thought (by the hospital) to be intoxicated for the second time. Even the interpreters were shocked. Similarly, her disinhibited dress, swearing and generally assertive and rude conduct would be profoundly shocking to those who understand the cultural values of the family. For this reason in particular, Mr M has resisted the use of Pakistani interpreters. Recently, he said that he preferred my male Pakistani co-worker to stop visiting, although they had got on well together and had had useful discussions. I have insisted that the co-worker remains involved, although he too has been embarrassed by Mrs M's language and reported behaviour.

The following case illustrates the work of a white social worker in helping a little girl, born in this country of Afro-Caribbean parents, to come to terms with being black. Virginia spent the first three years of life with white foster parents who, in their kindly attempts to minimise racial differences, unwittingly led her to deny her blackness. When, for example, she spoke of wishing she were white – an indication of the identification she had made with her foster parents – her foster father responded that he spent a lot of time in the sun to go brown, and that she should be pleased with her colour. It might have been more appropriate to explore the feelings behind her wish to be white; but the foster parents seemed unable to do this, possibly because of an understandable reluctance to face up to unhappiness related to so basic a factor as skin colour. In a sense, they denied the visibility of her black skin, and this may have created a confusion of personal identity for this little girl: she liked to talk about how nice it was to be pink, and would search her body for areas where the skin colour was nearer to pink.

The social worker was concerned, therefore, to alleviate the child's unhappiness by helping her to identify with black adults: she had moved to live with her grandmother a year ago following an application to Court. The following are extracts from the social worker's case study.

Virginia (aged nearly five)

Virginia is a black girl. Her parents are Afro-Caribbean: Virginia was born in this country.

Virginia moved to her paternal grandmother last year following a six day hearing in the High Court. Custody was contested between her mother, her white foster parents with whom she had lived for most of her life, and her paternal grandmother.

Grandmother impresses as a sensitive, caring, warm-hearted woman who has a charismatic effect on people she encounters. The foster parents consistently opposed her care of Virginia, and delayed this happening by appealing to the Director of Social Services, and then, when this failed, putting in an application to adopt Virginia. This delayed Virginia's move by eighteen months, and resulted in a long Wardship hearing in the High Court. During this period Virginia was very aware of the conflicts over who was to care for her. The situation was further complicated by Virginia's mother and father separating during this time, and Virginia's mother desperately trying to get him back to live with her and their older son.

Virginia moved from living in a predominantly white suburban area to a multi-racial inner city area with her Grannie.

The task at the outset of this piece of work were as follows:

(1) To enable Virginia to separate from her white foster parents and re-attach to Grannie.

(2) To enable Virginia to gain a positive identity as a black child.

M, Virginia's grandmother, only became significant in Virginia's life in the eighteen months prior to her move there. Virginia was taken to visit her by her mother approximately fortnightly from that time, and started having staying access (after a court hearing over access) in the four months prior to the hearing. Virginia had picked up the strength of feelings against her grandmother from her foster parents, and talked about not liking her. When she was with her, however, she clearly enjoyed herself.

Virginia had picked up a negative image about being black. The foster parents, while claiming not to be prejudiced, were not able to deal with Virginia's needs to have a positive black identity and claimed that Virginia's need to be placed with a black family was the only reason that the Department wanted to move Virginia. Consequently, they saw this issue as over-emphasised. They had a view of themselves as doing a better job of rearing Virginia than anyone in her family could do and that they were essentially 'rescuers'. The foster mother in particular spoke of 'West Indians not knowing how to stimulate their children'. This was communicated to Virginia in subtle ways. She came to view the conflict between the adults in her life as due to her being black, and frequently tried to deny her blackness. In sessions with me, prior to her move, she would get very angry with the black toys, throwing them across the room and saying, 'I hate black people'. As stated previously, the area where the foster parents live is predominantly white, so the only contact Virginia had with black people was with her family members.

In summary, my assessment at the commencement of this piece of work is as follows:

(1) Virginia's power position was suddenly lost. She was moved, against her will, to someone of whom she had built up an image of being like an ogre.

(2) She was moved from a white suburban environment to a multi-racial inner city area.

(3) She lost her parent figures, to whom she had built strong attachments, having been placed with them for most of her life. She would suffer major grief over this loss.

(4) She saw me as all powerful, since she knew I supported the move to her grandmother and it was actually I who moved her. She had not been able to express any anger towards me.

Once Virginia had been with her grandmother for about two months, it became clear that there was a need to clarify expectations, and a written agreement was drawn up between myself, the foster parents, and grandmother. Access up to this point had proved difficult, since it was allowing Virginia to continue the emotional split between the principal adults in her life. Similarly, it was necessary to clarify with Virginia's mother the purpose of her access and to emphasise the control that the Department had over her access. She was initially unable to accept this control, and sought support from her solicitor, my area manager, her community psychiatric nurse and psychiatrist. Fortunately, they all gave her an united response, and she has since given a clearer message to Virginia that she supports her being with her grandmother.

Direct work

Virginia had experienced a major change in her life, losing her routine, her playgroup and friends, as well as the care-givers who had been central to her life. I felt it appropriate to take my cues from Virginia, and tried to establish an atmosphere of openness and trust. I thought that she may need to work through strong feelings of sadness and anger. When we were talking about her move, she showed a surge of energy by banging hard on the table with her hands. On my next session, I took some hand drums and encouraged her to drum her anger. In one session when I was talking to Virginia about her move to her grandmother, she said that I had 'robbed her'. (She explained this as being that I had moved her from her foster parents.) On my next visit I referred back to this, to acknowledge to Virginia that I acknowledged the hurt I had done. I also wanted to demonstrate that I valued what she had said.

The process of the work

I have visited Virginia approximately fortnightly. I usually spend some time with grandmother before walking to the school with her and then having about one hour with Virginia at her grandmother's flat. In these sessions grandmother is not present in the same room, but I try to inform her at some point of what I have been doing.

I prepare for each session by having some sort of plan about what we are going to do, but also being flexible to cues from Virginia.

Below is a brief summary of the eight sessions I have had with Virginia.

As equipment for our sessions, I brought some models of kings, queens, magicians, and poor people to explore ideas of power. Virginia chose the weakest and poorest model to be the most powerful. We then did self portraits, and Virginia showed much anger as she drew big black circles round the outside of her picture.

She chose to draw herself in pink: her grandmother and I talked to her about her skin and hair colour, comparing her with Grannie and other members of her family. I drew myself as pink, and Grannie drew herself as black.

I also brought a mirror so we could look at ourselves and we spent some time cutting and sticking pictures of black and white people. In the third session I brought a story book and this proved to be evocative for Virginia. We talked about sadness and anger, and she said to me, 'You robbed me'. When I asked her how, she talked about how I had taken her away and it was like robbing her. I saw this as the beginning of her expressing anger to me. At the time her hands were pounding on the table, and she said that talking about this was hurting her.

In the fourth session I brought some drums. We spent some more time on Virginia's story, and I reminded her of her saying 'You robbed me'. We talked about anger, and banged it out on the drums.

I invited grandmother into the room to share in this, and she beat out some rhythms. We sang some songs from their church, which Virginia obviously enjoyed. When I asked Virginia what made her angry, she said 'black'. She asked me about what made me angry, and I talked about how my children sometimes make me angry. I explained the different ways my children show me they are angry. We talked about different shades of colours, using a range of pinks and browns.

In the fifth and sixth sessions, I brought some play people and a doll's house. I had used these before in sessions with Virginia prior to her move, and she had identified figures to represent her family, her foster family and other people in her life. There are black figures and white figures. She talked about how she sometimes makes up stories about things she'd like to happen, I asked her for an example, and she said 'Daddy took me to see mummy'. There is a wide rift between her parents, and I talked to her about how her mummy and daddy do not live together any more and how her granny looks after her. She talked about having secrets from Grannie.

In the seventh session, therefore, I brought a children's book about secrets, which is aimed at Virginia's age group and talks about how babies are born. Virginia was fascinated by this, and asked lots of questions. I shared it with Grannie and left it with her to read again to Virginia. We went on to Virginia's story, and she said 'My mummy says I am to stay here until I'm grown up'. We then did some portraits again. She now sees herself as brown. 'Now, what colour am I? Brown.'

She told me a story about people shouting at each other. She took some toys and arranged them like a committee, which then ordered other toys about where to go. We talked about her sadness at being taken from her foster parents, and their sadness too.

Evaluation of the intervention

The feedback I get from Virginia is such that I believe she benefits from our sessions. She asks questions and pursues things, and seems to be making sense of what has happened to her. She now calls me her 'friend'. Grannie sees my work with Virginia as of value. She has been able to express her anger about me and to look at the issue of power and how decisions are made. She is learning that adults are in control, and that she is a child who does not have the power of an adult. She has experienced a positive release of anger in her sessions.

The loss that she has experienced is going to take time to come to terms with, but I see the work that I am doing with her as drawing on her own resilience, enabling her to move on and build.

She is now far less negative about her blackness, she no longer expresses dislike of being black. The most significant influence on her black identity has been that she is now amongst other black people. Her grandmother has frequent contact with black friends and relatives both socially and through her church. Virginia's school reflects the multi-racial community and is committed to multi-racial education. I hope, however, that my sessions have also helped Virginia to accept her black identity by exploring and acknowledging our differences. The change in her two self-portraits over the period covered by this piece of work is significant.

Peter (aged 13)

Here again, a white worker seeks to help a black client – an adolescent boy whose parents have separated and whose mother feels that his behaviour is beyond her control during school holidays. The presentation demonstrates how a programme and content of intervention may be planned in an orderly way yet may still misfire: the problems of transracial work are illustrated and addressed by the social worker, but she has difficulty in finding black foster parents for the boy, and this is without doubt an important factor in the work being unsuccessful in outcome. But perhaps it did achieve something of value to the boy.

This case study considers work undertaken with Peter (aged thirteen). The programme of direct work with him has been placed within the context of the ongoing case work.

Position at the outset of the work

Peter is a black West Indian child. His mother came to England from St Vincent when she was in her early teens.

Peter's father left his mother when Peter was aged three, and ceased contact until last year. Peter has been known to this Department since he was three years old when his father reported that he thought Peter was being mistreated by his mother. Peter's mother reported that he was a difficult child to manage. When he started First School, the school needed to appoint a welfare assistant to help with his management. Peter was statemented as having behavioural difficulties and placed as a weekly boarder in a residential school when he was seven, but his aggressive behaviour continued to cause problems.

At aged nine, Peter spent four weeks in care as his mother felt she could not cope with him during the long holiday. After a violent attack on a teacher he was transferred to a Steiner school as a termly boarder. Peter was the only black child there. The extended holidays started to present a problem for Peter and his family. His mother seemed unable to supervise him and so he drifted around the town. The Department offered help during the holidays with day care, sponsored activity holidays, and on one occasion Peter spent a week with foster carers. His housemother at his school also helped by caring for him during part of the holidays. Although Peter's mother was happy for other people to have some responsibility for his care, she did not want him received into Care and there seemed insufficient grounds for a Care Order. The department had no black foster parents available for short term placements.

Last year Peter was suspended from his school, and although the school eventually readmitted him Peter did not return and spent the summer drifting; no-one was certain where he was and his mother lost interest in him. He came to the notice of the police during this time and his father made contact with him. Although his father had not seen him for ten years, he offered him a home and Peter spent three months living with him, his co-habitee and their baby son. This arrangement ended when Peter's father was remanded in custody for an alleged armed robbery; Peter was said to have acted as look-out on this venture. At this point his mother requested reception into care. She did not wish to care for him herself and was certain that she did not want to transfer custody of him to his father.

Peter was received into care and placed in a children's home. He was moved after a week to a Children's Resource Centre after a violent incident.

At the initial planning meeting it had been agreed with Peter and his mother to seek a black foster home and an appropriate school. In January there had been a response to an advertisement for a foster family and this was being followed up. However, Peter was still waiting for a school place.

The last few months have been extremely unsettling and unsettled. He had been violent to members of staff and had been charged with numerous burglaries. He was suspected of dealing in drugs.

At the outset of this particular piece of work Peter still had no school place and was living in a Children's Resource Centre. His contact with his mother had been fraught and she had made it very clear to him that she did not wish to see him. His father was preoccupied with waiting for a trial date.

Assessment

My assessment of Peter's situation indicated clear lines of action. At this point he presented as a child without a home or school, both prerequisites for a normal childhood in our society. His behaviour so far, and adults' reactions to it, have excluded him from both home and school and have effectively marginalised him. Starting from the premise that children should be able to expect to be part of society and its norms, it seemed to me that these two areas in particular needed addressing.

He had become satisfied with his autonomous existence outside such structures and he found the notion of a school regime and education irrelevant.

Peter himself recognised that he needed a family. At first he hesitantly apologised for being 'racist' as he said he wanted a black family, but towards the end of the period of work he was able to be confident about wanting what he needed and was able to say with conviction that he wanted a black family to be 'safe'. His assessment of this need coincided with mine.

Although the practical tasks seemed very clear – find and approve a foster family and help Peter move to a new school and family – they also seemed very hard. Intervention needed to be on several levels. I needed to be an advocate for Peter within the department in the hope that funding for a school placement would be made available. I also needed to follow through the response to the advertisement for foster carers.

Peter's needs, as a black adolescent apparently rejected by his black family, were acknowledged by the department. He was allocated a black keyworker at the Resource Centre; however, my generic team has no black social worker in it, so I needed to prepare myself to work transracially. Paradoxically, I needed to offer support to a black child who had been failed by the white system of education, Social Services and law. The aim of the direct work was to help Peter use this transition period to prepare for a foster home and school. I perceived him as a child who knew little about forming attachments and who had little experience so far of adults who were committed to him.

My assessment concluded that Peter needed a change to develop an attachment which was safe within understood boundaries to enable him to go on to make attachments within a new family and with school staff. I was conscious that I needed to focus on how Peter's needs as a black child could best be met; he identified himself as black and openly expressed his anger and contempt for white authority figures.

The process of intervention

One of the main aims of the process of the direct work was to achieve the balance between offering Peter a consistent structure and enabling him to use the time in the way he found most useful. I knew that Peter had two main ways of expressing himself; these were aggression and drawing. Peter's rage with life was so immense I did not feel it could be contained within a work session. He enjoyed drawing and wanted to make pictures. I knew that he felt that no one person had a commitment to him – his black woman keyworker had been replaced by a black male keyworker because of his violent behaviour – so I chose to present Peter with a typed programme of five sessions as a way of formalising my commitment to him and also my expectations of him. I hoped that this would give him a sense of structure amid his personal chaos. Although I presented Peter with a programme which progressed through work which I considered necessary, I offered a range of means that he could use to make the movement. These included designing a personal life flow chart, plotting his life journey on a map of Britain, involving a chosen family member in producing a genogram, reminiscing and producing a transitional object, and rehearsing the changes ahead.

I knew Peter needed to discover that he could influence the content of each session without resorting to violence and learn that his views had value. I carefully chose a time when the sessions were most likely to succeed: Tuesdays are Juvenile Court day and Peter has been appearing there weekly, so I knew that I would be able to contact him on this day. I chose late afternoon when he would be out of Court and would also be waiting for tea at the Resource Centre. We used a private room at the Resource Centre.

Each session started on time and we always started by reminding ourselves of the programme, where we were on it and how we could work with that day's agenda. I made space if there were any issues left over from the morning's Court hearing to be discussed. Frequently, there were times when the only sound was of Peter's felt tip pen on paper. The issues addressed were very painful but the privacy from his peers meant that he could cry when he needed to and talk about his grief without embarrassment.

This direct work was carried out in the context of Peter's ongoing behaviour and situation. He was repeatedly in Court charged with a variety of offences ranging from assaulting a policewoman, using cannabis and stealing washing from a line. During the direct work he had clearly stated to me that he did not feel that he was his mother's child anymore. His father could not function as a parent due to his own criminal activity so this left him effectively parentless. As a result of this information and also the high level of attention that Peter was receiving from the local Juvenile Court, I called a case conference which included the County Solicitor.

A black woman had responded by telephone to my advertisement in *The Voice* for a foster family for Peter. After this initial contact I heard nothing for four weeks. I left messages on her ansaphone and wrote saying that I understood if she had changed her mind about fostering Peter but that I needed to know either way as he needed a home. It appeared that the woman's grandmother had died in Jamaica and she had been away for six weeks to sort out family matters. I made an appointment to see her at her home. I was impressed by what she appeared to have to offer Peter. She was a youth worker, well accustomed to dealing with adolescents, and very aware of the problems that black children encounter. Her home felt comfortable and comforting. I left the application forms with her; she said she would complete them with her husband and return them so that the process could begin. I heard nothing for a month, and so sent another 'Are you sure?' letter. I received another telephone call saying that the couple were still wanting to proceed and would put the form in the post, but as yet I have not received it.

The direct work with Peter offered him space and a chance to make an attachment. The series of sessions with Peter seemed to provide him with some respite from the tough image he portrays to the world. As a method of gaining and sharing information it was effective and efficient. He has telephoned me a number of times when he has been missing. On these occasions I reassure him that I am pleased to know he is safe, tell him that I have his possessions safely and that he will have to return to school. He listens, tells me he is safe and says 'Bollocks' when I remind him of where he should be. The mildness of this expletive and his wish to check in every so often makes me feel that he is less of an 'unheld' child now, although the situation is obviously still very far from satisfactory.

As a result of an interview Peter was offered a place at residential school. He said he was keen to go and this seemed to represent a change for him.

Peter learnt important things from his father when he shared the genogram with him. A previously sketchily explained scar on his forehead is now a painful symbol of his relationship with his mother. She had apparently thrown a saucepan at him when he was a toddler. During the work he learnt that he had value and was interesting, that he could cope with change and that admitting vulnerability is acceptable.

The limitations of such a short programme are self evident. Peter is a very damaged child with a thirteen-year-old history of emotional deprivation and loss. His contained rage is immense and I felt unable to address this directly, as I was not prepared to put myself at risk. I needed to feel secure within the boundaries of the work so that I could give Peter some of that confidence. He has, however, committed three major assaults since the end of the work.

I enjoyed doing the work and I think Peter enjoyed it too. I think I was able to offer a useful experience to this black child. He has intuitively engendered a sense of protection in me, I have responded to his willingness to show me his vulnerability by wanting to find security for him. This in turn has made me very angry about the resources that have been lacking for him.

Programme of work

My expectations of the content of each session.

(1) The agreement:
Our agreement – the agreement between Peter and me about the plan for the sessions. What is the overall plan for Peter? Who agrees to this? – case conference, i.e., authority, also grandma/grandad – mum/dad.
Permission has been given to Peter – Does he agree?
Genogram to show graphically who agrees, also identify Peter within his family.

(2) What happened:
Trying to make sense of situation, drawing a flow chart. Finding out where things went wrong – identifying age where emotional development faltered. Was it anyone's fault?
Who is caring for Peter now?

(3) The traveller:
Draw route on map of Southern Britain.
Also do chronological history of main carers with addresses.
Use photos if any available.

(4) Wishes:
Whom Peter wants to keep in touch with – how, when?
Also, what will foster parents/school wish of him?

(5) Getting ready:
What jobs have to be done in preparation for move? Rehearsing cognitively how leaving will take place to reduce stress.
Compiling Peter's life book.

Actual content of programme

Peter owns the book that was created by him and will take it with him to school. This is a summary of the work.

(1) The agreement

The agreement about the sessions was made. Peter drew a genogram of his mother's family, identifying key people. Also drew a life flow chart, quite spontaneously said that he had chosen the bad way when his father left, but wanted to be a 'very good young man'. Acknowledged his break with his mother 'I am not her child any more'. He found it very painful that no one in his mother's large family wanted him, started to think about need to move on.

(2) What happened

Father remanded on bail, so visit to him to do his half of genogram. This was a treat for Peter – the affection between the two was immediate and warm. Peter's dad was able to give him snippets about his babyhood, including an explanation of his head scar. Father gave Peter permission to move on to a residential school and a new family. Arrangement made for Dad to visit him; his father is likely to be sentenced to five to seven years' imprisonment so all this is also about saying goodbye. This session was very positive for Peter; he was very childlike.

(3) The traveller

Peter plotted his route on a large map of Britain; he enjoyed doing this, also ringed places visited on holidays or day trips. He was able to discuss the next possible stopping places. He also listed in order all his addresses; which I have typed up for his book.

(4) Wishes

Peter was able to talk about who he would like to keep in touch with, but defended himself when thinking about all the rejection by drawing a bubble picture of himself lying in the Caribbean sun – he has never visited St Vincent – and counting out his money – he says he has funds from selling stolen goods; this is likely.
This was elaborate and defiant. Peter finished by saying 'I don't need any psychiatrists'. He was unable to give himself permission to be vulnerable in this session.

(5) Getting ready

Peter spent a lot of time thinking about what comprises a school uniform – trainers, tracksuit, shirts and so on. He had visited the school and so this was becoming more real for him. He wrote a school uniform shopping list. He also wrote a list of people he needs to contact. We spend a lot of time discussing who would take him to school – (I will) and when.

Finally, in this section, we have a case where a social worker of mixed race seeks to help a family group. We are, once again, reminded of the difficulties of comprehending what a family tragedy really *means* when culture, religion and colour differ between clients and worker. Initially, the referral problem certainly implies the relevance of family therapy: the social worker is experienced both in the kind of problem and in the conduct of family therapy.

To her credit, she recognises that, across the cultural divide, this technique of work is unacceptable and inappropriate; she avoids the temptation of fitting the clients to the theory (rather than vice versa) and of blaming them for its irrelevance to their situation.

This is followed by reversing the issues: a black social worker offers family therapy for a white family, as a means of offsetting the risks of physical abuse to a child. This case study provides a useful illustration of how parents' experiences of deprivation in their own lives may tend to increase the risks of their abusing their children. So far as can be judged from the record, the black worker has fewer difficulties in relating to white clients than white workers to black clients. It is useful to consider why this might be.

The Patel Family

Families are dangerous places: the arena for our hopes and fears, loves and hates, constructive and destructive actions. They are places where we take our achievements and our disappointments. We are nurtured by them, and we can express hostilities in privacy. Such great expectations from a social institution are likely to cause difficulties. This is my framework for work with the Patel family, referred when Ritika upset the equilibrium by overdosing. What was she telling us about the family and could a family therapy approach contribute to a restoration of family functioning?

The family is large (parents and four daughters); they are Moslems, who have lived in England for fifteen years and are engaged in the process of finding a way of living in British society; father works from home and shares the care of the children and mother works in the hospital where Ritika was treated. Two years previously an elder daughter had been admitted to the Children's Ward complaining of 'breath holding'. Attempts to work with the family by the social worker fizzled out as follow-up appointments were cancelled.

I hoped to engage the family in therapeutic work, but as on the previous occasion when the family had demonstrated stress through the 'medical route', it was not possible to do more than short term work. Nevertheless, I believe that the work can be seen in a positive light in that mother did engage with me; she did change her life style and role within the family; and as yet there has been no rereferral. I have addressed the issues chronologically under the following headings:

(1) Interdisciplinary work

(2) Crisis theory

(3) Use of self

(4) Choice of method with particular reference to ethnically sensitive practice and racism.

Interdisciplinary work

It is the practice at the hospital where I work for all overdose patients to be interviewed jointly by a registrar and social worker before discharge. Teenage overdoses occur at the rate of at least one per week. As duty social worker, arrangements were made by the administrative assistant for me to interview Mr and Mrs Patel and Ritika jointly with the registrar. The assessment took over two hours, having two distinct parts, the first being explorative and with Ritika's participation; the second being a four way meeting between the professionals and the parents. The session involved both assessment and crisis intervention.

I was unfamiliar with this kind of joint assessment and had only five minutes to discuss with the registrar (whom I had not met before) how we were going to work together. I heard myself assuring him twice that I was a qualified social worker. We agreed that he would start the interview by focusing on finding out what had happened and on the medical implications. The parents looked anxious, keen to cooperate and able to communicate with each other. Ritika was in a wheelchair, one arm attached to a drip, the other to a large machine which kept bleeping and needing attention from a nurse, who had to be called in twice.

The initial discussions centred on moving the frame of reference from 'accident' to 'overdose'. (Ritika had said she had taken the pills for a headache.) The registrar focused much of his questioning on Ritika and it seemed to me that he was harsh in manner. The effect was to make her tearful and to vomit. It was impossible to know how far this was caused by the nature of the questioning and how ill she was feeling (she looked very ill to me). Mother was tearful and Ritika acknowledged that her mother feared that she might have died.

I moved the focus to a social assessment: family size, siblings, relationships, schools, employment and family patterns. Ritika asked twice to be allowed to go back to bed and after saying a little about her quarrels with school friends there was a break when her mother took her back to the ward with all her machinery. It was noticeable that, despite the distress, the parents were able to communicate with each other. Interestingly an identifiable trigger had not been found. Therefore *either* the trigger was so painful that it could not be shared, for example a family secret like sexual abuse, *or* the trigger was so trivial as to be forgotten in the drama and distress of the illness, for example a squabble with a sister about not going to school, *or* a trigger could not be openly acknowledged as this would mean that everyone knew Ritika had taken an overdose deliberately. The consequence of such open admission is guilt and blame and, I suppose, ultimately punishment: such an attitude would be incongruent with the feelings of relief that Ritika had survived and their distress for her suffering. Whatever construction is put on this, we proceeded on the basis that we were there to discuss issues more complex than an accident caused by carelessness in leaving pills around and ignorance of the consequence of taking too many.

The second phase of the interview was shared between the registrar and myself. We felt more comfortable with each other and were able to take clues from each other (we did not need a structure for taking turns, nor were we fighting each other for space). The seating arrangements were interesting:

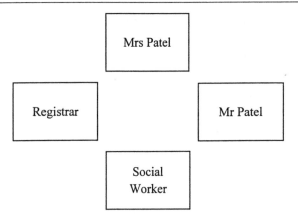

At one point the registrar was discussing education with Mr Patel (who tended to blame the school). Mrs Patel was stroking her face, and indicating to me that the problem at school was racism. I was intrigued by the use of this gesture to identify skin colour as a problem. White social workers in the Department said that they would not have understood this nonverbal communication. (It was a gesture used by my mother to explain to me as a child the racism experienced by my father.) Other interesting points were that this was a communication woman to woman, and that she thought I might be Indian. I have never been identified as non-white before in a professional situation. It has therefore interesting implications in terms of the choice of ethnic backgrounds of workers apart from the personal resonances; food for thought in terms of anti-racist practice issues.

On reflection, the registrar and I complemented each other well, he focusing on the medical aspects of the situation and I on the social and emotional side. We talked in detail about relationships, schooling, working patterns, tensions and family functioning. By the time the registrar suggested that he and I should take some time out, we had some feel of the processes in this family and had established some trust with Ritika's parents. I only thought later about the consequences for Mr and Mrs Patel of being left while we talked about them in another room afterwards. How did they feel and how did they use/spend the time? For us the time was useful in sharing perceptions of the material received. It is worth noting that there was a wealth of information (e.g. Mrs Patel had wanted an abortion after Ritika was conceived: Ritika had taken an accidental overdose at age three which the family remembers even if she only remembers being told about it; Ritika had had seven stitches in a leg injury when her father had swung her round and cut her leg on a glass lampshade).

We agreed that Mrs Patel was not 'mad' (this was how she was described by the casualty doctor). She was distraught by the events and loss of sleep. I was surprised that the registrar was still considering the view that perhaps the whole thing was an accident.

I identified the issues to be addressed in subsequent family work as:

(1) Attention to the feelings of individual family members about the overdose, in other words, feelings of fear, shame, guilt and what the family was going to tell others about it, and the implications.

(2) I suspected that the trigger may have had something to do with how the four girls relate to each other and to other adolescents, Ritika experiencing puberty earlier than her school friends, and their relationships with the 'baby sister'.

(3) Racism in schools is a cause of anguish for parents. There are no easy answers or prescriptions to ease the pain. What might be helpful would be for the girls to share their experiences together and to think about strategies and share their understanding.

(4) Was there a family secret?

It is worth pausing to think about why I decided at this stage not to suggest offering Ritika help in her own right. What I knew about this family so far suggested that the parents might be able to use help. Admittedly, I had not met the girls. Ritika seemed to be telling us that all was not well in the family. She had managed to obtain what she appeared to need at this stage: her mother's undivided attention as she stayed in hospital with her for the three nights she was an in-patient. I saw her on the ward on the following day. She chattered about school on a superficial level. There were few signs of engagement with me. I am not ruling out that she might need help in her own right in the future but I felt at the initial stage of involvement with this family that expecting her to continue to carry and express difficulties being experienced by the whole family would be counterproductive. People can only be helped by social workers if they want to be. Ritika had obtained the extra nurturing from her parents that she had asked for. Her family seemed to me 'good enough' in terms of protecting her in the future.

Crisis theory

It is the essence of crisis theory that at a time of disequilibrium it is possible to effect change quickly. I think we were able to shift the focus from 'accidental overdose' to a plea for help without exacerbating guilt to such an extent as to make the parents uncommunicative. The issue of guilt is important and required sensitivity in order to involve the parents in an assessment which revealed details of how the family functioned. On reflection, I regard our professional task as to be assessing Ritika's safety in the future. Was the parenting good enough to avoid self harming and the use of dangerous means to express needs, ensuring that they would be met in the future? The shock of this overdose made this family look at itself. I believe that our assessment interview helped the parents to appreciate the interrelationship of factors involved. In consequence, Mrs Patel ultimately decided to change her role in the family by giving up work to spend more time with the children. It would have been easier to allow understanding of this overdose to become stuck on one factor, racism at school for example.

Use of self

Social work involves professional conduct, but without self involvement, work of a therapeutic nature cannot begin. This case tested my professionalism at the same time as enabling me to use my knowledge of local schools and sibling rivalry to the advantage of my clients. My daughter attends the same school as Ritika's elder sister. There were issues of confidentiality; my knowledge of the school enabled me to empathise with the family more closely.

Having daughters of a similar age to the Patel family meant that I could see their conflicts as meaningful, although raising the issue of separating the subjective/resonance issues from the objective reality of this *different* family.

Choice of method with reference to ethnically sensitive practice and racism

The family did not engage in family therapy. The roots of the failure lie, in my opinion, in the ill-fitting nature of the family therapy method for a Moslem family in the hospital setting. I thought a lot about the tone of the letter inviting them to meet with myself and another social worker whom they had not met. To me it seemed authoritarian, but the social worker thought that the serious nature of the overdose needed to be stressed. On reflection, I think it was unrealistic to expect them to be able to use help offered in this way. They may have agreed to a home visit but this was against agency policy.

I learnt much about ethnically sensitive practice in terms of the suitability of what is essentially a Eurocentric treatment for this family and indeed for others who have distinct cultural identities, but are living in Britain and having to make adjustments to institutions in particular schools and the NHS. Racism, too, is a constant cause for concern and my knowledge of the ways of local school playgrounds suggests that schools have a long way to go in finding strategies to confront this. I think there is also a need for parents of ethnic minority children to obtain help in helping their children to develop strategies of coping with racism – something I confront with my own children. I do not have the answers, nor does society, but at least Mrs Patel knew I had heard her (we talked about this at our next meeting on the ward).

In this next case, we follow the work of a male Asian Social Worker with a white family. Interestingly, the possible impact of this cultural difference is not addressed by the worker, possibly because he has identified closely – by education and employment – with English life. There is no internal evidence, however, that problems were encountered.

Family composition

Mother	Sheila, 28 years
Mother's cohabitee	George, 33 years
Children	Jason, eleven years, Daniel seven and three-quarters years, Shane, five years, Simon, two years

(Jason's natural father is Desmond, aged 50 years. The other three children are of the present relationship)

Introduction

The family became known to me in 1980 on receipt of a referral of physical abuse to Jason by George. After a case conference, Jason's name was put on the 'At Risk Register'. As the other children were born to the family their names were subsequently added to the register.

Intensive work was done for a time with the family (the family then being Sheila, George and Jason) but concentrated on George, who had spent his entire childhood in local authority care (from two months to eighteen years), had little experience of stable family life, and was being too severe in his manner of disciplining Jason.

Over the years, social service involvement was associated with handling various crises: for example, when Daniel nearly died from dehydration, financial problems, marital problems and George's desertion of the family and enforced absence through imprisonment on three occasions. Family therapy has not been used hitherto as a way of helping this family.

Background history

Sheila was the seventh of nine children. Her mother died in childbirth when Sheila was five years old. She remembers very little of her life with mother. Her father remarried and the stepmother disliked Sheila from the beginning; she was made to feel unloved, misunderstood in spite of her numerous attempts to please her, but got some affection from her older siblings.

At the age of 16 years, Sheila met an older man, Desmond, started a relationship and was six months pregnant with Jason before she understood what was really happening to her.

She was unsupported, and relied upon her siblings for help. She was homeless after Jason's birth and lived with one of her sisters before moving to halfway accommodation, then being rehoused in 1979. Jason and mother lived alone until early 1980 when they were joined by George.

George was placed in care by his mother at the age of two months. He thinks he has about 17 half-siblings, but only knew one sister, who was later placed with him. They have had no contact with each other since childhood.

George did not know his father, who was sent to prison for bigamous marriage to his mother, whom he met briefly when he was in the army. George's experience of 'Care' was of unhappiness, insecurity and instability. He never felt wanted; by the age of ten years he had lived in thirteen different families and institutions. There were large gaps in his memory of early life, but these were bridged when his file was obtained from the Local Authority and he was informed of its contents. George could be described as hard, aggressive and very rigid in his manner.

He married once but the marriage was of very short duration. Thrown out of the army because of his wife's behaviour, he drifted from place to place, in and out of employment.

Sheila and George and the children

The relationship started in early 1980; he was the lodger. Their first child, Daniel, was born at the end of 1980 and two others in 1983 and 1986 respectively.

Their relationship has always been volatile. There have been violent rows, constant friction, separations and reconciliations, George's imprisonment, financial difficulties, long periods of unemployment, and mother's constant threats to run away.

Jason, who was physically abused by George, always resented his presence in the family. He more than the other children was adversely affected by the family situation and his position became precarious. There were threats of expulsion from the family and school, where his behaviour cried out for attention. He became aggressive, isolated, eager to please and watchful. Daniel was beginning to be at home what Jason was at school. The other two children were increasingly unruly and unmanageable when mother was alone with them.

The parents knew that this state of affairs could not continue and agreed to working with me as a family group.

The objectives

(1) To create a change in the family dynamics and interaction which will improve the quality of family life.

(2) To create a happier atmosphere in the home for Jason and his brothers.

(3) To help the parents to understand each other better, to show respect for each other.

(4) To gain the parents' cooperation in helping Jason to change his self-image in the family and at school.

(5) To help the family to identify and draw on their positives and strengths.

The first session

On my arrival to escort the family to the clinic they were all dressed and waiting. Sheila announced that she would not be attending as she had taken on the care of three children for a neighbour. George felt her action was deliberate and made a derogatory remark to Sheila 'You can't even manage your own, yet you take on more'.

Sheila's explanation was she really wanted to come, but felt obliged to help a friend.

The children were eager and excited as we left with their father. On arrival at the clinic, introductions were made, and the family was given the opportunity to familiarise themselves with the room and equipment, after which we settled down for the first session.

The family seated themselves and left an empty chair for Sheila. It was interesting to note that Jason sat next to George (in the next session, with mother present, he sat farthest away from her) whom he dislikes and away from mother, with whom he has a closer relationship.

Each member was asked to say why they came to the clinic.

George said he was unsure of what Sheila wanted from him, nothing he did pleased her. When he was at home he did the housework because Sheila took too long. He and Sheila quarrelled in the presence of the children. She would follow him to see if he met another woman. He was not at home enough.

Jason said he played mum up, was naughty.

Daniel said he was naughty, would throw a wobbler, refused to do as he was told.

Jason was nominated to play the role of his *mother*. She would need help because Daniel and Shane threw butter all over the place, she swore at them and would hit them with a stick which she doesn't like doing, it made her feel bad; she wanted help to stop the children winding her up. She complained and also reinforced George's behaviour.

Shane said he made mum angry, played her up.

Problems to be worked through as the family saw them are:

(1) George taking over Sheila's role (parental).

(2) Control problem (Sheila/children).

(3) George not spending enough time with the family.

(4) Sheila's insecurity in her relationship with George.

Note: The children's behaviour was secondary. The main difficulties were the relationship between George and Sheila.

Jason was praised for role-playing his mother so well, and looking after his brother, and George was praised for keeping such good discipline. Jason with dad's help was to tell mum of the session.

The contract

The contract between the therapist and the family was that:

(1) All the family should attend the sessions

(2) If for any reason the parents were unable to attend, they should notify me.

(3) I was to see Sheila alone with the children while George waited outside.

(4) It was already established that sessions would be on a weekly basis – dates fixed so family knew well in advance.

The evolution of the first interview

This could be divided into four stages:

(1) *A social stage* in which the family was greeted and made comfortable; all the members should be involved in the actions in order to define the situation as one in which everyone is involved and is important.

(2) *The problem-defining stage*

(3) *An interaction stage* in which the family members were asked to talk to each other about the problems, changing seats around in the process if necessary.

(4) *Goal setting stage* where the family was asked to specify what changes they seek; finishing with making the next appointment.

Second session

George was absent from this session (gave prior notice) because he was doing community service.

Since one of the agreements at the last session was to see Sheila alone with the children at some point, the session was not cancelled. Using the same format as before, Sheila's reasons for attending the clinic were:

(1) To find out why Jason had difficulties at school.

(2) Control problems, giving double messages to the children and her inability to carry out discipline, where she was pushed to the point of hitting the children, which she doesn't like to do.

(3) Strong feelings about being told what to do by George, who undermined her role as a mother; although there was strong resentment about this, Sheila submerged her feelings to avoid an argument.

This was well demonstrated in the session. At the end of the last session George told the boys they were not to play with the toys because of the distraction. Sheila knew this and was given the opportunity to make her own decision; she decided the children should play with toys, but before long suggested George was right and stopped their play.

Although George was absent he still controlled the family.

Other areas of difficulties which were highlighted were:

(1) Lack of meaningful communication between George and Sheila.

(2) Jason's parental role within the family, which stemmed from his desire to make life easier for his mother.

(3) Sheila's wish to separate Jason from the rest of the family, especially from George and make him her responsibility alone.

This session ended with an agreement that the couple would be seen next without the presence of the children.

The third session (the couple alone)

Fourth session with the children and parents (in their home)

The problematic areas which needed immediate attention were:

(1) The relationship difficulty of the parents which was affecting the household.

(2) Jason's position in the family, and as a spin off his problems at school, and improvement of his self image, and self esteem.

The family skills needed to be made known to themselves as well as to me. This was achieved through questioning, interaction and observation of the couple and the children.

Communication

(1)*Between the parents*: an evaluation of this showed the couple able to talk to each other honestly and quietly, but when a third party was involved (the therapist) they shouted angrily at each other. In both situations, although they communicated, they were unable to agree on anything, mainly because they misinterpreted what each other said and did.

(2)*Between the parents and the children*: Daniel and Shane appeared more comfortable and relaxed and had no trouble in saying what they thought the other members of the family did which upset them; but Jason was unable to do this. He could not respond, but kept looking for approval from his mother. This triggered off George's anger, and he screamed at Jason, who by then was weeping. George continued to shout about boarding school being the answer to Jason's behaviour. When Jason was comforted and George was calmer, Jason said he was frightened of George's temper, was afraid of being hit by him. Sheila was immediately on the defensive, accused Jason of trying to get George into trouble with social services.

While not wanting to appear to sanction Sheila's attempt to isolate Jason as her responsibility alone, it was important to get her to see that:

(i) Jason had a right to say how he felt.

(ii) She misinterpreted what he said.

(iii)She needed to take a more central position, not take sides, and to view the situation through Jason's eyes – in other

words, that George wants to get him out of the family
and Sheila, whom he felt supported him, lets him down.
He felt out on a limb and on his own.

After some deliberation, George and Sheila both suggested that
Jason's behaviour reflected problems within the family itself.
Viewed in this way the focus was removed from Jason and put back
within the family generally.

George, Sheila and Jason agreed to 'role play' their interactions, with
Jason being asked a question and alternative responses substituted
for the old. They were able to see how George's screaming and loss
of control directed at Jason forced him to retreat into himself and
Jason was able to see how this frustrated George.

George spoke of the gaps in his knowledge of his childhood, so for
the next session it was decided that family scripts might be useful.

The family was advised that if there was a shift in Jason's relationship with George and his position in the family, someone else had
to make room for this. It was acknowledged by the parents that
Daniel would be the one affected. Ways of combating any adverse
reactions and accommodating Daniel were discussed.

Sessions five, six and seven

These three sessions were devoted to looking at family scripts and
compiling a genogram. Time had to be spent first on giving information to George about the missing links in his childhood, particularly during the first eight years of his life.

Sheila was aghast at George's background history as a child and
teenager. There were areas of Sheila's life which she did not share
with George before this, and he too registered surprise.

This gave the couple a new understanding of each other, and
helped them to realise that changes were possible in their relationship.

There were such similarities between George's experience in foster
care and Jason's, he made the statement 'I am responsible for
Jason's behaviour'. Positive use was made of this to promote
changes in the relationship between George and Jason.

Several of the issues raised in this chapter are crystallised in the following extract from a project on bereavement counselling:

> Is it appropriate to offer bereavement counselling to somebody who comes from a different religion, culture and race?

> One professional I spoke to felt that Asian culture and religion is so different from her own white Christian culture that she is alien to them and would only be seen as interfering. She thought that this is how she would feel in their position. Anthony and Bhana (1988) conclude their study of Muslim girls by suggesting: 'To counsel outside the religious belief system of the person concerned, may be far less comforting and cause greater anxiety than helping can alleviate' – when referring to counselling for dying people.

> I think that there are two separate parts to this. There is the outward accepted behaviour and ritual and the inner experience of grief and death: first the help that people need to enable them to manage the rituals of dying, and second the help needed to provide personal support. This can only be provided by individuals who know the culture and religion well.

> Wikan's (1988) research into Egyptian and Balinese Muslims' approach to death, loss and bereavement emphasises the importance of knowing not only the religion but also the culture. Wikan argues that each of these cultures has its own conception of calamities that would occur if the accepted way of grieving is not followed. Behaviour that in Bali is 'sanest of the sane' is seen as a threat to health and life in Egypt. For example, amongst Egyptian Muslims it is necessary, for one's own health, to express feelings of anger and unhappiness, whereas in Bali sadness is avoided, there is no word for grief and people who are sad are laughed at in the belief it will stop them going mad.

> However, Wikan argues that the different ways of coping with loss do not mean that grief is experienced in different ways. There is a common cross-cultural dimension to bereavement and loss. Thus, Firth (1988) found that the stages of grief, as described by Murray Parkes and others, may be relevant to the processes of mourning amongst Hindus, even though they are culture-specific.

> I would therefore argue that cross-cultural bereavement counselling is possible, so long as the work is done in a way which acknowledges the important influences of race, culture and religion. I have increasingly realised that the way people grieve is closely related to the general ethos of their lives: grief is not some-

thing separate from the context in which it is experienced. Previously, I think I saw grief as somehow separate from the rest of a person's life. The loss of a loved one induces a crisis in people's lives, which challenges or threatens them; but the crisis can be resolved by using the strengths of the person who is facing it, provided these strengths are genuinely understood, and are recognised as cultural as well as personal.

I have also changed my approach to the way in which people grieve. I increasingly believe that people need to be given space and permission to grieve in their own way at their own pace. A counsellor can do this by letting them know, for instance, the range of feelings they *may* experience; but there is no clear pattern as to the order in which they will experience these feelings or whether all the possible feelings will be experienced. For instance, following a neonatal death, there are several means of helping parents emotionally to move on; for example visiting the grave, visiting the neonatal unit, seeing the paediatrician and openly acknowledging their loss to others. However, this can only be done at the parents' own pace, and sometimes this means not at all.

This approach to grief counselling applies to work with different cultures, religions and races, as it involves an ongoing negotiation between the counsellor and the counselled and it does not make assumptions about how people should grieve. As Lawson (1990) writes 'Exotic skills are not necessary to provide culturally sensitive care to grieving parents. What is required is only to accept each grieving parent's unique qualities and means of expression and to demonstrate a willingness to listen and support them...' (p. 79).

Having said this, it is important to examine issues of racism and power relationships between a white social worker and an Asian client. Huby and Salkind (1990) argue that it is the professional's responsibility to make sure that the service provided does not add to the client's experience of being devalued because of skin colour, language or origin. Professionals should not believe, still less base their practice on, negative generalisations about minority communities.

To work in a 'culturally sensitive' and anti-racist way involves being aware of one's own cultural background, religious beliefs and race. To acknowledge our own place in society, the privileges we have, the oppressions we may experience, enables us to move on to working in a way which is less likely to abuse our power.

Lawson (1990) suggests that 'The first step toward providing culturally sensitive support to a grieving family is to explore your own attitudes about grief. Ask yourself what death means to you, how the death of an infant affects you and how you expect a person to grieve.' But then, one must recognise that these attitudes and feelings are culturally determined, and that they should not lead to assertions about the 'proper' and 'actual' feelings and attitudes of others.

CHAPTER FOUR

Administrative, Professional and Interprofessional Processes in Child Protection

This chapter contains four case presentations which illustrate a range of administrative and professional issues in ensuring the protection of children at risk. The first concerns the daughter of a woman suffering from periodic psychotic disorders; case conferences are beset by disputes about how far the child continues to be at risk, and the weight to be given to parental rights. To some extent, the replacement of parental rights by parental responsibilities (by the Children Act 1989) offers some guidance to professional workers, but this distinction is not an easy one for distressed parents to comprehend; and the uncertainties of assessment and diagnosis inevitably leave a degree of uncertainty and anxiety in the minds of professional helpers, especially when they are drawn from different disciplines. In the event, the social worker aimed at the rehabilitation of the whole family, but was forced to the conclusion that individual help was needed by the members individually.

The second presentation takes further some of the difficulties of working in partnership with parents as a means of protecting the child. It is included here because it clearly demonstrates the dilemmas of statutory powers when seeking parental co-operation. Reference may be made on this topic to the case of Don and Linda (Chapter 5), where Don associates professional powers with suspicions that the hidden agenda of the social worker is to smooth the way towards the removal of the child.

The third presentation is again concerned with the exercise of professional powers and responsibilities, although in the somewhat unusual situation where a handicapped child – by reason of his handicap – is over-protected by his temporary foster-parents, and where the aims are to encourage his social development with a view to adoption.

The fourth presentation sets out the context of preparing a Divorce Court Welfare Report, and the distortions of professional intentions in seeking to help a family. It illustrates the work of an Asian social worker with a family of mixed races.

Helen (12)

Position at the beginning of the work

I was asked to take over this case, following the decision of a Case Conference a month earlier, to register Helen on the Department's Child Protection Register, in the category of Confirmed Physical Abuse.

On reading the minutes I was concerned to learn that the Case Conference had not addressed the question of access between Helen and her mother, or considered taking any legal action to safeguard Helen. Helen's mother was a voluntary patient at a local Psychiatric Hospital, and the Consultant Psychiatrist had expressed the opinion that he had no grounds for detaining her against her will should she decide to leave. Furthermore, the Psychiatrist had said that in his opinion Mrs S would be ready to be discharged next month; he could see no reason why she should not return to live with her husband and daughter. Mr S had told the Case Conference that 'Mrs S was a loving and caring wife and mother, and that Helen idolised her'. He did, however, acknowledge that Helen had asked not to see her mother in hospital, and appeared apprehensive about a future meeting. Mr S had not expressed any concern to the Psychiatrist or the Case Conference about his wife returning to live with the family. The two Social Workers present at the Case Conference had expressed their concern for Helen's safety, should Mrs S return home, and reminded the Case Conference that it was Helen's safety and welfare they were there to consider and not that of Mrs S. This statement appears to have been made in response to the Consultant Psychiatrist's view that it would be very helpful to Mrs. S if Helen would visit her in hospital to bring about a reconciliation.

Assessment of situation and negotiation of intervention with the relevant people

My initial assessment was that this was a dangerous family mirrored by dangerous professionals. Mrs S had killed her daughter Ann, aged three, in 1984. She had returned to live with the family 12 months later, after spending seven months in prison and five months in hospital. During this period neither Mrs S nor her husband nor Helen had been offered any therapeutic help. There had been no assessment of needs of the family, in order to prevent future violence. Dale *et al.* (1986) have written:

> 'The operation of the family system at the time of a child's death, or serious injury, is of crucial significance. Such families have simultaneously produced two sets of dangerous transactions: (1) the transaction of assault between perpetrator and victim: (2) the failure to protect, or lack of action, by the parent who is not the aggressor. In our experience serious or fatal child abuse is rarely a simple transaction between one adult and one child. During the assessment a clarification of the transactions behind the injury provides an important baseline against which to view changes in the operation of the family system.'

Seven Case Conferences had been held during the 12 months Mrs S was absent from home; all recommended that there was no need to add Helen's name to the Child Protection Register. At a Case Conference held three weeks before Mrs S's planned discharge, the Case Conference 'expressed the general opinion that it was not necessary to enter Helen on the At Risk Register, given the close network of support the family had'. The next Case Conference, held three weeks after Mrs S's return home, again decided not to put Helen on the At Risk Register. The Key Worker said that 'she did not think it appropriate to place Helen on the Register, feeling that Mrs S's new found confidence would be undermined to some extent by such action'.

Although the question of Helen's safety had been raised by the Chair-person, she agreed with the Key Worker's recommendation on the basis that 'there were regular contacts and outlets which, if Mrs S needed help, would be aware of the situation and respond'. This view was supported by all members of the Case Conference.

In total, ten Case Conferences had taken place over a 21 month period, indicating some anxiety by the professionals, but on no occasion did the minutes reflect any concern that Helen might be at risk.

Six years later Mrs S attacked her daughter Helen, aged 12, and her intent, in a statement to both the Psychiatrist and the Police, was to fatally injure her so she could join her sister in heaven.

In spite of Mrs S's history, nothing was done to secure Helen's safety at the subsequent Case Conference. The Psychiatrist maintained that this was an isolated psychotic episode and that it would be safe for Mrs S to return home after completing her treatment, which mainly consisted of anti-depressants and talks with the nursing staff. Both the Psychiatrist and nursing staff had made it clear that they felt the Social Services Department had shown an unnecessarily harsh attitude when they expressed extreme concern for Helen's safety.

I was requested, therefore, to carry out an assessment. It soon became clear that any effective work would depend on forming a better working relationship with the Mental Health Team. When it was mentioned that an assessment would include Mrs S, the Psychiatrist had questioned whether it would be in his 'patient's interest' to participate in such an assessment. It became apparent that considerable effort would be required to engage with this part of the professional system before work could commence with the family. I therefore approached the Mental Health Social Worker responsible for working with Mrs S and asked if he would be prepared to do a joint assessment with me, as I had little recent experience of mental health work, and he agreed to this. We met twice to discuss the case before seeing the family, and considerable progress was made in agreeing how we would carry out the work. We planned to see the couple for four to six sessions initially.

In order to attempt to engage the Psychiatrist, we discussed our plan of work with him, and his reaction was positive and encouraging; he said that he shared our concern about the child's safety, and would play a background role during the assessment period. Unfortunately, this improvement in our relationship with the Psychiatrist did not extend to the ward staff, who continued to be hostile, believing we were keeping the family apart for no good reason. This was demonstrated by their refusal to engage in casual conversation with me on my visits to the ward, and in comments made to Mrs S telling her that they thought she was well enough to go home if it wasn't for the Social Services Department.

Last, we needed to introduce ourselves to the family to explain the purpose of the assessment, and to get their agreement to undertake this work with us. Mr and Mrs S were told that if they agreed to work with us a recommendation about Helen's future would be based on the outcome of the assessment. Mr S had already told me that he had no objection to this, and Mrs S was extremely enthusiastic, saying she had all to gain and nothing to lose.

The first joint session was used to negotiate the assessment, our respective roles, the family's responsibility for the work, the duration and frequency of sessions, and where to meet [in this case at the hospital]. Both Mr and Mrs S appeared keen to get on with the work, particularly Mrs S, who said she did not feel she had received any real help whilst she had been in hospital, and realised that she needed some. My colleague and myself were struck by Mr S's 'flatness', and apparent lack of emotion; he often said, 'There is a logical way to solve all problems'. There was an incongruence between what he said and how he expressed it; for example by saying to his wife 'Of course I want you to come home, you know I love you', in a flat monotonous voice without looking at his wife. Equally, she talked about how upset she had been and how much she missed Helen, and although her eyes were moist, there appeared to be a lack of feeling. In debriefing after the session, we decided to pursue this seeming lack of ability to express emotion in the next session.

By agreement, my first 'individual' session was with Mr S and Helen. We had agreed it would be appropriate to involve Helen in this session, as she was old enough to understand what we were talking about, and had expressed an interest in being involved, as it did not include her mother, whom she said she did not want to see. It transpired, however, that she had seen her mother during the preceding week. When I enquired about this meeting, Helen broke into tears and said she did not want her mother to come home until she was much older, or much better, as she would not feel safe with her mother in the house.

She also said that she had only visited because she felt it was her duty, and both parents had asked her to go. As I was doing some individual work with Helen and was due to meet her the following day, Helen asked that we should talk about this later.

Both Helen and Mr S became very involved with this session. It transpired that Helen did not have much knowledge of her father's childhood; he had suffered physical abuse at the hands of his step-father, until his mother separated from him because of his violence, when Mr S was 12 years old. Mr S showed little emotion until we spoke of Ann's death, when both he and Helen started crying. Mr S comforted his daughter, who said it was the first time they had talked about Ann's death together, as her mother had not wanted Ann talked about, and they had all complied with her wishes. I suddenly realised that I was meeting two people who had never openly been able to express their grief. I encouraged them to talk, asking them where Ann was buried, and they spent nearly an hour talking about Ann, about how much Mr S missed her, and missed talking about her.

The following session was spent with Mrs S in hospital. Mrs S appeared very anxious and agitated, and when I asked about this, she said that she had been worried that I would not turn up, as she had misunderstood the time of our meeting. I wondered if, in fact, she was worried about the session ahead, and made a comment about how many people find it difficult to talk about the past, and she smiled and said 'yes'.

Mrs S was the eldest of four children. She described her mother as always busy; she was a school cleaner, and she did not see much of her. She said her father was dominant; he worked at the local Army Camp; she was not sure in what capacity, as he wanted to pretend that he was a higher rank than he really was. She thought he might have been a Storekeeper.

Her father had high expectations of her, she was 'the apple of his eye', but she never felt she could live up to his hopes for her. She then said that her father had sexually abused her when she was 12 years old, which she had never spoken of before.

Mrs S relayed her past in a flat voice saying she had spent all her life trying to please others. I asked her if she was angry with her father for what he had done to her, and she looked at me in amazement and said 'Of course not, I love him, he was a good father'. She went on to describe how he had continued to kiss her on the mouth until she left home at 28 years, and how she had hated it. I was struck by the incongruence between her positive and negative feelings about her father, who had been responsible for what she described as 'doing horrible things'.

About her marriage, Mrs S said she had married Mr S because she was worried that she would soon be too old to marry. She had always found him rather distant and quiet, but had thought she could change him. She added that her father would never have approved of him, had he been alive, but then he had never wanted her to marry anyone, and it was only after his death that she felt free to do so.

When she spoke of Ann's death, she appeared to minimise her responsibility, saying things like 'I didn't mean to do it, and I am the one who has suffered the most'. She also added that she would never do it again. Mrs S showed little emotion throughout this session until the end, when she started talking about going home, saying 'No one understands how much I have suffered'. She did not mention Helen other than in the context of 'she needs me to look after her'.

In our next joint session, Mrs S spoke of lying in bed as a child listening to her parents arguing, and being terrified that one of them would leave, and how she believed it was unsafe to argue and express feelings, as it may lead to being deserted by her husband, which she dreaded. I, therefore, said how frightened one would feel in this situation. Mrs S became tearful and said that Mr S had never supported her, he was always working; that she felt lonely and had no confidence in herself as a mother; she had always tried to please others, especially her father and husband, and was confused about who she really was. She started talking about her fear of desertion, and how, if her husband left, she would be unable to cope with looking after Helen, whom she might also lose. She became angry and raised her voice at her husband, saying that if he had only understood how she felt this would never had happened; that she had killed Ann to protect her from the world, and she still thinks sometimes that Ann is better off where she is in heaven.

Mr S showed no emotion throughout this; he just said 'It wouldn't help to shout', and that he had told her when they married that he had a demanding job which would keep him away from home for long hours. We took this opportunity to explore how emotions were expressed in the family. Mr S replied that he believed that everything could be worked out logically, and if only she would talk there was no need to get upset about anything. Mrs S replied that she wanted to talk, but that he was never there to listen, and she also wanted to be angry but could not, because of the way she had been brought up.

She then expressed surprise at her angry outburst, saying this was not like her, although she thought it was a good thing. Mr S disagreed, saying it was unnecessary. We fed back that anger was a natural feeling, and that we felt that it needed to be expressed appropriately, rather than suppressed. Scott (1973) has made the observation that 'It is the quiet over-inhibited individual who is the most dangerously aggressive. The unexpected violence in the otherwise passive personality is certainly a feature of many fatal cases of child abuse'.

We started the following session by asking Mrs S to help us understand what she meant by 'Ann is better off in heaven'. She repeated what she had said before, that Ann would be protected from the world, and also that she, Mrs S, had been worried about what would happen to Ann if she had not been able to look after her because she was very depressed at the time. Mr S did not respond to his wife's statement, in spite of encouragement from my colleague. Mrs S asked about returning home, to which he replied that he was worried about Helen's safety. 'I don't know why you keep saying this, she is safe with me'. 'Ann wasn't', Mr S replied. I asked Mrs S to ask her husband how he felt about Ann's death, which she did. He broke into tears saying he missed her so much, and that she was a very lovely little girl. This was the most emotion Mr S had shown in a session. Mrs S told her husband she had never realised how he felt, as she had been so bound up with her own feelings. But they did nothing to comfort each other.

In the next session, Mrs S continued to say that she felt sure Helen still wanted her to come home, as she needed her mother to be with her. We therefore placed an extra chair in the room, asked Mrs S to sit in it and imagine she was Helen. I asked her how she felt about what had happened to her when her mother had attacked her. Mrs S looked confused momentarily and then 'I don't know, I still love her, she's a good mother'.

I asked her if she was frightened or angry with her mother, and she replied 'No because she wasn't well, and she didn't mean to hurt me'. Mr S spent most of the session looking at the floor in front of him and had very little eye contact with his wife. He did not respond to her statements about Helen, other than to say 'You have said all this before'.

He then confronted his wife with not taking responsibility for Ann's death. She replied that she had never harmed any of her children. 'But you killed her, it doesn't matter whether you think it was for good reasons or not, she's still dead'. Mrs S shook her head in disbelief, saying 'I don't agree with you, I did it to protect her'. 'How do I know you won't do it again to Helen'? 'Because I am so much better now,' she replied.

After this session, it seemed apparent that Mrs S had not changed her position. She continued to minimise what she had done and had taken little responsibility for her actions. We concluded that Mrs S needed intensive help, possibly psychotherapy, and that we could not recommend that she should return to live with Helen.

The following day Mr S telephoned me to say he had decided to start divorce proceedings, and would, if necessary, take out an Injunction preventing his wife returning home. He was seeing a solicitor the same day. He said he had reached this decision following our sessions at the hospital, where he had drawn the conclusion that Helen would not be safe with her mother. (I also suspect that the marriage had been in difficulties for some time, and that this had influenced his decision.) Mr S wanted to cancel the last session, but I persuaded him that it was important to see it through in order that he could tell his wife what he had decided, and why. We all met the following week and Mr S told his wife of his decision. She was remarkably calm, saying that she thought she should perhaps spend some time living on her own to build her confidence, but that she was concerned about how Helen would manage without her.

We agreed that further consultations were necessary between me and Mr and Mrs S, either together or individually, to discuss how we could best help Helen to adjust to this new situation. I would also continue to be involved with the family in my capacity as Key Worker, and continue to work with Helen.

Evaluation of intervention

Our assessment focussed mainly on the relationship between the parents and their attitude to the abused children. Dale et al. (1986) believe that the spouse relationship is invariably a crucial dynamic behind child abuse, and positive changes in this relationship, often as a result of therapeutic work, holds the key to the potential rehabilitation of the child following serious child abuse.

In this case, I believe the work was hindered by the lack of a common goal among the professionals involved. Professional assumptions differed, and may have affected the clients' ability to focus on the task. The Child Care Model was based on working towards the client acknowledging responsibility for the injury, and demonstrating willingness to engage in therapeutic work to promote change. The Mental Health Model appeared to be based on assigning Mrs S to a sick role 'from which she had sufficiently recovered to be able to return to live with her family in the near future'. In a letter three weeks prior to Mrs S's discharge, the Consultant Psychiatrist wrote 'Mrs S has recovered significantly from her depressive illness, and we feel that it is time to start normalising the situation by attempting reintegration with the family'. The two perspectives did not work together: the hospital was telling Mrs S 'You are better now', and we were saying 'There have to be some changes, and this will require you to do some work before we can make a recommendation about you and Helen living together'. To what extent this affected the outcome is difficult to evaluate, but it is clear that the professional system did not give the family members a clear statement about what they needed to do.

Mrs S has not been offered any therapy (in spite of a request from the Child Care Team) in the belief that she no longer requires it. This is of major concern, both for Mrs S and for Helen, as it is unlikely that all future contact will be severed between mother and child. 'The fact that mother is showing no remorse or anxiety about what she did, and taking no responsibility for her actions, suggests that the risk to Helen in future is high.' Equally, concern has been expressed by other professionals and by Mr S that Mrs S may attempt suicide.

Mrs S needs help and support as an individual. She will have to face a lonely and difficult future, and her needs have not so far been addressed. Helen has suffered a double trauma. She has been attacked by her mother, who intended to kill her, and has lost a parent, because of her mother's behaviour, and because of her parents' divorce. Further work will need to be done with Helen to ensure that she does not feel responsible for the breakup of the marriage, or for her mother, should Mrs S harm herself in future.

Mr S has been offered, and has accepted, bereavement counselling, and Helen is seeing a Psychotherapist. However, the family may need some help to build up a social network, as they are relatively isolated in the community and have little contact with their extended family and have few local friends, other than acquaintances through their church.

Lyn

This is an account of my work with a young white woman, named Lyn.

Background

Our department first became involved with Lyn in October 1988, when she and her family moved to Lewisham from Glasgow, Lyn's home town. Initial concerns focussed on:

(1) Lyn's request that the second child she was expecting should be placed for adoption.

(2) The appalling home conditions the family were living in – one bedsit in a large bed and breakfast hostel predominantly used for probation referrals.

(3) Generally poor level of care offered by Lyn and her partner (Tony) to baby Lauren.

Lyn's second child was placed for adoption immediately after her birth and Lyn was offered counselling from a social worker in the Adoption Team. Lyn would only see the social worker when accompanied by her partner, Tony, and often missed appointments. A social worker from our office offered short term help with practical issues (housing, day care) but closed the case after two months when she left the Department.

Lyn next came to the Department's attention in May 1989 when she was pregnant again by a partner other than Tony and wanted help in arranging a termination. Lyn was referred to the Brook Advisory Service for counselling and a termination was subsequently offered. Further concerns were raised about the deteriorating care of Lauren, who was grubby and unkempt and very silent, and also about Lyn's heavy drinking. I was allocated the case in June 1989.

Assessment

It was apparent at an early stage that Lyn had not grieved properly for the loss of her second child through adoption. This unresolved grief was now being expressed through an increased dependence on alcohol, depression, and confusion about her personal relationships. I expected that her third pregnancy and termination were closely linked with these issues and would increase the sense of despondency she felt. The external pressures of bad housing and poverty were further factors which needed to be addressed.

The deteriorating care of baby Lauren was an indicator of the extent to which Lyn had 'switched off' from her because of her absorption in her own sorrow.

Purpose of the Intervention

The purpose of my intervention has been twofold:

(1) I aimed to help Lyn address some of her past losses in the hope that this would relieve her depression and enable her to take more control of her life. I expected that an improvement in her mental health would also enable Lyn to improve her care of Lauren by being more open and responsive to her needs.

(2) I have been aware throughout my work with Lyn of my responsibility for monitoring the level of Lauren's care. I have had to ensure that this did not deteriorate to such an extent that she would be at risk, and at one point had to intervene to protect her. This has occasionally felt at odds with my therapeutic work with Lyn and I have addressed this issue further in my review of the process of the work.

Methods used

I have used one-to-one counselling in my individual sessions with Lyn. These are contract-based, in that we agreed to meet for six sessions initially and then plan to review the progress of our work. I felt it was important that we should have space and time on our own, given the past experience of workers only being allowed to see Lyn with Tony, and the sessions take place in my office. I encouraged Lyn to arrange for Tony to care for Lauren at these times, which she has successfully done.

In terms of my child protection role, I have made regular visits to the whole family, and have assessed the relationships between the parents and between the parents and Lauren. I have also been involved in advocacy and liaison with other departments (Housing/DSS) in resolving practical issues.

Before starting my individual work with Lyn, I explained the child protection aspect of my role to her, specifically my duty to monitor Lauren's welfare.

Theoretical Base

I have aimed to use a feminist perspective in my counselling with Lyn. This has involved acknowledging the specific life stresses she has experienced as a woman (caring for Lauren, caring for Tony, the termination of pregnancy) and encouraging her to recognise what her own needs are so that she can care for herself better. I have also aimed to underline the voluntary nature and equality of our relationship through the negotiation of a contract and open discussion of topics we wish to raise. This needed very careful handling, however, when dealing with child protection issues.

Process

I concentrate here on my direct work with Lyn and have referred to the other aspects of my work only in so far as they influenced this.

Lyn was initially reluctant to see me for individual sessions, stressing to me that if she could move from where she was living, she would no longer feel depressed. I persisted, and on my third visit to the family, when Tony was absent, Lyn became very tearful and said she had to talk to someone about her worries and would like to take up my offer of counselling.

This was set up and Lyn made good use of the first two sessions, in which we explored difficulties in her relationship with Tony and her past history. We constructed a family tree and Lyn talked about her teenage years in care and her sadness about the subsequent loss of her relationship with her mother. She also expressed some anger towards her family for not supporting her and for contributing to her current sense of isolation. We discussed the possibility of Lyn re-establishing contact with her mother and I encouraged her to write to her and send pictures of Lauren. An exchange of letters followed and Lyn subsequently spoke to her mother on the telephone for the first time in eighteen months.

It was after these first two sessions that my concern for Lauren grew to such an extent that I had to invoke child protection procedures. Lyn presented at the office with Lauren, who had a very prominent black eye. This had been preceded by a week to ten days of concern about Lauren being left unattended and rows at home. After detailed child protection investigations, with which Lyn and Tony fully co-operated, it was decided not to place Lauren's name on the child protection register. One positive outcome of the procedures was that the family were moved from their hostel, which the conference considered was a major contributory factor to the family's stress, to much improved homeless families accommodation.

Obviously this whole procedure was very stressful for Lyn and counter productive to what I was trying to achieve in our individual work. The process of medical examination and checks seemed to emphasise Lyn's passivity and despair and forced me into the authoritarian role of demanding certain things of her. I expected it to have considerable implications for our individual work in terms of re-establishing a trusting and open relationship; but apart from a delay in schedule, when I had to concentrate on discussing the child protection issues with the parents, our sessions have continued.

We have had two further sessions so far, and in the second of these Lyn began to talk of her adopted child, who she had named Catherine. She became very emotional when telling me, shaking and shivering in the process but was anxious to explain all the details of the birth, her very brief contact with the baby, how she felt afterwards and her reasons for requesting adoption. These were overtly related to the practical stresses in her life, particularly housing; but she also expressed some ambivalence about her relationship with Tony, both then and now. This has re-surfaced recently, largely due to pressure from him to have another child 'to replace Catherine' and to get married. Lyn initially talked of these as joint decisions, neither of which is she ready for. She is uncertain of her commitment to Tony and has talked of the pressures another child would bring.

Problems in her relationship with Tony have been a regular theme throughout our work, with Lyn expressing resentment at his inability to meet her emotional needs and to share the care of Lauren, but also expressing her fear of losing him. At her request, I have planned a session with both of them to explore some of these issues further.

Evaluation

Lyn is now beginning to function more positively than when I started work with her. She is caring for herself properly, looks well and has not resorted to drink for some time. As a result, her care of Lauren has improved significantly. She is clean and well groomed and interaction between her and her mother is improving. One factor in effecting this change has been the move to better housing. The family are realistically hopeful of being offered permanent accommodation soon.

However, I consider that Lyn's regular commitment to our sessions indicate their importance to her and recognise that we are beginning to address significant issues concerning choice and responsibility in her life. Lyn has made good use of our relationship, which was not affected by the child protection investigation, largely because of initial clarity about my statutory role and Lyn's willingness to accept this.

Peter (three and a half years)

Peter was placed for adoption at birth. His mother had a history of manic-depressive illness, and the heavy doses of drugs taken during pregnancy caused Peter to suffer foetal drug syndrome. He required careful nursing and medical care in the first two years of his life, and was assessed as having both mental and physical retardation. He was placed temporarily with very experienced but elderly (68 and 61) foster parents.

At the age of two and a half years, Peter was unable to walk unaided, was still eating baby foods, was very quiet, continually gazed at his foster-mother, and was not toilet trained. He had never been left and had never played with children of his own age, only with two much older grandchildren of his foster parents. He had never been to a toddler group, on a swing, to feed the ducks, or for a walk. He went to bed about 7 pm, woke at 11 pm and every one to two hours throughout the night until 6 am. He did not sleep in the day. When he woke in the night, he cried to be brought downstairs to be given a drink and shown around the house, switching the lights on and off. He was then taken back upstairs, nappy changed and back to sleep for another couple of hours. Medication was not advised because of his early birth history.

His relationship to his foster mother caused me concern. I felt she treated him like a baby, spoke to him like a 12-month-old and played with him like an 18 month old – that is, very simple picture books, building up a tower of bricks, pointing and naming things in the room, very much as one might do with a very young baby to encourage early development.

The foster mother stated – 'He is not ready for meeting children'. She regarded him as a baby and we could do 'untold damage if we interrupted his stability'.

There was a NCH Nursery for handicapped children nearby – that would be ideal – a sheltered environment, with independent developmental assessment and teaching expertise available.

This had to be arranged through the Community Medical Officer. She strongly advised against it, saying that Peter's relationship with his foster mother was important, and to damage it now would be disastrous. The Doctor was feeling that Peter was very dependent and insecure and very emotionally delayed. My own impression and it *was only an impression* at this time, was that

(1) Peter was not being encouraged to grow, and there was no stimulation for him.

(2) Therefore, because he was not growing, he was not getting gratification from growing and doing things.

(3) He thus regressed and clung and became miserable and played games to get attention and gratification.

(4) I also *felt* and noted on the file that 'this little boy is not mentally handicapped: his problems are a result of the way he is being handled'.

The Department went along with the Doctor and did not push for a Nursery place until Peter was three, when he began to go in three days per week.

After eight months, the teacher spoke of Peter at a case conference: he had taken a long time to settle, but he had made a lot of progress. He was, however, vulnerable to new relationships. He was now eating proper meals at Nursery and drinking from a cup, and he was totally toilet-trained by day. The speech therapist had also said that his language was greatly improved. The Medical Officer, who had been charting his progress for the last two to three years, commented that she saw Peter on his third birthday and noted that he had made considerable progress. The GP wrote urging great caution in moving Peter, since the separation from his foster mother would be traumatic. However, the picture now, in the light of his attendance at the Nursery, was of a little boy who had made great strides as a result of this introduction to a new environment, and had, in fact, separated from his foster mother, without any drastic consequences, although the medical profession had always advised against this.

The Chairman concluded that leaving him with the foster parents was delaying a constructive move. The atmosphere at the Case Conference was tense. There were those who believed that Peter should stay where he was, despite his progress and the beginnings of evidence that he could separate. The Medical Adviser to the Adoption Panel felt that Peter should be moved before he was due to start school in 18 months' time.

I was given the task of moving Peter.

Intervention

I was very aware that, before I could do anything about searching for a home, I had to have clear in my mind exactly at what stage of development Peter was. My concerns were as follows:

THE FOSTER FAMILY

The foster family were against Peter being moved and, in any case, did not think we would ever find anybody who would cope with him, especially at night. With such a stance, how was I to help this little boy separate, and would they ever let him go?

THE POSITION OF THE NURSERY

The Nursery was the pivot of this case. Peter made progress there and had relationships. Therefore, if at all possible, it must remain a feature in his life.

THE SEARCH FOR THE FAMILY

We had not been able to find Peter a home and hence the referral to BAAF. Why should I be any more successful?

WORK PLAN

(1) *Regular meetings with Peter's teacher* to build a relationship both with her and Peter. She would be vital in my move plans.

(2) *Get to know the foster parents better.* Work with them towards letting Peter go. Involve them totally in the plans, but bear in mind the foster mother's very strong character, and inherent in that, a capacity and probable desire to sabotage plans.

(3) The actual search. Plans were made to do a postal drop for the Nursery catchment area – a total of 34,000 households. I also wrote to every approved adoptive parent within the appropriate area and every foster parent within the county, whether they had been approved for this age group or not.

The postal drop brought 24 enquiries and the circulation of adoptive parents and foster parents brought in one set of approved adopters and one set of foster parents. All were visited within the next few weeks and, in October, we looked set to ask the Adoption Panel to approve a placement. The present foster parents did not approve of our choice, because they were a childless couple. The foster-mother felt that Peter needed a family with children older than himself and certainly parents who would be able to cope with the sleepless nights: she did not think this couple would be able to.

The teacher had been saying increasingly that she thought Peter's problems were behavioural and that they had been able to shape his behaviour a great deal by responding appropriately and consistently. She felt he could fairly quickly become adept at manipulating adults and was, in fact, doing this with the foster parents and probably had been doing so for some time.

The prospective parents had met the teacher, the doctor and had seen Peter in the playground. We had talked to them at length, giving them every possible piece of information. The next stage was to meet the foster parents and Peter at home. The prospective parents withdrew just before that meeting.

This was quite a blow. Three months had passed and, in effect, no progress had been made. My despondency increased, and I felt sure now that we would have to re-refer to BAAF, but one of my colleagues had been doing a review with some adopters who were waiting for placement and who had been circulated with Peter's details. It seemed they were intrigued by Peter, but felt that the method, that is, a leaflet through the door, a bit unusual! I pursued them. Fortunately, I had been involved in their approval, so they were not strangers to me.

I laid the position out to them clearly – the problems, the pitfalls, the possibilities. Peter's latest assessment had just come through – at three and a half years. his progress was increasing. I was feeling more and more sure that Peter was manipulating his home environment to get lots of adult attention because this was the only way he could get gratification.

Finally, the adoption panel selected this couple; they have two children, David (nine) and Emma (seven). The adopters then met the foster mother.

Planning the Move

We were aware that the foster mother was hostile towards this move. She was convinced that no one else could handle Peter. I had spent considerable time with her, but to no real benefit. During the past five months, I had probably seen her on ten occasions. The foster mother had, by now, accepted that she could not realistically do anything about preventing Peter's move. What concerned me was would she help Peter move? She tried desperately to be in control, (in effect, she had been, for the past few years) and felt that it should take about *three years* to move Peter! She was visibly shocked when I calmly, but firmly, suggested three months. As time was going by, I had three strings to my bow:

(1) Peter was progressing rapidly under the firm guidance of his teacher.

(2) The adopters were experienced parents, and respected, agreed with and got on well with the teacher. They would be able to carry out her work plans with Peter.

(3) The foster home was set against progress. The foster mother did not agree with the Nursery's methods. In a sense, he had been stuck in babyhood. The basic psychological task faced by every individual is to find a balance between autonomy or self reliance and dependency or trust in others. Peter did not have this bal-

ance. The foster mother made Peter over-dependent: he was a little boy who could not grow up. She had fostered many babies previously and possibly had unmet dependency needs herself. Her 30-year-old son had never left home. Peter showed marked stranger-anxiety behaviours. He had never been encouraged to make relationships, that is, to take risks, and it was constantly mentioned in front of him that he did not like strangers. In fact, what we were beginning to see in this relationship between Peter and his foster mother was a reflection of her own family – a closed unit.

I knew by now that Peter had to move quickly and I obviously wanted to do that properly and hoped that the foster parents could be grandparent figures to Peter. I had discussed this with the adopters and they were willing. The foster parents did not believe that once Peter was moved they would be allowed to see him.

Here is an extract from the adoptive parents' notes when they first met Peter.

Peter prior to March, 1985

'When we first met Peter in January, we found an anxious little boy who, nevertheless, was pleased to meet us and play with us. Our first impressions were that he was a bright child who was accustomed to a great deal of attention. He was very obviously behind in his physical development, looking more like a toddler in the way he walked, slowly and without much balance.

During the two months following, we had more frequent meetings, both in his old house and elsewhere. In this time, we had a chance to observe the way he related to his foster family. Although nearly four, he seemed to be treated very much as a baby by his foster mother. He was dressed and undressed without being encouraged to help. Because he did not walk very well, he was taken out mostly in a pushchair. At the same time everything he asked for was provided for him. A typical routine was "I want milk", but as soon as the milk was brought, "I want tea", at which, the milk was exchanged for tea. This was then followed by "I want milk", whereupon the tea was taken away and a cup of milk brought back.

If his foster mother did not respond quickly enough to his requests, he would get frustrated and several times we saw him kick her legs very hard, without any punishment. His foster mother complained to us that he had never been a loving child and did not care to be kissed and cuddled.'

The Move

The adoptive parents had been selected at the November Panel and the foster parents and the adoptive parents had met. The adoptive parents got a cool reception. I laid out my plans quickly, aiming for as early a move as possible, hoping, and praying too, that it would be possible. We all armed ourselves, including the foster parents, with Fahlberg's (1991) *Helping Children When They Must Move*. I felt that the close attachment that existed had previously been misinterpreted. However, he had been going to the Nursery for three days a week for a year now and was making a lot of progress and could make more, if the home environment was compatible with the Nursery's methods.

I recognised the need to

(1) plan very carefully and make watertight plans;

(2) involve the foster parents as much as possible;

(3) introduce the adopters gradually, but establish them as part of 'Peter's world', along with the Nursery and home;

(4) make his experience with them

(i) pleasurable, i.e. fun with opportunities to do new things, but

(ii) realistic, i.e. carrying on the discipline he was experiencing at the Nursery.

Work with Peter

The foster mother did much of the preparation with Peter, talking about his move, but his teacher also spent time with him, using figures and cars to show what was going to happen to him. I think Peter had overheard a lot of conversations at home as well, and was well aware of what was happening.

Our task with Peter, then, was initially to help him separate (we did this gradually because we feared repercussions), and then to help him attach to his new family. We did this by making sure that the adopters were firmly part of his world, that their responses to him were predictable and that, gradually, the outer predictability of their responses was becoming an inner certainty to Peter and, therefore, he began to build up a basic trust in them.

During the introductory period and the two months that have followed, we have had in mind the following issues which have been identified by Fahlberg.

1. Responding to the arousal/relaxation cycle

    (i) The adopters and their children shared Peter's excitement when he enjoyed new experiences or did things for the first time.

    (ii) They talked to him about coming to live with them.

2. Initiating positive interactions

    (i) They touched and cuddled Peter and held his hand a lot, told him they loved him and looked forward to the time when he could live with them.

    (ii) They played with him and read to him and responded positively to all his overtures.

    (iii) They looked at his photographs with him.

    (iv) They included him in all family outings and activities, i.e. picking the children up from school.

3. Claiming behaviour

    (i) They encouraged Peter to call them 'Mum and Dad' once he had moved. The foster parents are referred to as 'old Mum and Dad'.

    (ii) They had a new family group picture taken to include Peter and sent copies to grandparents and relatives.

    (iii) They took Peter to visit relatives.

    (iv) They took him out to buy new things and let him choose his own birthday present (a bike).

By the time Peter moved, he had built up a very positive relationship with his new family, and was well on the way to becoming attached to them.

Work with the foster parents

I continued to spend a lot of time with the foster parents, helping them to let go of Peter, helping them grieve for Peter, supporting them and enabling them to give their permission for Peter to move and transfer his attachment. I involved them in all the plans and met them more than half way on many occasions because I knew it would be important for the success of the move for the foster parents to take Peter to the adopters.

They did that, and did it very well. As the days passed, we observed none of the 'Protest', 'Denial' or 'Despair' responses that Bowlby (1980) describes.

Peter moved with all his belongings, even his bed and bed clothes, and several photograph albums of his early life. With the foster mother, I helped prepare a story for Peter, giving reasons why he was going to move. They were also assured by me and the adoptive parents of a continuing role in Peter's life if they wished.

Two months on

Peter has been seen by the Medical Officer and she is pleased with his progress and feels that entry to normal school is appropriate – six months early.

We are making plans for him to discontinue at the Nursery. The stimulating, lively, consistent environment of home has meant that he has outgrown the Nursery environment, and is finding it frustrating being with handicapped children. In addition, he is becoming increasingly anxious at home-time until he sees his adoptive mother, when he runs joyfully to her. (We feel he has memories of being picked up by his foster mother and is not fully convinced that he will be staying in his new home.)

At home, he is, to quote the adoptive parents, 'a very different little boy to the one we met five months ago'. He has matured a great deal, and has lost that 'baby look'. He also walks well and will now walk for long distances. Peter can also run, jump and ride a tricycle, and obviously delights in these achievements. He eats well and almost anything. He now normally sleeps through every night. 'We simply refused the night-time drinks and he soon got the message. In the mornings he gets out of bed himself – something else he never did. He used to wait for his foster mother to pick him up'.

Peter has seen his old family twice since he moved. The first time was a month after placement. This was a difficult visit for the grown-ups, but fairly relaxed for Peter. He did not ask to go with them and held on to his adoptive father's hand. Two weeks later, the adoptive parents held a belated birthday party for Peter. The old family would only come as long as no playmates of Peter's were invited. The party went well, but Peter was disturbed after this visit and regressed to babyish ways – thumb-sucking, wanting to go in the pushchair, in other words, behaviour that was associated with his old home. It passed in about two weeks.

Conclusion

The problems in this case

(1) The social workers had been blinkered by the Medical Officer's assessment and had not recognised the shortcomings in the foster home environment or in the relationship between Peter and the foster mother.

(2) No other professionals had been called in.

(3) There was a problem because the social worker did not recognise an abnormal attachment.

(4) Peter was regarded as handicapped first and a child second, and was therefore not looked after by the Child Care Section.

- We should plan for children. Planning should be creative and be work- and time-focussed.
- Children need a family setting where they can thrive and grow – preferably their own family; if not, the least detrimental alternative.
- We must make thorough assessments of children, and must involve other professionals.
- Management must be involved in making major decisions.
- Work must be carefully supervised, monitored and kept going.

The following case study illustrates how legal and administrative processes may combine with the emotions of conflicting clients in such a way as to distort professional intentions and patterns of work. The case concerns the preparation of a report for divorce proceedings. The conflict between the partners is intense, exacerbated by diverse expectations of gender roles, and religious and cultural differences. As the author recognises, these important dimensions were not (and probably could not be) dealt with in the limited time available to her; but other pressures on the worker – arising in part from the impact on herself of various gender conflicts – meant that these fundamental dimensions were overlooked during the early part of the work. Thus, it is a useful study of the emotional involvement of the worker in a situation where there are no ideal answers.

The work was undertaken shortly before the implementation of the Children Act 1989, and the author usefully indicates how far the outcome and the social work task might have been different in response to subsequent legislative and administrative changes.

Mr and Mrs M and son Paul
Divorce Court Welfare Report

'This is a very sad story.' Mrs M's opening words at our assessment meeting set the scene for a complex piece of consultancy work within a legal context: Mrs M's solicitor had requested an independent welfare report for County Court divorce proceedings. The dispute concerned the custody, care and control of Paul, aged 12, whose welfare seemed to be tangled up in a bitter divorce dispute as a 'spoil of his parents' war'.

In effect, the work was validated by the legal profession and Mrs M, but I continued to have a grumbling unease about my understanding and handling of the work and hence about the recommendations. This case study provides an opportunity to explore uncertainties and possibly to shift perspectives with the benefit of hindsight.

Family

Mr M	Iranian, born in Iraq. Muslim. Languages – Arabic, Romanian, English. Refugee status: Medical qualifications not recognised in UK. Employed as night watchman.
Mrs M	Romanian, Orthodox Christian. Languages – Romanian, English. Refugee, qualified as beautician in UK and employed in a central London store.
Paul (12)	Not strongly attached to any one church. English language only.

Family History

The marriage took place in Bucharest after a five year courtship. Mrs M was pregnant but later miscarried. Her Romanian family gave permission for the marriage to Mr M, an Iranian born in Iraq and studying medicine in Romania as a refugee. They moved to Algeria where they lived for six years.

Stresses within the marriage were experienced in the early years, resulting partly from Mr M's refugee status, and from the religious, cultural and language differences between them. Marital violence preceded Paul's birth in Bucharest in 1978: Mrs M had returned to Romania for the birth and described herself as very unhappy. Mr M's parents took refuge in Sweden but Mr and Mrs M decided to go to America, coming to England initially to obtain an entry visa to the States. Living at first in homeless family accommodation, they obtained political asylum in 1981 and subsequently moved to a council flat. Mr M attempted, but failed, to pass medical examinations to allow him to practise as a doctor in Britain. He became depressed and spent their social security income in amusement arcades. Mrs M cared for Paul and undertook training as a beautician. Success enabled her to obtain employment, and with savings they bought a comfortable semi-detached house. Mr M obtained work as a night watchman. Throughout this period there were serious episodes of marital violence, and on two occasions Mrs M's mother came from Romania to stay and seems to have acted as some sort of spur in encouraging Mrs M to shed her husband.

At the time of the referral, a truce seemed to have been reached, whereby Mr M worked at night and looked after Paul after school. Mrs M worked by day and attempted to care for Paul in the evenings, although she made no secret of being unable to control him. Mr M had stopped paying the mortgage so that inevitably their working relationship could not continue unless Mrs M withdrew her divorce petition. I never fully understood why Mrs M felt strong enough to stand up to her husband at this time in their lives when the family was living in circumstances more comfortable than ever before. It felt destructive, but possibly it was an expression of her employment success. The family system was failing to meet her personal needs and her gender identification had shifted too fundamentally for her to remain in a patriarchal household where violence seemed to be both impulse-driven and primarily expressing intimidation.

Work undertaken

(1) *Telephone negotiation with Mrs M's solicitor*

A principal focus was clarifying the inherent conflict in the request. An independent welfare report had been required by the court because Mrs M was dissatisfied with the report prepared by the Divorce Court Welfare Officer. I was not to see the report, but it was reasonable to assume that the recommendation was for Paul to be cared for by his father. It was uncertain whether Mr M would co-operate in this second report – in the event he was advised by his solicitor to be present. The hidden agenda seemed to be that I should champion Mrs M's case, since the work was being financed through her legal aid. On reflection, this dilemma contributed considerably to my subsequent unease.

(2) *Separate interviews on the same day with Mr and Mrs M and Paul in their home*

Stage two seemed equally problematic. Using *The Welfare of Families in the Process of Divorce* (Curnock and Bayley 1988), I noted the importance of meeting both partners together and a principal 'task of the welfare officer being to bridge the communication gap between them'. Attempts to interview jointly failed...the previous worker had failed too.

The next hurdle was the ease with which Mrs M engaged and communicated, using the interview as both an attempt to obtain an ally and as a therapeutic process. Mr M, in contrast, was co-operative, polite and reserved, with the intention of providing minimal involvement to satisfy the court. Paul seemed to have his prepared statement so well rehearsed that any attempt to topple it might have uncertain consequences with his father (who was probably listening in).

(3) *Brief telephone contacts with Paul's Year Head at school, the Education Welfare Officer and Mrs M's GP*

All these expressed outrage on Mrs M's account and provided a consistent message of Mr M's evil influence over his son. Interestingly, Paul's school performance and behaviour seemed to be of minimal concern, giving a slight glimmer that Mr M might actually be doing an effective parenting job. (My own assessment of Paul during our short meeting reflected a similar, though intangible, feeling.)

(4) *Attendance of Court*

A full day wheeling and dealing between solicitors in an attempt to reach a solution agreeable to both parties to present to the judge. Through this stage I gave Mrs M considerable support and comfort. The issue of alliances by now was clear, in the sense that she was bullied by both male solicitors and needed guidance.

On reflection, I was doing a different task from that for which I was recruited. It felt valid at the time, but now I feel I made a mistake in terms of establishing an alliance rather than achieving professional independence in my consultancy.

Discussion

Out of the many themes which present themselves in this case material I have selected the following for closer consideration:

(1) Consultancy

(2) Paul's welfare

(3) The Children Act 1989

1 Consultancy

On reflection, I veered towards seeing the consultancy task as that of an 'authority' or even an expert, meaning that I felt I ought to be able to find a solution. To see consultancy more in terms of advice, which may enable a deadlock to be broken, the range of choice to be extended and movement to occur is a more comfortable task, bearing in mind that 'special cases' usually seem intractable. This is the reason for a consultant being sought. Seeking 'advice' should warn the consultant that the road will be hard and labyrinthine, not necessarily offering a satisfying outcome: this is the challenge of the work.

If I had seen more clearly Mr and Mrs M's situation in terms of a conflict orchestrated in such a way as to alter power distribution within the family, it might have been possible to remain more detached. Mr M received through the post an unexpected divorce petition. His tears, pleading and violence did not weaken Mrs M's resolve to split the family. He therefore exerted the only powers he had left, which were to destroy his wife's potential gains: their son and their house. He stopped paying the mortgage and began a careful education and fathering process with the son whom he was reputed to have ignored previously.

Whatever triggered and empowered Mrs M to take divorce proceedings at this stage is uncertain, but she wanted to reduce her husband's power, punishing him for her unhappiness by securing their son and consequently the house. Paul, for whom the divorce petition was also a cruel surprise, could only side with his father, who had begun to treat him well and was likely to be able to continue to keep him in comfort (including holidays abroad); and at his stage of emotional development, identification with his father was the obvious choice. His mother represented the risk of poverty and the experience of deception.

Among the dilemmas for any female worker with her own family are the resonances and empathy aroused by this marital situation. Mrs M's wistful and punished manner were hard to resist in terms of the formation of an alliance.

Perhaps the lessons are that the consultant needs to be constantly mindful of 'dangerous liaisons'.

2   Paul

> 'Divorcing couples often take up entrenched positions, each spouse seeking to enlist other people who will take up the cudgels on their behalf and help them defeat their former partner...children may be left to make their own way backwards and forwards across the emotional minefield which divides warring couples and their supporters'. (Dale *et al.* 1986)

Paul anchored himself to his father, provoking outrage in his mother and her female supporters. Paradoxically, it was difficult not to lose sight of him because he was so certain of what he wanted and his mother seemed so needy: 'keeping him in mind' was one of the most challenging tasks as the 'destructive forces' within the marriage reflected on the worker and induced a kind of paralysis.

It seemed from his behaviour and Mrs M's account, that Paul had experienced a warm and secure relationship with his mother so that, apart from what outsiders viewed as unacceptable (his adoration of his father), he presented as a friendly, happy, out-going 12-year-old.

Kellmer Pringle (1980) writes of a child's need for love as 'a stable, continuous, dependable and loving relationship with his parents, who themselves enjoy a rewarding relationship with one another'. This is what Paul craved for, but he had been betrayed by his mother, who did not warn him of her divorce intentions because she feared it would upset him.

Wallerstein and Kelly's (1980) research into how children and parents cope with divorce indicates that a parent's distress and depression makes it difficult for the parent to offer a child consolation at the time he most needs it. 'Children who were accustomed to feeling comfortable and secure would suddenly be set adrift.' No wonder Paul sought shelter with his father.

> 'Young people were particularly vulnerable to being swept up into the anger of one partner against the other. They were

faithful and valuable battle allies... Not infrequently, they turned on the parent they had loved and been very close to prior to the marital separation. A child between 9–12 has the capacity for unswerving loyalty.' (Wallerstein and Kelly 1980)

To outsiders, Mrs M presented as a martyr...wronged by her husband and now punished by her child. Looked at another way, Paul's anger and disapproval of divorce initiated by his mother was to be expected: 'The anger of the older children that was generated by the divorce was not related to the quality of the parent-child relationship before separation.' (Wallerstein and Kelly 1980)

The outcome of the Court case was a supervision order and a referral to child guidance 'which should have been made yesterday' (the judge). These results were in my view more likely to be symbolic than effective in the sense that attention was drawn to 'joint parenting responsibility' and the need for joint care and action on Paul's behalf. I doubt whether the local authority would prioritise this case or whether Paul would be responsive to therapy at a child guidance clinic. Acknowledgement in the court of the trouble in store (should alliances be maintained) and the placing of responsibility on both parents were, in my view, the best that could be done at that stage.

A final consideration is how Paul managed to remain apparently resilient in the face of adversity – one recalls the effects of his international mobility, constant violent conflicts in the home, mixed racial identity, religious conflicts, difficulties with language. Indeed, diversity rather than harmony seemed to be the pattern of his life. There are warning signs indicating conflict in Paul's inner world and the areas of his identity he will need to resolve as he approaches manhood.

3 The Children Act 1989

It is ironic that, after October 14th 1991, the battleground for this dispute would have been fundamentally changed in view of both the philosophy of the Act and the legal framework. In a sense, one of the major battles could not have happened since, in divorcing situations, both parents now retain parental responsibility. Parents do not cease to be parents because they are divorced. By insisting on 'shared care' arrangements at the court hearing, the judge was clearly mindful of the imminent changes in the law. It is a pity that neither Mrs M's solicitor nor I were fully aware of the implications of these legal changes.

Other important considerations are that Section 41 of the Matrimonial Causes Act 1973 has been radically amended to absolve the court from its duty to make the 'declaration of satisfaction' before making a decree absolute (Sch 12 para 31). Only in exceptional cases (this may be one of them) may the court exercise its power to postpone making the divorce absolute because further time is needed for consideration of welfare matters. Since there is no case law to draw on, it is not possible to know whether Mr and Mrs M's divorce would have been a special case.

A further principle: Avoidance of delay (Section 1(2)) potentially alters the handling and outcomes in this enquiry. By the time of my involvement, the entrenched positions adopted by the parents owed as much to legal tardiness as to the seemingly intractable nature of the problem.

It is realistic to assume, however, that Mr and Mrs M's bitterness would have been as acute despite the expectation of 'reasonableness' in the new Act. I would expect S.8 orders to be required in this case, a cause for concern being that, where parental responsibility is shared, each person in whom it is vested may act independently in meeting that responsibility. The Act has not created any rights of consultation before action is taken. It is conceivable that this may give rise to some difficulties in practice: a parent may not discover a proposed action until it is too late. In this case, where Mr and Mrs M had not spoken to each other for six months, communicating through solicitors while living in the same house locked in their own rooms, tactics seemed to take the form of wounding the other party as deeply as possible, usually by taking Paul out of the country for long periods without consultation or information. In Bainham's (1990) words 'the failure of the Act to incorporate rights of consultation may well impede one of the central objectives of the reforms which is to achieve a norm of parental co-operation following divorce.'

Finally, the centrality of the welfare of the child in the Act must change the focus of this dispute. Instead of a parent having rights of access to the child, the child is to have rights of contact with his parents. In Paul's position at the time of the enquiry, he would have refused contact with his mother. The ascertainable wishes and feelings of the child concerned (considered in the light of his age and understanding) and his physical, emotional and educational needs are crucial elements to this case. Although the wishes of the child are not to be a determinant of the outcome, the Act attempts to provide a legal framework in which the child's alternative claims to independence and protection may receive proper consideration. It may be argued that a child should not have to bear the burden of having to choose between one parent or the other. For Paul this may have produced an immediate shift in allowing himself to communicate with both parents, and may have reduced Mr M's 'brainwashing' tactics.

Postscript

This chapter, perhaps more than the others, suffers from a lack of sufficient material to provide adequate illustrations of the range of administrative and interprofessional issues encountered in child protection work. Nonetheless, it provides material for some discussion; comprehensive coverage of the subject would require a book to itself. Implicit in these presentations is the view that there is both scope and need for public debate and public recognition of the limitations and boundaries (legal, administrative and professional) of social work practice. These boundaries and limitations usefully constrain the scope of practice, which might otherwise be seen as over-intrusive and, in its complexities, beyond the scope of any practitioner, however skilled. But boundaries (if they are to be useful) require recognition and endorsement by the parties on both sides of the divide. This chapter illustrates how boundaries are not always seen as lying in the same places by the professionals concerned with them, and that, as a result, there are aspects of clients' lives and experiences which professionals run the risk of worsening rather than improving – by overlapping yet divergent intentions, or by leaving clients and colleagues bewildered by lack of help at critical points. Certainly, clarity is needed in public debate about what social workers are licensed to do, where the limits of their intervention should lie, and about the distinction – if there is one – between professional confidentiality and professional secrecy.

CHAPTER FIVE

The Stresses of Social Work with Children

At several points in this book, contributors have referred to the stresses they have experienced in their work. In Chapter 3, we observed how stress (particularly associated with feelings of uncertainty, risk and failure) is increased in work which attempts to bridge differences of language, race and culture. But in all work involving the care of sad, bewildered and hurt children, social workers inevitably experience stress: the fear of making situations worse rather than better; the absorption of a child's unhappiness; confronting choices in making a professional interpretation of a child's welfare and 'best interests' – should he stay with his parents? should he be fostered or adopted? how will he interpret the events of his life? does he stand any chance of a happy and worthwhile life? Supervision which is challenging, orderly, yet emotionally supportive is clearly desirable – and, in the hurly-burly of work in the social services, sadly seldom available to many social workers.

In this chapter, several of these themes are brought together by the presentation of two case-studies written by one social worker. He comes from the Indian sub-continent; his clients are a black child and a black adolescent. He is diffident of his ability to provide effective help, and sensitively aware that the demands of the work (and of the course in which he was a student at that time) are awakening uncomfortable and sometimes resentful feelings in himself. He recognises his need for personal support, without which there is a risk that the helpfulness of his intervention will decline.

Ostensibly, this chapter starts with the needs of two children. But because of the honesty of the social worker's account of his work, we are drawn to an even greater interest in the worker himself – his feelings, his needs and his aspirations.

Direct work with Jermaine (aged six)

Introduction

I had not undertaken any direct work with a child prior to starting the Goldsmiths course. There had been times when the need for such work was high, but somehow was not met, by me at least. When I think back to why this was, two reasons come to mind. The first is to do with the context in which I work. This is a local authority generic team. Many workers will recognise the 'feel' of this context as being rather like an accident and emergency clinic where stress is high, time is limited and changes in personnel happen frequently. Roughly packaged bundles of need are often presented, with immediate crises being responded to very well at times, but longer term needs not receiving as much attention as they deserve. Children *are* protected but may not be cared for therapeutically. Where there is lack of containment and continuity for workers, it is hard to provide these for children.

The second reason is to do with my own history, the story of my childhood, in which lack of continuity as a theme emerges power-fully. Separation and loss, through emigration, by being a stranger in a strange land, through death, have created a sense of 'unbelong-ing', compounded at times by racism.

Personally and professionally, much as I wanted to, I found it hard to tolerate the idea of direct work with a child, especially when transitions were involved – the child coming into care for example, particularly a Black child being drawn into a 'White' institution like a Social Services Department.

It was not until my daughter was born two years ago that I began to feel part of a family again. Slowly, since that time my confidence in being able to tolerate and contain the pain of separation of children that I have worked with has grown. There has been no sudden, magical transformation, personally or professionally. As I have struggled to understand the demanding nature of parent-hood, I have struggled also to comprehend the complex nature of the professional task.

These parts of my own history and work context impinged on my involvement with Jermaine, a six-year-old African–Caribbean boy with whom I met over several months. His history is briefly outlined in the next section. I am going to concentrate on one episode out of a number of times that we met. It illustrates Jermaine and me struggling together to make some sense of what was happening, particularly in relation to transitions, change, and loss. The themes that are highlighted are of continuity and containment.

Planning

'The Social Worker is the 'bridge' from the child's old life to his new one. He must trust the strength and safety of his bridge before he can make a crossing and the bridge must remain intact so that his past is not lost to him...'

(Horne 1986, p.87)

Jermaine is the oldest child of three in a family where the mother, Cora, is the sole parent. He has two siblings, a brother aged two and a half and a sister aged six months. All the children have different fathers, with whom no contact is maintained by Cora or the children.

Before I began working with Jermaine and his family there had been considerable Social Services involvement, including six other allocated social workers. Cora's first child had been removed by a Care Order when Jermaine was an infant. He had subsequently been adopted and the family had no further contact with him. The maternal grandparents saw family members from time to time and Jermaine was used to spending some weekends with them when Cora wanted a break from caring for him.

This break was necessary, she said, because he was regularly wetting his bed at night, hitting his brother, destroying his toys – she found him uncontrollable. She was pregnant, her blood pressure was high and she could not cope. Jermaine's schoolteachers described him as fundamentally a likeable boy but expressed concern about his unpredictable behaviour. They had difficulty containing him within the classroom and said he had an impaired sense of danger. He would often come to school smelling of stale urine, feeling hungry and looking tired.

The school's expression of concern and Cora's request to the Social Services Department for help with Jermaine led to an assessment of his educational and social needs. Cora appeared depressed for much of the time. A strong pattern emerged of an ambivalent relationship between mother and son, where Jermaine's behaviour demanded a lot from a carer and where Cora's behaviour towards him suggested she could offer very little. Separation was recommended. The maternal grandparents were identified as potential substitute carers. Jermaine moved to live with them two weeks before his sister was born. He transferred schools. My direct work with him began shortly thereafter.

In helping me to feel that the work was contained and indeed that I could be a 'container', I arranged supervision with Alan, a Team Leader in my area. My perception was that Alan was experienced in supervising direct work with children. I felt he could help me shape my work and help in making connections between my work and my 'self'. Furthermore, Alan is Black, and he and I had often spent time together sharing experiences of being Black, talking about belonging and unbelonging. I felt safe with him because I knew that we could talk at some level of complexity about these experiences, without jargon, without translation, but with meaning.

I planned to meet Jermaine once a week over three months. His new school offered us a room to meet in, with free use of a range of art materials and toys. Jermaine and I agreed to meet on the same day of each week, at the same time, for one hour. His school helper had been able to transfer over with him. In my meetings with her she said that Jermaine quickly latched on to the idea of regularity and would remind her each week that I was coming.

With regard to issues of race, I was aware that the world Jermaine and I were entering needed to reflect the multi racial world which was part of our daily reality. Lego people of various colours, sizes, shapes, male and female, were used as a normal part of our sessions. There was less disturbance in Jermaine's life in relation to racial identity than has been described elsewhere in work with Black children. His move had been within the context of his own culture, family, and community. My being Black and having a Black supervisor *may* have bolstered that sense of continuity. In any case, Jermaine quickly demonstrated his awareness of his own identity in our work (for example by regularly identifying a Black Lego person to be him in play), as well as his comfort with this. The main carers were always Black Lego people, although friends were identified at random from the assortment before him.

Some continuity was available to him and some containment was provided for him in the planning and implementation of our work. Jermaine's play, to start with, was full of what seemed to be the most awful violence. Vampires existed, giants ate up people and crushed houses, Jermaine rescued his mother from robbers. I asked him once, directly, early in our meetings why he had gone to his grandparents' home. 'So I can belong', he said. Usually such directness was ignored by him. My initial confidence began to ebb. I thought he thought I was clumsy. I thought I was clumsy. But I began to realise as time went by that most of his communication with me happened not in the form of grown-up conversation, but through play. During our fourth session Jermaine told me his story about 'the happy hoover'.

Process – 'The happy hoover'

'This is the happy hoover', he said, building a construction with many components clamped together. It looked like lots of railway carriages with many wheels. 'It will suck up little people; it's got hundreds of wheels. It's going to be happier (he attached more wheels) and happier (yet more).' He swung it round his head and wheels began to fall off and land on the Lego people who had been 'sunbathing'.

'The people are trapped. They think they are safe but the hoover can mash them up with its wheels.' He placed some of the people on a bed – a 'hospital bed'. I asked him why people went to hospital. 'Because they are injured or to have a baby. I can't wait, I'm going to Brighton with my mum.' (Cora had recently come out of hospital after giving birth to Jermaine's sister.) For a minute or so, he was silent, looked 'bored'. He walked around randomly looking out of the window. Slowly, he came back to the play people tray and picked up a child-shaped Lego person. 'I wish I could always be little people.' Holding the figure he made him fly around the room, landing him back in the tray containing lots of other people. He picked up a crocodile which no longer had an upper jaw, a casualty of our previous session. He put the crocodile on the hoover and both took off into the air together.

'The people don't know it's danger that's coming to them.' The crocodile attacked the person on the hospital bed. The hoover shed more wheels, it 'destroys people'. 'Some danger is coming, it's coming to suck up our kids', Jermaine shouted. The hoover and crocodile dropped to the floor 'this croc has sharp toes'. He trapped the crocodile between two pieces of wood. 'Now it's dead, now it's trapped.'

He walked away back to his Lego, spending some time making a 'space ship', with a single figure who sat in it, 'the driver'. The space ship took off, landing high up on a shelf. It had propelled Jermaine along with it and he climbed a chair and then a table to keep up: 'here he can see the world'. What could he see, I asked. Jermaine named his mother and his brother and sister. 'He's got poison, he's lost.' I asked that if Jermaine was lost and somebody asked me what he looked like, what should I tell them? 'Just tell them he looks like a boy, he's six, he goes to a new school.' I asked him what Jermaine liked doing. 'He likes playing and eating.' Where does he live, I asked. Jermaine gave his mother's address. Who does he live with? Jermaine said his mother, brother, sister, grandmother and grandfather. What if people said they thought he had moved? Why did he move? 'First because my mum was having a baby...'Jermaine curled up on the chair, fell onto the carpet, and lay there for a while.

I reminded him that our time was nearly up for this week. I would see him next time. He sat up. 'Have you seen a baby crocodile?' he said. He picked up the crocodile from his trap and deconstructed the hoover. 'The hoover sucks up all the people...can you take me back to my old school, to Mrs C (his previous classteacher)?' I promised that he and I would go back together to his old school, and I would speak to Mrs C about it. He helped me tidy up the room, I returned him to his classroom as usual.

Evaluation

For me, this session highlights the struggle Jermaine and I were engaged in. Here both of us, sometimes together, sometimes apart, were attempting to make sense of transitions and loss. Imperfectly, without much reference to our relationship with each other, small steps were being taken to test out containment and to offer continuity. I had moved away from attempts to ask questions directly and bluntly, but felt little confidence in exploring the dynamics of the relationship between the child and the worker. It was almost as if I was absent from what was happening for quite a lot of the time. Having said this, I feel now as if a beginning level of competence was emerging during these sessions. The overall aim of offering a professional adult relationship to the child where his feelings can be borne, thought about and talked about was to some extent being met.

Critically, this process and its development was facilitated by detailed supervision within which I felt contained, professionally and personally. Also, I would have found the work difficult to tolerate without personal experiences which were part of the process of change.

Overall, I feel more confident as a consequence of working with Jermaine. Technically, I feel less clumsy and more fluent. It feels like a good beginning.

Work with an adolescent

'What became of the people of Sumer?', the traveller asked the old man, 'for ancient records show that the people of Sumer were Black. what happened to them?' 'Ah', the old man sighed. 'They lost their history, so they died.'

Introduction

Samson is a 14-year-old boy. He is Black. His mother and father are from Ghana. He was born in a South East London suburb where his family lived until he was 11. He has two sisters, one of whom is 16 years old, and one nine. His parents separated when he was five years old, at the time of his younger sister's birth. His mother says that his father was violent towards her but never to the children. The family was subject to racist violence for a number of years prior to being rehoused in the area where I work. The family home had been fire bombed and gutted. They had no possessions to speak of at the time of the move.

Sometime after the move Samson and his older sister started offending. Both were charged with deception. Samson received a one year Conditional Discharge. I had written his Social Inquiry Report and over a number of months came to know the family well. During our initial encounters I noted that Samson was quiet and withdrawn, offering monosyllabic answers to any questions, and making little eye contact. His mother, on the other hand, gave graphic accounts of his misbehaviour at home, his challenges to her authority, and expressed concern about his staying out late and mixing in 'bad company'. The school gave a simple picture – 'good at sport, bad at study', a little caricature of a troubled Black adolescent, an 'extremely aggressive and disturbed pupil'. In the presence of his mother and teachers, it was hard to reach him. I offered to meet him on his own and he readily accepted.

Initially, we met regularly. He was invited to say how he wanted to spend our time together. We played cards. He taught me a new card game. Then for one meeting he was late. He said he had been suspended from school. A boy had told a racist joke and he had retaliated. We talked about his experiences of racism. A sudden animation emerged in him combined with anger, not only focused on those who had been racist to him but on his parents – why had they come to this country? Why didn't his Dad stay and look after them when they were being attacked? He could not speak his parents' language, had no contact with the extended family, could not recall where his parents came from in Ghana, what his grand-parents were called, what they looked like or did... A sense of dislocation from his past presented itself powerfully. I asked him whether in our meetings together he would like to talk more about these feelings and experiences. 'Maybe', he said.

He did not keep the next appointment and was 45 minutes late for the next one. In the meantime, he stole some running shoes from a shop and was caught and charged by the police. He received a one year Supervision Order in court and I became his supervising officer.

After the meeting where he had talked so much, my initial reaction was a combination of wanting to rescue him and thinking that I could not cope. His dilemma, a sense of unbelonging, resonated with my own experiences in adolescence, certainly that single accusatory question to my parents in the face of racism, 'Why did you bring me here?', often said in English without an Indian accent. I scraped through my adolescence. Even now, not far beneath the surface, I feel the dilemmas I experienced then, sitting unresolved, a bundle of contradictions and rebellion which I can barely touch. Because of this I find it difficult to work with adolescents.

Samson began to attend irregularly and was often late. We tried to construct a genogram in which significant figures remained name-less; we tried an ecomap where many relationships were described as weak or stressful. During late Summer, Samson stopped attend-ing altogether. I made no contact with him for about a month.

I wrote to him again recently asking him to come and see me. The Supervision Order still has several months to run. Interestingly, when he came to our last meeting a few days ago, Samson said that he had regretted not seeing me and that he thought I had not written to him because I no longer wanted to see him. Ghana, apparently, did not go the way of South Africa because Black people did not cede power to White settlers. They were organised. I know this because Samson told me. He knows because he asked his father, with whom he has re-established regular contact. The prospects of being able to work together look brighter than they did.

Thoughts about the work

Boston (1983), in writing about technical problems in psychotherapy with severely deprived children, mentions instances where the client is very hard to engage or takes flight before he has really begun. She says:

> 'There may be overt abuse...or more subtle expressions of it, not turning up to the next session, for example. Mistakes and confusion over appointments are frequently enactments of feelings of being unwanted which are unconsciously thrown back to the therapist. It is the therapist who is left, abandoned, not knowing if the client will come. This difficulty can make it very hard to know in advance what frequency of treatment would be most appropriate.' (Boston and Szur, p.61)

In my attempts to work with Samson, this comment provides a distillation of some of my experiences and feelings. But as I write, one of the things I am struck by is that the mistakes and confusion, and feelings of being unwanted, were not confined to my contact with Samson, but re-enacted with my Supervisor and Practice Coordinator in different ways.

I had begun this piece of work at a time when my Practice Coordinator was leaving. His departure created a lot of turbulence and I was left with a feeling of not being wanted. Anger arose, which was re-enacted with Alan, the Supervisor for this piece of work, where I made arrangements to meet, cancelled at the last minute, confused appointments, or saw him in passing only to explain breathlessly how busy I was with other pieces of work. Ultimately, what should have been a series of meetings to consider the detail of my work, was reduced to a single meeting within which the parallels of Samson's behaviour with me and my behaviour with Alan were drawn out. These circumstances were compounded by pre-existing feelings of uncertainty about work with adolescents, referred to above. I felt as if I *had* to work with an adolescent, but did not really want to. Leaving this work to be done towards the end of the course was in itself no accident, but partly a product of a silent rebellion against my tutor's expectations, an expression of ambivalence, and a symbolic representation of non-conformity.

Coleman and Hendry (1980) say that in adolescence, non-conformist behaviour reflects the ambivalent attachment to parents, as the process of disengagement from the family gathers momentum. The adolescent surges powerfully between infancy and adulthood, history and future, dependence and independence. The matrix of experience which defines his current identity remains labile, its edges rough, fist-shaped and fragile. The adolescent seeks and resents containment (Kroger 1989) and displays uncertainty about where he belongs. Continuity is threatened as roots are severed in attempts to fashion a new sense of self. For Black children, living in a hostile environment where being Black is bad, socially unacceptable, and historically marginalised (Fryer 1984), the risk of severance from roots is high. Many writers stress that maintenance of a positive sense of racial identity (Maximé 1986) and cultural identity (Anderson 1982) is essential if the Black adolescent is successfully to negotiate a coherent sense of self, founded in part on a sense of history. Ways of retaining continuity are variously referred to, for Black Afro–Caribbean children at least, as 'psychological nigrescence' (see Cross 1971). Anderson says that one aspect of this is the provision of positive historical connections for Black children, as a counter to 'cultural corrosion' (Hazareesingh 1979) in an alien land.

> 'In order to feed Black children with more wholesome 'foods' and to clear centuries of stigmatisation and stagnation, we need to 'go back and fetch it'. Many people are educated to believe that Africa past and present, held or holds nothing. Black people, as a result of this racist education, feel little or no kinship with Africa and other Africans. The proverb 'you have to go back before you can go forward' is important for Africans who seek to re-educate themselves… Such seekers recognise that a people without true knowledge of their history are like a tree without roots. To go back is to repair and rediscover the foundations of a collective identity and to show self respect, a pre-requisite for group respect.' (p.4)

In this context, the task for Black adolescents, caught as they are in the process of oscillation present for all adolescents, is to learn about and positively value their history. The thesis is that one arrives at a newer and better understanding of oneself through developing and understanding of where one has been.

Stating the thesis in its purest form, it could be said that the turbulence and power an adolescent brings to a psychotherapeutic encounter could, if the 'container' is strong enough, lead to a (safe) explosion of awareness.

I say 'in its purest form' in an attempt to distinguish reality from fantasy. The reality, as many writers on therapeutic work with children and adolescents attest, is often marked by hurtful explosions, slow change, premature disengagements, and uncertainty. It is a pity that in accounts of therapeutic work, issues of race and culture are often not explicitly addressed. When they are addressed, some of the common features mentioned by a variety of writers are a sense of bewilderment and fear experienced by White workers and their task of helping Black children to understand their roots. A lack of understanding emerges, unconsciously felt or explicitly articulated, a combination of 'not knowing enough about their culture' and 'not feeling secure enough about being anti-racist'.

In my work with Samson I think what happened was that equal and opposite gaps in my capacity to contain were present – almost a feeling that I knew too much, and was too close to Samson's experiences. It is difficult to gauge but perhaps for other Black workers similar feelings may be engendered. I have not been able to find any written accounts of this from the Black worker's perspective. This may in part be due to Black workers and writers currently finding themselves being prescriptive in relation to work with Black children. There is a need for prescription, but I wonder how easy it is, in the process of meeting the need for certainty and expert opinion, for Black workers to talk about or write about being uncertain or inexpert.

The following two case extracts illustrate the usefulness of working with *both* child *and* parent in a crisis. This is basically a happy and united family; but the young mother has contracted leukaemia, and her son is distressed by the uncertainties of her going in and out of hospital. Matthew is not a victim of parental neglect or abuse, and perhaps there is no proper place for him in a study of child protection; but it is to be hoped that, despite the burden of statutory responsibilities and priorities defined by politicians, administrators and accountants, professional social workers may still find time to respond – however briefly – to simple human suffering.

The social worker presents here her separate pieces of work with son and mother.

The story of Matthew and his mother is included here not only for its intrinsic interest but because of the stress it imposed on the social worker. As she says at the end of the case, she finds it hard because of her own feelings to evaluate the work she did. We have a further indication of this stress in her work with Matthew, when she feels that other children (themselves in need of help) are somehow intruding on her work. The more a social worker feels a sense of identification with a client, and the more the client's feelings and experiences echo those of the social worker, the greater the likelihood of stress. Amy is a good mother; her suffering is, by any reckoning, 'undeserved'; it raises the primitive and fundamental anxieties about 'why do these things happen to good people' – the issues raised, though only tentatively resolved, in the Book of Job. Thus, it can be argued that, *in emotional terms,* neglectful or abusive parents are easier to help than 'good' parents, although the work may be difficult in terms of achieving positive behavioural changes. Similarly, with neglected and abused children, the social worker can derive some support from a feeling of coming to the rescue. But in Matthew's case, rescue from what? Not from another human being, but from the kinds of stress which have affected and will affect us all. A parallel situation arises in the work involved in marital reconciliation or conciliation; here too social workers often feel a greater sense of risk and 'loneliness' than in undertaking their statutory responsibilities – partly because there is no supportive legislative duty and no clearly defined 'agency function', but partly also because of the sense, in many instances, that this is a situation we fear as a possibility in our own lives. In this present case, the social worker skilfully avoids display of her own sadness and anxiety – she cannot be accused of over-involvement – but her honest comments about evaluation indicate the stress she experienced.

Direct work with Matthew (aged three)
Initial outline of the situation

In 1988 Matthew's mother became extremely ill with severe headaches. Initially it was thought this was due to the early stages of a
second pregnancy, but following hospitalization in 1989 she was
diagnosed as having a leukaemic type condition of poor prognosis.
Long periods in hospital followed until Sally was born in August
1989.

At the point when I became involved directly, June 1990, Matthew's
experiences of his mother were that she would usually be tired and
lethargic with frequent and unpredictable periods of hospitaliza-
tions for blood transfusions. Under consideration then, and
throughout the following summer months, was a bone marrow
transplant, the consequences of which would be a separation of
Matthew from his mother for some four to six weeks. The family
had an allocated area social worker, Matthew had a full time social
services nursery place and Sally was cared for during the day by a
childminder. Father continued to struggle with shift work as a bus
driver.

The nursery staff described Matthew as an anxious child, who on
one particular occasion had withdrawn into a corner sobbing and
talking quietly to himself about mummy for some 15 to 20 minutes,
so inconsolable that he was beyond the comfort of his usual cuddle.
Mother said Matthew was waking a lot at nights and coming into
their bed, whilst father recalled a time when he had told Matthew
mummy was back in hospital and 'it had really thrown him' and
how much he himself had cried because normally he sees Matthew
as 'okay'.

Purpose of the intervention

A young child is totally dependent on the love and approval of his
parents, without which he feels he cannot survive. Because Matthew was experiencing separation from his mother during his years
of 'magical thinking' ('step on a crack, break your mother's back'),
he could in some way assume that he is responsible for the loss. He
may have decided that 'he was so bad' (in some particular way) or
was 'so unlovable' that even his own mother didn't want to be
around him. These self-imposed labels deal the child's self-esteem
a blow from which many children are slow to recover, resulting in
the loss of a sense of self and identity. Miller (1987) describes

healthy narcissism as being in touch with one's own emotions and having the ability to take them seriously and express them spontaneously.

The purpose of the work with Matthew was therefore to encourage him to bring his feelings of insecurity, bewilderment, confusion, fear, frustration and aggression to the surface, helping him to live and work through these emotions as they presented. If he could be helped with his inner world, he might make some sense of his outer world, and have a healthier start to the possible grieving process which lay ahead.

Methods used

Initially, it was essential to gain the consent and cooperation of everyone in the system. The nursery staff had identified the need for such work. The family's social worker expressed great interest and has joined with me in the experience. The idea was put forward to the parents by the social worker, following which we did a joint visit. It was interesting to learn that mother had discussed 'the work' with her health visitor, who had confirmed 'what a good idea it was, as children tend to get neglected in these circumstances'. Indeed, mother herself wanted to be involved in the work, and my sessions with her are more fully outlined later in this chapter.

The work was organized in three strands. First, my assessment of, and getting familiar with, Matthew. Second, the direct work with him through play. The third stage was my withdrawal, and the nursery staff taking over my role.

Process of the work

My first task was to assess for myself where Matthew was at, and for both of us to get to know each other. Initially, I met him in his own home with mother. It was important that mother was seen to regard me as an 'okay person', as the relationship created between Matthew and myself would be a deciding factor in the outcome of the work. I then met Matthew ten times over a three week period at various times of day in the nursery. This allowed me to see, and be involved with him in different activities – creative play with paints, glue, and so forth, imaginative times in the home corner, at meal times and being collected by father. Matthew has a favourite car in the nursery and initially he would drive up to me, stay close as I sat on the ground, and/or attempt to push the car through me.

Gradually he began to recognise that I was there just for him, his face would 'light up' when I appeared and he would invariably seek a cuddle. I was therefore surprised during the second week when I arrived and made myself comfortable on one of the small nursery chairs to find he had disappeared. However he re-emerged carrying a chair for himself which he placed next to mine. In order to facilitate a dialogue and working relationship with Matthew, I used some of the format in *All about Me*, a written record of personal development and progress devised and piloted by Sheila Wolfendale in association with the Under Fives Unit, National Children's Bureau (1987). Towards the end of this period Matthew was getting on well with me, telling me through the toy 'phone that mummy wasn't well; it was becoming increasingly difficult to have any discussion without other children competing for attention.

Whilst it was recognised that some of the larger equipment, such as the home corner, sand/water trays, and so forth, would be good media through which to work with Matthew, it seemed more important that we had our own private space. With the help of the nursery staff, toys were selected for imaginative play and creative activities, and placed in a box labelled 'MATTHEW'. Amongst the toys we chose were:

a puppet	• could be used as an extension of the child's self
a telephone	• talking to or through, helping overcome inhibitions
hospital people and equipment; a doctor's set	• affording a chance to go through family situations of his own experience
dough	• encouraging imagination
books	• relaxing, with the opportunity of giving the child some close and comforting attention

Thus equipped, Matthew and I started a 'special time' thrice a week between 12.30 and 1.30 pm (when there was a quiet period following lunch) in a small room in a cabin in the nursery grounds.

On the first occasion he became acquainted with all the contents of his box, playing for a short while with the doctor's set. He told me 'that's what the doctors do with mummy'. As the sessions progressed Matthew would from time to time return to the doctor's set and hospital people and equipment, but his main pre-occupation during the following three weeks was with the dough. Initially, he made butterfly cakes 'like mummy', but by the third session most of the time was spent making, destroying and re-rolling different coloured doughs representing mummy, daddy, Sally, Matthew, Nanny and Pops. On one occasion he made sure that the Matthew and mummy figures were put away together squashed in the same pot, to which I commented 'You want mummy and Matthew to be together'. Matthew's imagination later extended to all the dough people being piled together in dough cars, 'brum, bruming' around the room going to the park. In one session he mentioned driving to hospital. Matthew showed me the hospital bed and said 'that's what makes ladies better'. When I tried to draw him out he commented further 'mummy's not well, doctors have made her better', and with a shrug of his shoulders saying 'that's done', informed me verbally and in body language that I had gone far enough. Towards the end of the second week Matthew appeared very restless, to the point where on one occasion he couldn't cope with a whole hour of 'special time'. As always I was directed by him, only to learn later that mother had been discharged from hospital the day before. Towards the end of our sessions together Matthew started to bury a small toy baby in the dough, rolling it up, looking for it and (with help requested of me) retrieving it. It felt as if he was acting out the disappearing and coming back which were his experiences of mother, and perhaps were also about me as I attempted to prepare him for my departure. I tried to put into words how confusing people being there and then not being there must feel. The activity could also have been an expression of anger towards Sally, whom he wanted to disappear as with her arrival mother had become ill.

The final stage of the intervention was to hand over the work. Originally it had been planned to do this by co-working, with my lead gradually being taken over by a member of the nursery staff until my complete withdrawal. However, because of holidays and staff shortages this was not possible, and the work for my part was drawn to a conclusion by engaging the wider system in three individual meetings:

(1) The officer in charge, to whom Matthew was already attached, and who was to continue the direct work

(2) The allocated social worker and officer in charge, and

(3) The parents.

Evaluation of the intervention

The work with Matthew continues, and I hear he is presently displaying considerable anger towards his mother, as she attempts to prepare him for her bone marrow transplant, by banging and shaking her as he hides her in the dough: a healthy sign, as he seems to have overcome the fear that if he lets out some rage a calamity will result.

I have heard it suggested that it takes seven years to get over the death of a parent. A young child loses a parent over and over again – when they go to school, birthdays, and so on. Matthew's situation raises powerful emotions for all those who meet him, and there is a feeling of not being able to do enough and a desire to tackle the 'problem' as soon as possible. I feel the main value of the work has been to set in motion a *gradual* process in which helpful adults understand that his chances of a good life depend on taking a great deal of time and will involve some pain. There is no short cut and hurting is part of the cure.

Work with Amy (aged 28)

Assessment of the situation

Amy is Matthew's mother.

I first met Amy on 5th June 1990, with the family's social worker, with the intention of gaining her consent and trust in allowing me to do a piece of work with her son. Her immediate response was so positive that she also wanted to be involved in helping and supporting Matthew through the unpredictable and lengthy separations from her. Guilt and pain are inseparable from loss, and for Amy this showed in her taking on board all the responsibility, as she saw it, of 'putting Matthew through this'. Perhaps she also felt undermined, as through her illness she was now reliant on a wide range of people to help her fulfil her mothering role.

Purpose of the intervention

The outcome of a child's loss or separation experience hinges on how adults allow and even encourage the child to accept his strong feelings. My work with Amy would therefore support and complement my work with Matthew. However, Amy also had her personal agenda: that is, to bear the unbearable, the uncertainty about the future. There was a need to provide time and space for Amy to reflect on her experiences, understand what is happening, adapt to the reality of the illness and treatment, enable the expression of fear, anger, anxiety and sadness and provide a safe place and person – one who was not involved in the medical treatment, and so could be the recipient of unwanted and sometimes frightening feelings.

Theoretical base of the work

To do this work I needed to be in touch with my own losses, the impact of these and the unresolved issues in my own life. Of painful personal significance to me was the fact that I have a pregnant daughter of 26 years with a son, Matthew, of two years. In such situations the security of the onlooker is threatened, and the temporary feeling is that the 'shadow of death' can easily pass over one's own family.

Process of the work

Although I had already met Amy, I saw our first meeting in mid-August as the beginning of our working relationship. I started in a non-threatening way to get her to talk about how life had been for her before she became ill. I hope this showed that my interest was not simply because she was a mother. We discussed her family and she drew me a genogram. As she talked about her dead mother and father she did not display any fresh sadness; this gave a useful indication of how she had coped with previous losses and thus her ability to deal with the present stress. Amy had been told her diagnosis some eighteen months prior to my contact, and I was able to lead the focus of the session to the present time and to gain some understanding of her feelings about her illness. Out tumbled her feelings of frustration, self-reproach and sadness at not being able to share and take part in the day-to-day life of the family as she had done before. Within the extremely fine balance of her not feeling stripped of the means of overcoming the situation, whilst at the same time not wanting to deny her intense grief, we looked together at ways she could contribute positively. One of the most important of these for Amy was compiling a book for Matthew with photographs, postcards and messages from her, for now and during the anticipated separation.

Amy worked hard between my first two visits, and brought to the second session a level of self-awareness that isn't demanded from us when life is straightforward. I was able to draw her attention to the fact that she appeared to be carrying all the responsibility for the pain inflicted on the family, especially Matthew. This seemed to make it possible for her to mourn her own loss, that of her once healthy body. She talked about the procedure of a bone marrow transplant, and in particular the excruciatingly painful experience of a lumbar puncture and the anticipated loss of her hair. She talked about living daily with uncertainties, and how vulnerable and anxious she felt. There were subtle pressures, especially from her husband Alan, to modify the expression of feelings, and consequently there was a greater need for me to recognise, accommodate and accept her anguish as entirely normal. As I left this second session I carried my own sense of guilt at leaving the situation to go on holiday, when during this period it seemed probable that Amy would be starting the treatment.

On my return to work in mid-September I learnt that Amy was still awaiting a bone marrow transplant, and it was anticipated that she would be admitted some time in October when a bed was available. As already agreed I arranged my third and fourth sessions with a week's interval between.

All the family were together on my arrival for our third meeting – Matthew had a cold and therefore had not gone to the nursery, Sally was to go to the childminder's, whilst Alan was due at work in an hour after organizing Sally. The previous week they had been on holiday and there was considerable talk about what a good experience it had been. I formed the impression that it was important (in Alan's and Amy's eyes) to avoid perversely brooding over death. I left Amy and Matthew together sorting out materials for painting.

My fourth and final meeting with Amy found her extremely tired and lethargic and in desperate need of a blood transfusion. She was 'holding on' for the summons from the London hospital for the transplant rather than presenting herself to the local hospital 'just for blood'. She was lying on the settee in anticipation of my visit, after which she would retire to bed. We agreed how once the transplant process was underway she would need all her physical and emotional energy to concentrate on her own wellbeing. Alan was giving up work and we talked about how he would cope, and how during the present crisis they appeared to complement each other, in that she expressed and acted out the feelings in the relationship whilst he steadfastly put his energies into supporting the family in practical ways. I then invited Amy to tell me in detail what the treatment would mean for her, both physically and emotionally, so that together we could share the fears and the realities. Amy was very eager to share. She said that she would be undergoing very painful and frightening treatment and isolation with an uncertain outcome/prognosis. She was very calm and positive as she entirely aligned herself with the medical profession 'imposing' the treatment; that is, she saw herself as active rather than passive. Together we were able to touch on the possibility of her dying and at the same time to look for hope of remission.

Evaluation of the intervention

I was a small link in the professional chain that surrounds Amy. Amongst the complexities of feelings within the network is a continuum from denial to premature mourning. Amy knows how ill she is, and through the experience of feeling safe together, she went as far as she was able in sharing her feelings. A show of too much affection or too much concern could easily have smothered her openness.

It is hard to evaluate my intervention objectively, as my experience of working directly with Amy was an intimate, painful and frightening one. My emotions are still racing with the work that remains to be done, and the uncertainties of what that work may involve.

Finally, in illustrating the range and depth of the stresses involved in social work with children, there is the case of Brian. The social worker's plans of work are nullified by the vacillations of Brian's parents; their alternating and vigorous demands for and rejection of their son mean that there is no secure context in which to offer help; Brian is driven into regression and violent anger which – for lack of other outlets – focuses on the person who is trying to befriend him. Brian is a severely damaged boy, lacking self-esteem, stable affection, and realistic hopes for the future. Despite this, the social worker provides such security as she can; her work is characterised by resilience to Brian's changes of mood, by patience, and by finding ways of communicating with him despite his refusal to talk about matters closest to him and central to the social worker's responsibilities.

This is demanding work: the social worker has been able to contain the stresses she experiences and the despair she must feel about the tragedy of Brian's life so far. Sadly, good professional work of this kind receives no publicity, but here we can offer it some level of recognition.

Brian (aged nine)

Prior to my involvement, Brian had been living with his mother, stepfather, brother and three step-sisters. He was first received into care under Section 2, Child Care Act 1980 in January 1988. It had come to light that his stepfather, Mr S, had been sexually abusing his half-sister. Mr S was convicted and sentenced to serve a three months' prison sentence. Brian's mother rejected her daughter because she held her responsible for the sexual abuse and for causing her husband's imprisonment; and mother rejected Brian because his difficult behaviour had been a trial to her for many years. His behaviour in a foster home was also difficult to manage. Both foster parents totally rejected Brian and made no contact with him, and because of the problems in the short term foster home and the fact that long term plans needed to be determined, Brian was moved to another foster home.

It was while he was in this placement with Mr and Mrs B that the Area team consulted a psychiatrist who had seen the family in the past and was continuing individual work with Brian's sister. The psychiatrist recommended that Brian needed a period of individual work to provide an opportunity to explore and sort out what had happened to him. As she was not in a position to provide this it was agreed that I would take on this work with him.

However, the situation changed. Following a review where the mother and stepfather (now back with the family) were confronted with the plan for permanent substitute care, they expressed a strong wish for Brian's return and a series of trial weekends at home were arranged by the Area Social Work staff.

Brian is of low average ability with specific learning disabilities in reading and spelling. He is a sad, angry little boy, emotionally deprived and scapegoated by his parents. His self image is low and he sees himself as a 'bad' boy. In the past he has run away from home and foster home, stolen from shops, hoarded food; he plays with matches and can be destructive. The psychiatrist had found 'no mileage in working with the family' as they 'would not co-operate'.

Situation at the beginning of the work

My first two sessions took place in Brian's foster home, to prepare him for return to his parents. He returned to his parents shortly afterwards but within a week the parents requested his removal.

In the absence of the Social Worker, my role on my visit to the family became concerned in plans for Brian. Following a case conference, Brian was readmitted to care and returned to his previous foster parents, Mr and Mrs B. He and I met weekly thereafter.

Summary of work to date

Brian loves drawing and initially immersed himself in this, keeping to safe subjects. In the uncertain situation about his family, he presented as an anxious but friendly little boy, but unwilling to talk about the family, only once referring to his sister. Any encouragement to discuss this or to use drawing or play materials in relation to family life has almost always been blocked. Consequently, I have needed to be extremely patient and to listen, using non-directive reflective methods to help Brian to begin to reveal information and feelings. Gradually, he has become more creative in his use of materials, which have included pens, papers, magic board, cardboard, scissors, glue, finger paints, dolls, cars, dolls house, ghost house, puppets, reading books, modelling materials, water and clay. Gradually, he has been able to release some of his feelings. The foster parents have meanwhile required support to be able to deal with his regressed behaviour.

The day after Brian returned to care, he ran back home and was brought back by his foster father. His intention was to ask his parents if they were ever going to have him home again, but he was unable to confront them with this. In this first session he cried throughout but was able to be cuddled by me and was gradually able to tell me why he had gone home. In more recent sessions, Brian has been more adventurous, using modelling materials and clay and water, and these have been powerful media for him. There have been clear indications of his negative feelings about men and his insecure identity. Brian sometimes exhibits tremendous rage, defiance and severe regression, refusing to believe his parents' rejection of him. Whereas Brian and I have a relationship based mainly on non-verbal communication, this appears to be releasing increased verbal communication with his Field Social Worker, who is taking the brunt of his displaced anger. The present difficulty for workers is knowing how to allow ventilation of this overwhelming pent-up rage, and yet channel and control it to prevent external and/or internal destruction.

At one stage I felt very 'stuck' and yet on reflection can see the movement that has taken place and the gradual unblocking of suppressed feelings. Movement has felt very slow but powerful feelings are beginning to emerge and I am able to show Brian an understanding and acceptance of these. Brian has remarkable recall of sessions, remembers our arrangements and looks for the 'toys' and materials for us to use together. He enjoys the individual attention. Below is a note of one of our recent sessions together. Needless to say, the work continues.

My last session with Brian has taken a significant step forward. Brian chose to play with clay. His attention span has gradually increased and was remarkable in this session: he remained sitting calmly with the clay for almost an hour. I tried in various ways to encourage him to express his feelings and wishes, past, present and future. Sometimes Brian would 'move along' but always blocked when it felt unsafe.

After a period of feeling 'stuck', he started to talk about Darren, another foster child with Mr and Mrs B, who was returning home to his parents at the weekend. Brian was poking holes in the clay. He also talked about his forthcoming Review. Brian is insistent he will be there. He told me that this was to 'fight for his rights…his right to return home'. Gradually the holes in the clay became 'tunnels' and together we were able to use the analogy of the tunnels in the clay as a means for Brian to express his fears and feelings about (a) being stuck in the tunnels, (b) where he wants his tunnel to lead (e.g. home), (c) how tunnels can lead into new tunnels (e.g. another family). He talked about children who had seen the light at the end of the tunnel and I was able to talk about those who had taken another tunnel, including his sister.

The session ended with Brian giving me permission to use this analogy at the Review if he finds he cannot speak; and he asked me to share this with his foster mother. I acknowledged the pain he must have felt in this session and praised him for making his feelings and wishes so helpful and clear.

I was impressed at his ability to express himself so well, both verbally and non-verbally. Throughout, he demonstrated his words by using the clay. I knew that this was a session in which we had really 'communicated'. Hitherto I had used the method of reflecting back his words; but, for once, Brian had also allowed me to ask him questions, which he answered.

CHAPTER SIX

Being and Becoming an Adult

In adult life one carries the luggage of childhood experiences; the more disturbed those experiences, the more heavily the luggage weighs. It is frequently noted by social workers that abusing or neglectful parents behave as they do, at least in part, because of their earlier experiences as child-victims. In so far as the adult continues to perceive the world through the eyes of an earlier childhood, the social worker has two fundamental tasks in the pursuit of solutions to current problems:

- to help the adult to deal with the unresolved feelings of earlier life; and
- to recognise that the adult's response to the worker may often not be a wholly rational one, and that the emotions expressed – whether affectionate or hostile – may not be 'deserved'.

The extracts in this chapter enable some adults to speak for themselves in regard to these issues, and provide illustrations of the work done (and its emotional complexity) to help adults to express and resolve feelings which are ambivalently realistic and distorted.

The chapter starts with a man's recollections and feelings about his earlier life in the care of a local authority. This is followed by illustrations of families' responses to social work investigations. Finally, there are two examples of the difficulties of moving from adolescent to adult responses: in the first of these, an adolescent boy is helped to face up to the fears associated with leaving care; in the second, a young unmarried couple who were themselves in care, are helped to face up to the girl's pregnancy and to their obligations towards the new baby.

David (aged 21)

The Social Worker's perspective on David's life reads as follows:

> This is a study of David's life. It is a study of loss, lack of attachment, of isolation, disability, life in the Care System and limited After Care. David was born with Spina Bifida. His early life was spent in hospital, a nursery and a children's home. This pattern continued throughout the rest of his childhood. David had only the briefest of contacts with his own family. As he grew up, he suffered the loss of the few important people in his life. He also had to cope with his physical disability.
>
> David can be argumentative, sarcastic, cynical, surly and hard-hearted. However, he is seldom angry, seemingly finding it important to remain composed. He is intelligent and articulate. The top half of David's body is strong and athletic (he did weight-training); however, the bottom half is largely powerless.
>
> David had ten social workers (not including those responsible for his first three years) supervising him during his life in Care. Of these social workers, the longest continuing contact was three years.
>
> Approaching his twenty-first birthday, David began to talk about his family – something he had never voluntarily done before. As I listened more, David wanted to know more and I explained to David his rights to have access to his files.

Assessment of the Situation

The file made harrowing reading. It gave meaning to many of David's behaviour manifestations. His history was full of moves, changes, admissions and discharges from hospital. David appeared to have spent all of his life in some form of institutional style of living.

Where had David been given any opportunity to develop an attachment with a significant person in his life?

David's own family appears to have played a very limited part. I could discover no evidence of any attempt to re-introduce him to his family in early life.

Then at the age of 12 years, David experienced the loss of his own family by emigration, and the sudden deaths of the only people he had a meaningful relationship with.

If at the present time, one asks questions about David's feelings, e.g. '... what do you feel about this or that?', he either shrugs off the question or become defensive. He keeps the door on his emotions firmly closed.

I had a 'gut' feeling from my experiences of many circular discussions with David that he knew a great deal about his past. I felt, however, he had never attempted or had been able to address the feelings that accompanied his life experiences. I assessed this as being David's greatest need.

Influences that shaped my intervention

I was asked to contact David as part of an NCH service offered to people leaving statutory care provisions, the aim being to help them to come to terms with earlier experiences.

I have always found flow-charts to be particularly powerful and David and I compiled a flow-chart of his life. They are also frequently painful documents! The facts become nakedly exposed from lengthy narrative: the repeating cycles of rejection, of loss and of change, become clear.

Early rejection by David's mother was compounded by the medical necessity for hospital admissions and David's move from the nursery to other placements. No lasting strong, early relationships had been possible for David, within which to develop a sense of personal worth, or to contain the ambivalent feelings of love and hate.

In view of his difficulties in discussing feelings, we agreed to undertake joint practical tasks: a flow chart of his life, a genogram of his family. He became very interested in these, and in time agreed to tell me his story, based on this information. I hoped by this means to give David the opportunity of facing up to the feelings as well as the facts of his past life. David knew far more than I did and seemed to gain some pleasure from being able to put his social worker right.

The Work Process

I had six sessions with David, on a regular basis. I continue to see him, but at less frequent intervals.

I began by asking David how many social workers he had known during his years in Care. This gave him something factual and tangible to begin on; it also had the effect of taking him through the events of his life. David was able to list at least ten social workers, including myself, whom he had known. He believes he may have had others in the first three years of his life of whom he could remember nothing.

I was surprised to hear David say he had known me longer than any other social worker – for a period of three years. Once I asked David for his earlier memory, and he was 'away'. He suddenly became animated and lucid as he told me 'his story'.

I allowed him full flow. On this first 'interview, I made no attempts to clarify, nor did I try to rearrange David's story. He tended to move backwards and forwards with his story, sometimes at a bewildering rate. I found it important to find space to record interviews with David soon after they had been completed. The flow-chart I had with me, and which I shared with him, was very useful with recording. A pencil-mark by any incident on the flow-chart which David had spoken about proved a useful reminder.

The following interviews were never quite the same as the first, which I felt had a 'magical air' about it. I had found David ready to tell his story and I had tuned in with the 'right approach' to that occasion, to meet his needs.

Later interviews tended to be more reflective. Although they never had the force of the first interview, they were of equal importance to David. They enabled him gradually, and in the open with someone else to put his story in a sense of order he could handle. Here is his story in his own words.

'BUT IT'S UPSTAIRS'

My name is David. I am 21 years old. I was born in Slough, Berkshire.

This is my story of life in a children's home from about 1972 until 1988, and why I think I was put into the children's home.

The first thing I remember about the home is hitting a girl for calling me a cripple, then that person telling one of the staff. The member of staff told me I was a cripple and that I would never be able to walk, and then I was slapped. This was to prove right later on, but only through my own stupidity.

The thing I will always remember is the two people who ran the home. The person who owned it was called Mrs Arnold. For one reason or another, the other person was called Polly (Miss Jones).

The next thing I remember is all the strange people coming during the summer and only staying a few weeks and then going home. I asked one of the staff why I could not go home. She answered '...because your Mum can't handle you'. Then, even at the age I was, I resented my mother. A few years later I was to meet my so-called mother, at the age of eight years.

The thing I was to realise after leaving this home was that I was very over-protected. This is proved later on. The thing that I think I missed out on was the so-called 'love of a family'. This I would disagree with because I have never known any different, and what you don't have you don't miss. Then again, I think that being in a children's home has made me much more 'street-wise', which means I grew up quickly.

I think Woodcroft was run regimentally; by this I mean that everyone got up at 6.30 am, had a bath and went and had breakfast at 8.00; breakfast was always finished by 8.30 am. Then everyone was put on the bus which took us to school. Then we would be dropped off in the evening about 5.30 pm Tea would be ready by the time we were home. Then after tea everyone went for a bath, yet again. Then we would all sit around the television watching nothing in particular because the only people allowed to turn the television over were the staff. At 8 o'clock we were all told to go to bed. This went on for six days a week, the only difference was on Saturday when we were allowed to stay up until 9 o'clock, but everything else was the same.

1983 was to be my last year at Woodcroft. This was because on 21 March l983, Mrs Arnold died of a heart attack. This particular day, I got home from school at about 5 pm and everything seemed very quiet. This was very unusual because there was always someone around. That night everyone was quiet, but this was very uneasy. The strange thing was that I was not interested why. The only thing I was told during the afternoon was that Mrs Arnold had fallen down the stairs. After being told this I then thought that she had injured herself, so I wasn't worried. Then the next morning everyone was still quiet and we were all asked to go down to the dining room and sit quietly until Polly came down.

This she did, but she was crying almost uncontrollably. She did manage to say that Mrs Arnold had died the night before of a heart attack.

A few days later I was told that I was to have a Case Conference, which is a load of people telling you how and what you are going to do – this was to be the last time I cried. At this Case Conference it was to say that I was to leave Woodcroft within the next six months. After they decided this, Miss Jones tried and tried to get them to change their minds, but to no avail.

Then on the evening of 31 May, Miss Jones went horse-riding with a friend. We were all sitting watching the telly and it was about 8 o'clock when all of a sudden, the friend of Miss Jones, who she had gone riding with, came running up our stairs and said to the staff that Miss Jones had had an accident and was in hospital seriously ill. As soon as I heard this I thought to myself that she was about to go the same way as Mrs Arnold, which I thought at the time was selfish and that she was doing to die and leave me behind.

The next morning we were again asked to go to the dining room and told to be quiet. Then about 15 minutes later a doctor-friend of Miss Jones said that her horse had been frightened and had bolted and thrown her off. Then he said that she had been taken to the hospital with a broken neck and was put on some sort of machine and that it hadn't worked. She was taken off the machine at his request and died early next morning of her internal injuries. [I was then moved to another home.]

The first time I met the man who was in charge of the home was about a week after I was admitted. I was asked to go to his office, so off I went to meet this man who I thought would be the same sort of person as Mrs Arnold, who never seemed to smile that often. But when I got to his office, he was sitting by the window. He said '…hello Dave, I'm Steve, sorry I wasn't in when you came but I've been on holiday.' We then had a long chat about my needs.

The next thing I remember is Jack saying '…we are taking you on holiday with us to Devon'. So I asked him where in Devon we were going. He then said a place called Ilfracombe, which is only about 15–20 minutes from where I used to live.

Between the time I got to Briarleigh and when we were on holiday, the thing I thought was strange was the fact that I could choose my own birthday present.

During August I went on holiday to Devon, the irony of this was not the fact that I was again in Devon, but the fact that I was going on holiday to a place that I had to leave. On holiday I went back to Woodcroft, and when I got there it seemed like I had never lived there. The thing that hit me first was the fact that it was very quiet and there was no-one about. The thing that was to upset me the most was that the staff who were still there seemed very distant.

After getting back to the holiday caravan park, I sat for about the next two hours very quietly. Just thinking about why Mrs Arnold and Miss Jones had to die and why I had to move.

At the times of their deaths, I suppose I thought that they had deserted me. But even then I wondered why I could not stay at Woodcroft. This I found out was because obviously there was no-one to run the home, which I didn't understand.

After we got back from the holiday, I found myself just sitting around doing nothing, but watching the television and just sitting. This went on until the next May when I started at a new school in Hampshire.

On the day that I went for my interview at my new school, the Headmaster asked me to his office and I thought I would be in there for ages, but I was out again in about 30 minutes. Then at the end of this time the Headmaster told me I would be starting the following Monday.

On my first day I felt really lonely because no-one wanted to talk to me. The first thing I remember is being told the only thing that they were interested in was '...are you any good at sport?'

This is one man's views of his earlier life in care. The emotional content of his experience is, perhaps surprisingly, subdued; but it is tentatively present if one is willing to receive it.

What, on the other hand, of the feelings of parents whose fitness for parenting is under investigation by the statutory services?

Parents talking about being investigated

The following extracts are taken from a research project undertaken by a social worker at a Family Centre. Part of the study was based on group meetings with parents who had been referred to the Centre because of concerns about the neglect or ill-treatment of their children. The social worker tape-recorded parts of the group meetings: the following is an account of her impression of what the parents meant (as well as what they said).

Findings from the Taped Accounts

The dominant theme that emerged from the tapes was the sense of powerlessness experienced by parents. Three parents mentioned feeling humiliated, commonly when their child was examined:

> Hilary: But what really cut me up was then they stripped Sarah off and looked at her from head to foot.

Several felt wrongly accused, or not believed. Five parents said they did not understand what was happening:

> Nadine: They made me feel horrible really. I felt guilty and I didn't even do anything.

> Natalie: I didn't like the way they (Family Centre) took me to the office and I didn't know what it was all about, and they started questioning me.

> Emma: I felt left out of everything, everything was happening round me.

There was a feeling that they had no choice but to do as they were told or they would be seen in an even worse light. Hilary's account shows clearly the processes of being taken to the Health Centre and having to go to the Police Station. In two cases parents mentioned workers telling them they were lucky because they were not doing everything they were supposed to do by law. Natalie, for example, was told by the social worker that by rights she should also examine the victim's younger sister. Whether this was a way of the worker trying to demonstrate her own caring or to dissociate herself from the procedures, in reality it reinforced the power of the authorities and Natalie's own lack of power.

Decisions made at case conferences were recounted by parents as being made by others, and excluding themselves:

> Elizabeth and Keith: They had a case conference and after that they decided we should go to the Family Centre.

> Angela: ...we were told to wait outside... When we saw them they said they'd made a decision, that it was a risk...the baby would be removed from my care.

What happened depended on the convenience or willingness of others. After Angela's baby was born, 'they put her in another ward so we couldn't see her... I saw her about two hours a day...it depended how busy the staff were...'

As Hilary's account shows, seeking help did not always produce the support hoped for. Both Hilary and Dennis felt it did not pay to do the right thing.

> Dennis: The Social Services always get the wrong ones. Them that batter their kids, they're not stupid, they don't take 'em to school when they've got bruises...'

There were several issues concerning the Family Centre which seem important to consider. The open nature of the Centre meant that several felt everyone would know what had happened and that they would be labelled. Several considered not coming in again, and one couple decided to remove their son from the playgroup. In one case it was other users of the Centre who had reported marks on a child: 'They thought I'd burnt him with a cigarette...all the users knew what happened...them users was my friends..'

Nick was concerned about access visits at the Family Centre, feeling everyone would know their business. There was also a feeling of being monitored, although in no case had this been a planned role for the Centre.

> Nadine: I felt a bit funny after that about coming in and leaving the kids here after what they'd accused me of...

Hilary felt she had to bring her son to playgroup, or Social Services would think she was hiding something.

Thus the issues I would identify from this study would be:

(1) The balance of power in child protection investigations.

(2) The need for clear explanations about the process.

(3) The type of support and help available for parents.

(4) The need for a clearly identified role for the Family Centre.

(5) The issue of stigma at the Family Centre

In the light of this project, the social worker has made the following recommendations concerning work with parents in the precarious situation of suspected child abuse.

Balance of Power

In child protection work there is an inequality in the power relationship between parents and professionals, whether statutory or voluntary. It is important to acknowledge this, indeed not to do so can be seen to take away even more power from parents. The examples from the study where professionals tried to dissociate themselves from the procedures they were carrying out resulted in parents feeling more powerless. In the same way, the father who saw the Family Centre as pretending to be 'something else' felt cheated. An open acknowledgement of power gives parents knowledge and leads to less likelihood of abuse of that power. The concept of partnership with parents is a complex one and it may be more honest to use the term, 'participation'.

The study did, however, suggest ways in which the sense of powerlessness for parents could be reduced by being sensitive to their feelings. For example, when it is necessary to examine a child, acknowledging that it has to be done, if possible engaging the parent in the process and being sensitive to issues of culture, gender, age, and so on, could decrease the humiliation felt. In a similar way, showing respect and listening to parents, recognising their knowledge of their own child, can increase their self-esteem.

Information about the Process

Linked to the feeling of powerlessness was the feeling of not understanding what was happening. Although parents facing an investigation will inevitably be unable to take in all that is happening, it seems important to give as much information as possible, in jargon-free language, and to try and make available support helpful to the parents in facing the situation. Verbal information is often not heard when one is distressed or shocked.

Stigma

Several parents identified issues of stigma. This can best be offset by encouraging mutual support networks by means of, for example, family centres where individual counselling and practical help are available, and where non-abusing parents also receive help. (There is a sort of anonymity in numbers.)

We now turn to the experience of leaving care, of – in a sense – becoming an adult, seen through the eyes of a young man of 17, and recounted by his social worker. Alistair's reactions to attempts to prepare him for adult life show certain frequently found characteristics: a desire not to review the past but, at the same time, anxiety about discussing the future; and a

fear of turning into an adult with the same inadequacies as have been
found in his own parents.

Alistair (aged 17)

The following abbreviated record illustrates work done with a young man
faced with the challenge of leaving care and establishing an independent
life. For Alistair, the experience of care has been a positive one, but has
generated a fear of adulthood, particularly the risks of turning into
someone like his birth parents and the uncertainty of his abilities to
manage his affairs. Here again, the need identified by the social worker
has been to help him to reconsider his earlier life (neglect and dependence)
in the light of his personal strengths, and visual techniques have been used
to provide a foundation for discussions.

> This case study outlines the work done with Alistair in preparing
> a programme of work for Alistair, his foster parents and myself to
> prepare him for 'leaving care'. Alistair had expressed considerable
> anxiety about leaving care.
>
> At the outset of this work Alistair was 17 years 6 months old; he
> had been 'in care' for seven years, five of which have been with his
> current foster parents and with two of his three siblings. Alistair's
> placement with his foster parents has not been without its prob-
> lems. Three years ago Alistair's placement broke down. However,
> it proved possible to repair this within six months and since this
> time the bond between Alistair and the foster parents has strength-
> ened considerably. Indeed the foster parents are eager to offer him
> support after he leaves the placement. The bonds between Alistair
> and his siblings are strong and he is particularly influential in the
> life of his younger brother, Stuart. Stuart is 12 and exhibits some
> disturbed and disturbing behaviour (i.e., theft and pyromania).
> Both the foster parents and I have feared that, if Alistair left his
> placement harbouring feelings of anger and rejection, he would let
> Stuart use his flat as somewhere to hide stolen goods. An applica-
> tion had already been made for Alistair to a local housing associa-
> tion. Thus Alistair should be advantageously placed to maintain
> links with his foster parents, siblings, peers and some members of
> his extended family who also live in the area.
>
> At the outset of the work Alistair had just received confirmation
> that he had passed his B.Tec in Design and Engineering. Alistair is
> a sensitive young man who has many positive elements in his life

that could serve as a foundation for his move from foster parents to the community.

In the previous eighteen months I had broached the subject of leaving care with Alistair but he had always resisted the discussion, stating that he wanted to enjoy being in a family whilst he could. Indeed, the entire idea of growing up was one that Alistair found difficult to get to grips with. Alistair used to say 'Why should I want to be an adult when they have done me so much harm in the past'. As Alistair's eighteenth birthday approached, so his anxiety increased. At a review in March, Alistair announced that he was going to join the Air Force, when the subject of leaving care was discussed. When I asked Alistair why he wanted to do this, he replied that he would be 'looked after' for a further three years, have a job, and could get married when he left. This was obviously Alistair's strategy for negotiating the difficult transition from adolescence to adulthood. Whilst this institutional path would provide Alistair with both peers and a structure, something highlighted by his foster father, my misgiving was that this path would enable Alistair to avoid addressing his dilemmas about what becoming an adult meant for him. It was at this point that I asked Alistair if he would be prepared to do some specific work focusing on preparing for leaving care. I put it to Alistair that I felt that he had many resources on which to draw, education, family, friends, foster parents and social services.

Alistair's foster mother thought this was a good idea, for she was doubtful about Alistair's intention to join the Air Force. She thought it was more likely that Alistair would sabotage his independent living to ensure that he returned to the foster placement. The foster parents agreed to join Alistair and myself in accomplishing the tasks we identified as important in preparing Alistair for 'independent' living. Alistair was adamant at this stage that if he were to do this work it would not involve any counselling 'and going over what had happened in the past'.

The transition from care to being independent in the community is a difficult one. Alienation from past contacts and resulting isolation sometimes marks the lives of young people in this situation. It may negatively influence all areas of their lives, from their ability to hold down a job, to propelling some young people into 'criminal subgroups'. The problems of isolation and alienation were also found to be significant in Stein and Carey's (1989) study of young people leaving care. They criticised the dominant independence approach in that it expects young people who have experienced problems with relationships in the past and whose current relationships with family may be stressful or non-existent to achieve skills and maturity before their peers who do not come from a care background. This approach, they argue, is also insensitive to the complex psychosocial nature of the transition involved in growing from adolescence to adulthood. They argue the message of 'managing on your own and coping by yourself' subtly negates the significance of interdependence,

> 'that is young people giving as well as taking, getting on with other people and negotiating reality with the support of agencies, neighbours, friends and partners, the very important interpersonal and relationship skills that our young people needed all the time and which they found so difficult.' (p.158)

Godeck (1990) recognised that young people leaving care with a lack of good primary experiences and/or unresolved feelings about their families of origin are particularly disadvantaged in their negotiation of an adult identity. This point is emphasised again in the work of Stein and Carey who draw upon the work of Triseliotis (1988), who has suggested that the achievement of a clear sense of identity and enhanced self esteem for young people who have received substitute family care is dependent upon their experiences in three areas. First, the quality of care and attachment experienced in childhood. Second, knowledge about heritage, genealogy and personal history. Third, how young people perceive themselves in relation to the rest of society and how society sees them. As has been previously stated, Alistair was clear that he didn't wish to explore his past life in any detail or its impact upon his life in the present. However, exploring Alistair's future did lead him indirectly to ask questions about his past. In attempting to discover just exactly what Alistair was clear about and what he wasn't I used the technique of doing a road map as outlined in the BAAF publication *Making Life Story Books* (Ryan and Walker 1985).

In my first session with Alistair, I began by explaining to him how important I believed friendship, community and family contacts would be for him were he to choose to live in the community rather than join the Air Force. My purpose in doing this was to encourage Alistair to assess his social world. Which relationships did he see as important and enduring – who would he look to for support and friendship; and in looking to the future what were Alistair's best and worse fantasies? A good way of thinking about and illustrating these contacts, I suggested to Alistair, was the eco-map. Not surprisingly, Alistair did not know what one of these was so I volunteered to illustrate my social life with one. Alistair quickly grasped the idea so I asked him to do one of his present situation. It became evident that Alistair had a good network of friends and that his foster parents and siblings are of immense importance to him, though his relationships with his natural parents are tenuous.

I then asked Alistair to draw me two further eco-maps, the first illustrating the best position he could imagine himself in one year after leaving care, the second illustrating the worst position. There were four main differences that Alistair could envisage between the two scenarios.

(1) That Alistair's peer contacts would greatly diminish and he wouldn't be as close to his best friend as he currently is.

(2) That Alistair's siblings and foster parents would diminish in importance to him.

(3) Alistair's relationship with his father would continue to be distant rather than improve.

(4) In the worst scenario Alistair's grandparents had disappeared from the picture whereas in his best scenario they were accorded a position of great importance.

Having identified these differences, we discussed each of them in turn. Concerning his relationship with his peers, Alistair saw himself as involved in honest ongoing relationships, which would endure 'if they got on', in other words, they weren't 'care' friendships. He did comment that it made him realise just how important his best friend would be if he were to have his own flat. To continue to enjoy a good relationship with his foster parents, Alistair recognised that he would have to continue 'to put something in'. Alistair confirmed that his foster parents had spoken to him about how they wished to support him in the community but how the terms of this would change; that it would move slowly towards equality. They would expect him to behave responsibly towards his younger brother, and offer him help with tasks like decorating.

Regarding his father, Alistair and I discussed his extreme reluctance to talk to social services, but how Alistair has continued to see him. Again Alistair felt he could best determine the future course of this relationship. As regards his mother, she remains in all scenarios an anathema to him.

As regards getting on with his grandparents, Alistair and I talked a long while about the dynamics of his extended family and how he felt he had become scapegoated within it. Alistair stated that he felt that I could help him mend some fences within his extended family (many members of which I have met) and so help his access to some sources of support. We agreed upon how we could do this. I felt this was a positive session, enabling Alistair to focus upon what he could identify as future sources of support, and recognising that it would not involve a break with everybody he knew and the role he had to play in maintaining and developing these relationships.

Given Alistair's past reluctance to discuss openly the notion of becoming an adult, I felt that one way of potentially getting Alistair to engage in thinking about the transition would be to ask him to draw a cartoon about it for our session a week later. Alistair had agreed to do this but when I arrived he said he had not done it and really didn't fancy doing it.

Consequently, I asked Alistair to draw up two lists, those skills and attributes he felt he had as an adolescent and those he felt belonged to adulthood; they didn't have to be mutually exclusive. The object of this exercise was to engage Alistair in thinking about the transition from one status to another and the risks this might involve as well as the advantages.

Alistair saw the acquisition of adult status as bringing with it new freedoms such as going out with friends as and when he liked, but also new responsibilities, particularly financial. I put budgeting down on our list of tasks that we could plan to tackle with the foster parents. I was interested, though, to explore the concept of responsibility a little more. Initially, Alistair talked about how he knew that this would involve him taking responsibility for getting to college on time and having clean clothes. Alistair soon began to discuss what he felt was his greatest responsibility, namely, to himself – that he didn't end up on a park bench like his mother. (She is a chronic alcoholic who is sometimes to be seen in the vicinity paralytically drunk.) Alistair divulged that becoming like his parents was his greatest fear of adulthood. We began to discuss how adulthood was not a complete break with adolescence and how Alistair had already begun to take a lot of control over his life

– by his academic success. I was not able to say to Alistair that alcoholism was not a risk in his life, for clearly if he were to begin drinking excessively it would be; but the decision is his. Rather, I stated that Alistair might think what prompts people to become dependent upon alcohol and drugs, and what they might be able to do about this.

My fourth session with Alistair was opened by some significant news. Alistair had been successful in getting himself a part time job, something his foster parents had been encouraging him to do for some time. Importantly, Alistair had attended a family meeting with the child psychiatrist and child psychotherapist who are currently working with his younger siblings and foster parents about the past and future. Alistair had been previously invited to these sessions but had declined to go; his foster parents informed me that they had been surprised by the honesty and involvement of Alistair at the session.

I started the session by demonstrating to Alistair the principle of the road map. I then asked if he would like to show me what he knew about his life. Very quickly, Alistair became exasperated, saying he knew absolutely nothing. I suggested that perhaps he should work back from his current placement. Alistair was able to trace back to age ten. It became apparent that Alistair remembered little before this date when he was taken into care. I asked if he had asked his father about his early life but Alistair replied he was 'useless' – not even knowing the name of the hospital in which he had been born in Glasgow. Alistair asked what I knew and I told him what details I remembered. Alistair then stated that he wanted to go through his files. I explained to him the procedure necessary to do this and undertook to do this work with him. As regards any counselling, Alistair said he would 'probably' go to the family meetings.

My last session was with Alistair and his foster parents. In this session, with Alistair's permission, I presented the work we had done to the foster parents, making explicit the importance attached by Alistair to their continued involvement in his life. This they reaffirmed themselves and pointed out the expectations they had in terms of Alistair's influence upon his younger brother. Having gone through the work together, we identified the tasks that had to be accomplished to prepare Alistair for leaving care and who was going to do them. These varied from learning to prepare vegetables and planned weeks of self catering on a budget, to my undertaking to contact Alistair's grandparents as preparation for a joint meeting.

My work with Alistair has had quite profound outcomes. He decided to abandon the idea of joining the Air Force, has continued to go to the sessions with his siblings, foster parents and the psychotherapist and psychiatrist. He is now looking forward with understandable apprehension to having his own flat. My work with Alistair was in partnership with him as a young man who has opinions and agendas that have to be addressed – by him as much as myself. This mirrors Alistair's status as a young person who is preparing to leave care, that is, to live independently. However, our work together in drawing up an agenda of proposed tasks enabled Alistair to identify who he and I should seek to work in conjunction, or in partnership with. (Note Alistair's decision to engage with his grandparents and foster parents and not his natural parents.) In broad terms I believe that Alistair's movement may be seen as being one from defensiveness, ie his desire to go into the Air Force and his refusal to consider looking at his past experiences, to one where he has decided to engage in 'risky' enterprises, that is, having his own flat and exploring his own past and his feelings about it. Alistair is beginning the negotiation of an adult relationship with his foster family and siblings – moving out but connected by undertaking mutual tasks, particularly in behaving responsibly towards his younger brother. This process also prompts Alistair to have a qualitatively different relationship with social services. Their role, for example, by paying for Alistair's independent accommodation whilst he continues his studies, should be one that by 'advising, assisting and befriending' supports and encourages Alistair to undertake the risky task of becoming gradually independent from the social services department that has held statutory responsibility for him for so long.

I believe that starting from one of Alistair's strong points, that of his contacts within the community, was beneficial. This enabled Alistair to identify for himself, not only just how much support he has within the community, but also to think critically about the prospect of this continuing after his discharge from care. It was important that Alistair was able to identify the relationships that he owned, that is, that weren't just a by-product of his care experience.

Dan and Linda (17 and 16)

In this final study, we consider the help needed by a young couple, whose lives, both individually and together, are disorganised. The themes illustrated here are the emotional difficulties of leaving care and preparing for adult responsibilities; the importance of combining practical and emotional help; and the necessity for the social worker to clarify his role. As in the case of Alistair, the approach to the work is time-limited and task-focussed. Dan and Linda behave (and have behaved) in ways which could easily have provoked a moralistic stance in the worker. The professional task is certainly a moral one, but is – in this instance – refreshingly free of moralistic judgement; and the success of the work hinges partly on this finely balanced professional position.

The practice here draws upon certain theoretical formulations, particularly concerning the nature of partnership, the identification of adult roles, and the impact of stereotypical gender-role definitions.

The social worker's account concludes with an evaluation of what was achieved. (The writer is a male social worker; a female co-worker was introduced as the case progressed.)

The position at the Outset of the Work

Linda first came to the attention of the department when her living arrangements with her aunt began to break down. It was discovered that Linda's mother had asked her sister to look after Linda, because Linda and her step-father had for some years had a very poor relationship, and the family had decided to move to another town. Linda had declined to move with the rest of the family.

The social services department decided to accommodate Linda, and she was a found a place in a semi-independent unit for young people. While at the unit Linda revealed that she had taken an overdose earlier in the year, and it was noticed that she had inflicted a more serious cut to the inside of her wrist; she disguised this injury for some time as a sprain.

The placement broke down after two months. The residential staff complained that Linda was allowing groups of young men in her room overnight. Linda was not willing to change this behaviour, and staff felt that Linda was neither letting herself be looked after, nor looking after herself. She was asked to leave. Plans were made for Linda to live at home for the Christmas period.

In January it was discovered that Linda had in fact moved in with a boyfriend, Dan, who was living in private rented accommodation. Her mother knew this young man and approved of the arrangement. Subsequently Linda received a positive pregnancy test result from her doctor.

Enquiries made by social workers revealed that, until recently, Dan had himself been in care since the age of eight, and that he had exhibited threatening and violent behaviour while in care. He also had several offences of violence pending in the Crown Court.

It seems that at this point Linda and Dan's landlord asked them to leave their rented room. There were attempts made to accommodate Linda in a local family resource centre; however, Linda stayed only one night. Attempts to engage Linda in planning for herself and her baby quickly broke down. Linda and Dan went to stay with Linda's mother for a weekend, after which the couple presented themselves to the housing department and were offered temporary accommodation.

Due to the cases in Crown Court, Dan was remanded in custody for a short period, then granted bail with the condition that he reside at a bail hostel. Shortly afterwards, the housing authorities decided that when Linda and Dan left their rented room, they had made themselves intentionally homeless; Linda was given notice to quit the temporary accommodation.

Assessment of the Situation and Negotiation of Intervention

There appeared to be two main areas of work:

(1) Our duties to Linda under s24 of the Children Act 1989, as a young person who has been looked after since her sixteenth birthday; specifically, assistance with finding stable accommodation, and to think through what duties or powers should be exercised on Dan's behalf.

(2) Linda's recent history, and Dan's experiences throughout his childhood, led us to feel that an assessment of their support needs as future parents was indicated.

Linda and Dan were each very clear that they saw themselves as a couple, and that they wished to live together as soon as this was possible. Dan's offences had not been dealt with at this stage, and he and Linda were anxious about the possibility that the Court would give Dan a custodial sentence, making it likely that the baby would be born while he was in prison. (In fact Dan received 18 months probation, and we were therefore able to provide temporary accommodation for them together in a bed and breakfast hostel.)

We drew up a contract with Linda and Dan which is reproduced below. Linda and Dan understand that we are engaged in a piece of work clearly limited to three or four months, aiming to address both the areas of work outlined above.

Contract between Linda, Dan and two social workers (M and F)

(1) That we will meet together for eight sessions over the next two months.

(2) For two of these sessions Linda and F will meet together, and for two more Dan and M will meet together. What is said in these sessions can be discussed when the four of us meet.

(3) F and M will write a report in August which Linda and Dan can see and add their own comments.

(4) This report will be shown to agencies, such as the district office, Family Resource Centres, and the local National Children's Home project, to assist in making decisions as to what the best supports are for Linda and Dan once the baby has arrived.

(5) F and M will attempt to help Linda and Dan to begin to achieve these targets as part of an overall aim which is to be independent of social services:

 (i) a permanent flat

 (ii) being able to keep the baby healthy and well

 (iii) budgeting adequately

 (iv) good relationship with the health visitor

 (v) Dan in employment.

This contract was negotiated over two sessions. The targets set down under 5 above are as Linda and Dan expressed them. It was interesting to note how much more seriously they both took this document once they were invited to sign it. Linda's mother was not a signatory to the contract but was in agreement with the aims and methods of the work we planned to undertake.

Theoretical and Experimental Influences Shaping the Intervention

Theoretically, there are several sources which have informed this piece of work; I outline the main influences below:

Partnership practice was highlighted in this case by Dan's deep distrust of social services, and the child protection powers that social workers are invested with. Marsh and Fisher (1992) offer five principles of partnership practice.

(1) Investigation of problems must be with the explicit consent of the potential user(s) and client(s).

(2) User agreement or a clear statutory mandate are the only bases of partnership-based intervention.

(3) Intervention must be based upon the views of all relevant family members and carers.

(4) Services must be based on negotiated agreement, rather than on assumptions and/or prejudices concerning the behaviour and wishes of others.

(5) Users must have the greatest possible degree of choice in the services that they are offered.

We were conscious that adherence to these principles would be crucial in maintaining the confidence of this couple, particularly Dan. At the same time, we were concerned about the results of continuing instability on Linda's and Dan's chances of achieving adequate levels of parenting.

As our experience of this couple developed, particularly their inability to keep their living arrangements stable, I was reminded of Bentovim's (1991) thoughts about the conditions which can lead to disorganised attachments.

> *'There can also be a major disruption of attachment if, for example, the parents are unable to maintain consistency, predictability and a physical presence.'*

Fahlberg (1981) informed our thinking in relation to the benefits to the child of a strong attachment to parent(s), in other words

> *Attachment helps the child*

- attain full intellectual potential;
- sort out what he or she perceives;
- think logically

- develop a conscience
- become self reliant
- cope with stress and frustration
- handle fear and worry
- develop future relationships
- reduce jealousy.

The functions that Linda and Dan will need to carry out in order to foster such attachment are listed by Fahlberg (1981)

Things the family provide for children

- a primary caretaker for the child
- care by specific adults to whom the child can become attached
- continuous contact with these adults on a day-to-day basis
- continuous but changing relationships with a small number of individuals over a lifetime
- safety and security
- stimulation and encouragement for growth
- reasonable expectations
- experience in identifying and expressing emotions
- support in times of stress.

Goldner *et al.* (1990) also provided us with much food for thought. Although they were writing about couples in domestic violence, a phenomenon not to our knowledge present in Linda's and Dan's relationship, many of the observations they make are pertinent. Their thesis is that abusive relationships exemplify, *in extremis*, the stereotypical gender arrangements that structure intimacy between men and women generally. By adopting a 'both/and' position they allow themselves the freedom to explore domestic violence through multiple levels of description: psychodynamic, social learning, sociopolitical and systematic. They set out their intent as follows.

'Thus our attempt to discern and construct meaning in acts of violence does not overrule or substitute for our clear moral position regarding the acts themselves. Violence may be 'explainable', but it is not excusable, and it may or may not be forgivable. That is up to the victim. For us, as therapists, what is important is to make sense of the confusing circumstances of violence so that the parties caught in its grip can begin to stop it.' (p.343)

A view of the construction of gender is developed which refutes the idea that gender difference is an expression of a natural division, instead suggesting that gender identity constitutes a suppression of natural similarities. Men and women are both born of women, and women are the primary caretakers of both sexes. They have this to say about masculinity.

> 'Because of the primacy of the mother in early life, and the absence of an equivalent substantial relationships with the father, learning to be masculine comes to mean learning to be 'not feminine...'....For boys, this gender difference becomes the vehicle for separating from, and dis-identifying with their mothers. In other words, the boy constructs his sense of himself out of a negative: 'I am not like my Mother; I am not female.' In the view of most gender-identity theorists this childhood negation creates problems for the psychological foundations of masculinity, so that when the boy becomes a man, this gender structure is potentially threatened whenever experience calls up echoes of that early maternal bond, that early identification, that early separation.' (p.346)

They have this to say about femininity:

> 'By contrast a women's identity is forged within a feminine relational context and, in a sense, the girl remains a part of her mother's psychological space. Gender theorists have argued that this formative female bonding creates the conditions for a women's empathic orientation, and also for her difficulties in separating herself from relationships. Moreover, insofar as the daughter experiences herself as likened to, bonded with, and sometimes virtually part of a person of subordinate social rank, she must struggle to claim for herself what her mother was denied: a voice of her own, a mind of her own, a life of her own.' (p.346)

They develop their thinking as follows:

> 'Given this analysis, men and women under the best of circumstances form attachments in which they must seek in one another the capacities each has lost. This search often results in the problematic complementarities, that family therapists encounter in treating couples, and which are often

so difficult to change. In our view, it is only when both partners are committed to transcending the rigid categories of gender difference, and can begin to tolerate their disowned similarities, that real change is possible.' (p.361)

Men therefore struggle with premises that are in conflict with their psychological reality; they do feel dependent, sad, scared, and in need of protection. F and I have, looking back over our interviews with Linda and Dan, been able to identify stress points which have triggered Dan's angry and provocative comments. Goldner *et al.* (1990), observe of the men they saw:

'Indeed, it is when he is most close to recognising the feeling (of vulnerability) as his own that, we believe, he is most tempted to be violent.' (p.362)

We noted that Dan witnessed fearful scenes of life-threatening violence between his parents as a small child.

'When they are 'protecting' their women, it is as though they re-enact their fateful bond with their one-down mothers...'

We also observed that Linda, who we believe is denied a sense of personal power and agency by the processes developed in Goldner *et al*'s analysis, instead instigates a sequence of interactions in which Dan is instrumental in achieving her ends.

Commenting on the powerful bond that exists between the couples they saw, Goldner *et al.* suggest:

'Initially, and implicitly, the couple's bond is positioned against their families of origin and against the world at large.'

They go on to say that their couples described their relationship in similar terms to the way that Linda and Dan presented their relationship to us.

'This rebellion against oppressive gender roles creates a be-lief that the relationship is a unique haven from the outside world.'

The Process of the Work

So, referring back to our earlier contract, F and I had eight meetings with Linda and Dan in which we could between us think through what their needs as parents were likely to be. We also agreed to assist them in securing permanent accommodation.

F and I planned to divide our eight sessions as follows:

(1) Two sessions dedicated to Linda's early history and background, and her attitudes to past, present and future events

(2) Two similar sessions for Dan

(3) Two sessions dedicated to looking at the couple's relationship and to their interactions with their respective families of origin

(4) Two sessions for thinking ahead to the impact of the baby's birth on their present relationships and lifestyle, how they plan to cope with the baby, how and where to find support.

We met weekly. Linda and Dan were punctual and co-operative. We began with a session focusing on them as a couple. Then F and I were each due to take leave, so I saw Dan individually whilst F was on leave, and F saw Linda individually whilst I was on leave. When F and I were subsequently able to sit down and compare notes, we realised that our assessment was suffering in two ways.

The first was that this piece of work was dominated by Dan's suspicion that, whatever we said, our real intention as an agency was to remove their child. The problem, for Dan, is how can he receive the support he needs when, in his view, to be open with social workers about his and Linda's needs is dangerous? Our strategy was, as best we could, to work to a model of partnership practice, including the open use of recording, and setting clear aims and tasks.

As we progressed through our meetings, some of the processes at work became clear. Dan's response seemed to be to 'let us in' without actually 'letting us in'; he kept to the framework and agenda of our sessions without really making use of them to examine matters which might require any personal change. Once we realised this, we saw that it might be better to stop this aspect of work if Dan continued in this way. Otherwise, we risked participating in a sham which would only make things more difficult later on, both for Linda and Dan, and for the professionals that may be involved with them in the future.

The second issue was that crises of accommodation occurred frequently enough for F and me to feel that we were encountering resistance through chaos. We did our best to separate clearly the time spent with Linda and Dan sorting out practical details, which were usually accommodation issues, from our wider assessment sessions. If practical considerations could not be ignored, we would reschedule the assessment session rather than try to go ahead and then fail to do justice to the task. We needed to reschedule on two occasions.

It also seemed important to us that, in our work with Linda and Dan, we should ourselves provide a model of behaviour regarding those things that they will need to provide as good parents – consistency, age appropriate expectations, support in times of stress, and so on. Sometimes we managed this better than others. Between our fifth and sixth assessment meetings Linda and Dan were asked to leave their bed & breakfast accommodation because the manager claimed that Linda had changed a forged £50 note with one of his staff. Linda and Dan said that this was a complete fabrication, and would not think of making any restitution. Dan's uncle appeared with Linda and Dan, saying he had a flat he could rent them; Linda and Dan wanted us to pay for this rather than an alternative bed & breakfast. We agreed to investigate this possibility; however, these arrangements fell through, and we found ourselves needing to move them before 11.15 am one morning.

This scenario set up powerful processes which were hard to resist. Linda and Dan were victims. Their uncle was cast as rescuer, and F and I were joined with the bed & breakfast manager as persecutors. F and I found that a theme throughout this piece of work was that Linda and Dan would continually attempt to place on us the responsibility for solving problems which were properly theirs.

Linda and Dan disputed the reasonableness of our actions in relation to the move from one bed & breakfast to another, and at this point they wanted to withdraw from the assessment process.

F and I needed to check our mandate. At the outset we were providing two services simultaneously to Linda and Dan. One was a 'leaving care' process which was dominated by accommodation and resource issues. The other was our agreement to meet on eight occasions to assess Linda's and Dan's needs as future parents. These two services, however, were not negotiated separately, and were agreed in one contract. We clarified in our minds that one did not depend on the other; that is, we were not expecting their compliance in relation to the assessment meetings as our price for providing permanent accommodation and 'leaving care' grants.

When we met with them the following week, Linda and Dan were careful first to ensure that they were not jeopardising their leaving care resources by discontinuing the assessment. Then they told us to leave them alone.

F and I continued to be vigilant about avoiding rescuer and persecutor positions. Since there were two of us, this would have been all too easy to fall into: one feeling cross and rejecting, the other feeling anxious about how they were getting on.

We set about trying to keep them engaged in the processes of planning for their move into Housing Department accommodation, spending their 'setting up' grant, and so on. We accepted that, since we had only completed five of the eight sessions, and since Linda and Dan were declining to work with us on their needs as parents, we were not going to be able to write a report and use it as envisaged in our contract. We let Linda and Dan know that we would make use of the work that we had done together when we wrote our transfer summary; that they could see this summary and could comment on it, and that – once we knew where their permanent accommodation would be – we would then send the summary to the District Office that covers that area, requesting the allocation of a social worker to them.

This is where things stand at present. I envisage that our work with Dan and Linda will continue for at least another month. The birth of the baby is imminent.

I think that we have got the message over to Dan and Linda that we will not punish them by withholding their flat or their 'leaving care' grant. Dan, however, finds it very hard to believe that we are not moving against them in some other way, for example by 'secretly' putting their baby on the child protection register. The nearer we get to the birth, the more his fears magnify, and the more he 'shadow boxes' with invisible enemies.

Looking ahead, it will be important for F and me (and for future workers) to be clear about what mandate exists for intervention. Although there are clearly many factors in this case that provoke professional concern, our only mandate as things stand is in relation to helping this young family to find permanent accommodation. We cannot know whether Linda and Dan will somehow struggle through to achieve a level of parenting that will be 'good enough', or whether it will become appropriate to invoke statutory powers at some stage. Our experience of this couple to date is that it is easy for professionals to become induced into a position that is either over optimistic or over pessimistic.

An Evaluation of the Intervention

Evaluation of work raises questions of the criteria by which it is to be measured. The core questions I think are, to what extent were we honest and open with Linda and Dan in our practice, and to what extent were we able to share responsibility for Linda and Dan's decision-making with them. These are both aspects of practice crucial to working in partnership.

At the beginning, Dan was very mistrustful of us, and Linda was reasonably trustful. On occasion they felt very negatively towards us, but overall I think that they have held ambivalent feelings about us. Since Linda and Dan are good at dividing the world between those who are with them and those who are against them, I think that we have occupied a good position, paradoxically, because of their ambivalent feelings: not sucked into their view of the world, but not rejecting of them.

Returning to the principles put forward by Marsh and Fisher (1992), I think that at first sight we did well. We negotiated our mandate; set out the agreed aims of the work in a written agreement; and much of the work was task-focussed. What was not agreed so clearly was what the assessment work would involve. Linda and Dan, each in their own way, had a strong (and understandable) impulse to put their pasts behind them. They were at pains to portray a relationship between them that was conflict free. Dan considered himself to be 'cured' of his violence, and Linda became cross and defensive when her relatively recent attempts at self harm were raised by us. Our agreement began to fall apart once it became clear that our idea of how not to replicate the past (i.e., by working through those earlier painful experiences in a way which might allow each of them the choice to lead their lives differently) was not a shared one. To continue in such circumstances is neither productive, nor in tune with partnership thinking. If I were able to go back and do it again, I would be much clearer about attempting to build an agreement to do the emotionally painful work, as well as the task-focused work.

In terms of their world view, race and gender issues were both important. Linda and Dan both carry strong stereotypically racist views; black people take all the jobs and houses; black youths are responsible for street crime, and so forth. F and I made it clear that, while we could not alter their views in these matters, we could not tolerate their expression whilst we were providing services for them. Both F and I are white.

I have previously discussed the significance of gender at some length. In co-working the case we had a dilemma in how to model joint working successfully. One of the ways in which Dan tested F was by suggesting that I might handle things differently and better if I was there. I was careful not to reinforce such ideas.

Learning which has occurred during the work and thoughts about how this might be developed in future

By age, Dan is an adult and Linda is an adolescent; the problems presented were, in a sense, complicated by the fact that this couple are living through different lifecycle stages simultaneously.

For me this work was a mixture of the familiar and the new. The 'leaving care' and 'adolescent' focussed areas of the work were familiar ground on which I felt reasonably confident and competent. The assessment of this couple's support needs as parents was entirely new. Although adolescent work, and the acting out behaviour associated with it, is notoriously stressful, it was interesting for me to feel the extra pressure that accrues once the future wellbeing of a young life is at stake. Yet I found that there is room for the transfer of learning from one context to another, since the principles are the same. I have for many years in my work with adolescents been careful not to protect them from the consequences of their actions, and used my proximity to young people to assist them to make choices about their actions based on consequences that they are prepared to face. Much of our work with Linda and Dan was exactly this, with the principles applied to a parenting subsystem rather than to an individual young person.

As with everything attempted for the first time, I look back now and see opportunities missed and situations which I would now want to handle differently. I am much clearer now about the importance of establishing what my mandate is for each intervention, an issue that was critical during this piece of work; I also have the beginnings of a conceptual framework for working with parents when child protection is at issue. I appreciate now how powerful the forces are which act on professionals involved with abusing families, and how crucially important it is for workers to receive good supervision.

In thinking about this, I looked at Dale *et al.*'s (1986) writing on dangerous professions. They give examples which illustrate the same powerful processes that we encountered in this case, and also discuss dangerous professional responses which I recognised that F and I could easily have fallen into, had we been less well supported by each other and by our colleagues.

CHAPTER SEVEN

Themes and Questions

It is clearly not possible to summarise the wide and disparate range of activities and experiences presented in earlier chapters. Certain themes recur, however, and, in reviewing these, one is able to enlarge upon the purposes of this book.

One important theme is child protection; but the words are broadly interpreted – and, I believe, rightly so: it would be a pity if 'child protection' were seen as a response *only* to circumstances of abuse or neglect. I have also included a few cases where neglect or abuse, as conventionally understood, are not present but where a child is very unhappy (for example, because of the serious illness of the mother), and where parents are themselves so distressed, frightened or disturbed as to be unable to respond sensitively to the bewilderment and fears of their children. Such children, too, may sometimes need the support and protection of social workers and other carers; and examples have been given which express this concern to help. In a period of budgetary constraints in social welfare, service-users tend to become bureaucratically categorised according to the social problems they display (not their felt needs), and categories then compete for financial resources. Some of the children and parents presented here would not achieve high-priority categorisation, although their suffering is sometimes great and the contribution of social work is important to their wellbeing. This book implies the need for creativity and flexibility in professional practice – for practices which are as alert to human suffering as to the categorisations of problematic behaviour. 'Creative' is a hazardous word to use in social welfare: professional creativity sounds good, but 'creative accounting' smacks of dishonesty, and a 'creative bureaucrat' sounds (sadly and sometimes unfairly) like a contradiction. Yet all three areas of professional creativity are necessary to the public care of children. All the contributors to this book have, in various ways, emphasised the importance of professional creativity: in the skills they use and are seeking to develop, in their responsiveness to people's feelings as well as to their behaviour, and in the use of their own and their agencies' resources. Some social workers reading the book will envy the stance they adopted and the resources they were able to command. But the resources used – other than their salaries – were relatively cheap: some toys, paper and paints, and a room in which mess could be tolerated. A creative bureaucrat could provide these if the professional will and integrity are present and the work can be shown to be useful.

The outcomes achieved by the contributors in using their resources are variable – sometimes because of their levels of skill, sometimes because of the level of appropriateness of the methods used to the needs and problems presented to them. All contributors are, however, qualified and experienced social workers; they were at various points in postqualifying courses. The book may be said, therefore, to illustrate the current 'state of the art' in social work practice. None of the presentations claims to be perfect – what, in any case, does perfection mean in child protection? – but many are very good, and, most important, they represent performance which comes (or should come) within the capacities of all social workers if provided with appropriate training.

One of the clear messages is that social workers are (only) human. They work with people who, and problems which, are sometimes difficult to accept; people who do not always respond to conventional conversational signals; problems which sometimes defy rational solutions. The significant characteristic of social work practice is not its occasional blunders but its patient, unapplauded helpfulness in stressful situations. Sadly, in public discussions of social work (and even among readers of research reports) the perceived helpfulness is ignored and the blunders are emphasised. This book is therefore partly an attempt to demonstrate how social workers are and can be perceived as helpful. But, more important, it is also an attempt, in line with earlier studies, to give children and parents a voice: to show what events and relationships mean to them, how they define their feelings and needs, how their realities and fantasies need to be shared and recognised, and how, for them, short-term and long-term solutions are sometimes difficult to amalgamate.

In order to achieve understanding and constructive planning in partnership with young children, social workers need skills; we have here various examples of social workers seeking to develop these skills – working by means of play and games and stories; working through painting and drawing, particularly drawing families; making agreements – often written agreements – to set boundaries and purposes of work. As has been evident in several case studies, play is the child's work; but there are frequent difficulties in maintaining its purposefulness, especially when feelings are painful, ambiguous and ambivalent. Skills have been illustrated also of recognising symbolic levels of communication: what, for this child at this time, are the meanings of food, rituals, toys, ghosts and nightmares; how much physical and mental space does she need to feel safe without feeling alone; how much does she need to exclude the worker from her affections as well as to accept her within her affections? All these skills – diverse though they are – have a common purpose: to work in ways which transform negative experiences into realistic hopes for the future and jointly shared planning.

Several professional issues arise from the exercise of these skills and from the general processes of helping and protecting children. First, it is important to recognise the stresses involved in practice – stresses which increase as the worker attempts to achieve partnership with distressed people. The stresses are partly a natural outcome of sympathy; but partly also they arise from an essential tension in professional practice. The more sensitive a worker becomes to the feelings and needs of family members, the more she will recognise that there are several possible ways in which she could validly approach the situation, and that flexibility and adaptability need to be retained both in assessing needs and in trying to meet them. Yet both the resource-interests of the agency and the findings of social work research indicate that the work she does is most likely to be effective if work is time-limited, planned, and the result of an agreement. An important source of stress lies in the seemingly paradoxical demands of purposeful planning and responsive flexibility. Dr Johnson defined a paradox as 'a truth standing on its head to attract attention'; coping with paradox lies at the heart of satisfying and successful living, and it certainly lies at the heart of effective social work practice. But there are managerial and supervisory implications of this: a conscientious social worker needs time to plan, insightful supervisory discussions, a manager who is sympathetic to the need for working materials and rooms, and sympathetic team support in times when she feels inadequate to the tasks ahead, or adrift in the attempt to achieve consistency between professional integrity and legislated duties.

Finally, the case studies have illustrated several common problems in social work practice. They are listed below as I believe they offer potentially useful topics for seminars in social work courses:

(1) Issues in relationships between social workers and service users:

    (i) Manipulation may be present in both parties of the relationship: for example, a child may use the social worker or the

existence of a court order as a weapon against his parents;
an adult may comply with the letter but not the spirit of an
agreement; a social worker may strike inappropriate bar-
gains with a client – 'I'll help you with this is if you co-operate with me on that.'

How should one address these kinds of games?

(ii) Virtually all service-users feel ambivalent about receiving
help. Sometimes this ambivalence is expressed by dividing
the helpers/carers into wholly good and wholly bad.

How can this be resolved?

(iii) What skills does a social worker need in order to maintain
a balance between her assessment responsibilities (in, say,
a case of non-accidental injury) and her sympathies for victim or offender?

(iv) In cases of child sex abuse, is guidance possible on how far
to pursue investigations and at what point to stop?

The welfare of the child requires *both* a realistic understanding of his/her experiences and feelings about them *and yet*
avoidance of prurient and exhaustive investigation of all
details. Should the pursuit of a conviction against the
abuser always be maintained, or should prosecution be
sometimes abandoned because of the feelings and needs of
the victim? Where does one draw the line? And in what circumstances should confidentiality be breached?

(2) The issues raised in 1(iv) above prompt wider questions about the
powers and limitations of social work practice:

(i) Differences between the intrinsic power of the social worker
and the power of the client have appeared in several cases.
An example has been given of subtle ways in which professional power may be demonstrated by the worker or 'received' by the client. The exercise of certain sorts of power
in certain kinds of situation may be valid or invalid – and
it is useful to consider *both* the situations *and* the nature of
the criterion of validity…

(ii) …but one needs also to ask a more general question about
the legal, administrative and professional boundaries and
limitations of social work practice. It became clear in one
case study that the prior assumptions made by members
of particular professions affect their perceptions of facts

and their assessments of appropriate responses. This increases the difficulties of inter-professional and inter-agency collaboration. Should social workers be clearer about the scope and prior assumptions of their profession?

(iii)Some case studies have illustrated the issues involved in social work practice which crosses cultural differences and differences of language, and value has been given to working in ethnically mixed and culturally sensitive teams. It is necessary to recognise that some words and concepts do not readily translate between languages, and that some ideas are virtually unthinkable and unacceptable when translated. The importance and nature of family structures, the nature of marriage and the roles of women, the appropriate responses to mental ill health, the ways in which decisions are reached within the family, the content of child care and the roles of children, the acceptability of group work: all of these are specific to specific cultures, and thought needs to be given to how best to construct social work teams to reflect these issues and to work sensitively within them.

Social work with children and parents is complex and challenging and I wish to acknowledge my appreciation of the workers who have permitted their activities to be presented in this book and who have accepted the scrutiny of their readers.

Contributors of Case Studies and Projects

Jo Adams	Social Worker, London Borough of Hackney
Barbara Bittle	Children and Families Team Manager, London Borough of Waltham Forest
Isobel Bremner	Social Worker, London Borough of Wandsworth
Gillian Bridge	Lecturer in Social Work, London School of Economics
Sue Brookman	Service Unit Manager, London Borough of Lewisham
Dorthe Bucknell	Manager of a Family Centre in Dover, Kent County Council
Linda Charlton	Social Worker, London Borough of Tower Hamlets
Gillian Coates	Social Worker, NCH Action for Children
Susan Cooke	Staff Development Officer, Buckinghamshire Social Services Department
Viv Davies	Social Worker, London Borough of Wandsworth
Sarah Donlan	Commissioner for Children's Services, Kent County Council
Tess Duncan	Guardian ad litem, Reporting Officer and Panel Manager, Surrey Social Services Department
Barbara Hammerton	Senior Adoption Officer, Kent County Council
Eve Hopkirk	Senior Social Worker, West Sussex Social Services Department
Ravi Kohli	Lecturer in Social Work, Middlesex University
Kathryn Lambourn	Social Worker, Kent County Council
Robert McCandless	Manager, Services for Young People, London Borough of Wandsworth
Trudi McCullough	Team Manager, West Sussex Social Services Department
Judy Marsham	Housing and Social Services, London Borough of Sutton
Gabriel Parlour	Administrator, Quaker International Centre; formerly Specialist Social Worker, Kent County Council
Dianne Powell	Senior Social Worker, Gloucestershire Social Services Department
Jean Ross	Senior Social Work Practitioner, Kent County Council
Patricia Ross	Project Leader, Broxtowe Family Centre, NCH Action for Children
Anita Singh	Social Worker, London Borough of Newham
Bob Temple	Senior Social Work Practitioner, NCH Action for Children
Rita Wiseman	Assistant Regional Director, NCH Action for Children

References

ABAFA (1977) *Soul Kids Campaign Report*. London: BAAF.

Adcock, M. and White, R. (1985) *Good Enough Parenting*. London: BAAF.

Aldgate, J. and Simmonds, J. (1988) *Direct Work with Children*. London: Batsford/BAAF.

Anderson, P. (1982) Black cultural identity.

Anthony and Bhana (1988) In *Journal of Death and Dying*. USA, pp 215–227.

Axline, V. (1947) *Play Therapy*. USA: Riverside Press.

Ayalon, O. (1987) *Rescue*. USA: Nord Publications.

Bainham, A. (1990) Children – the New Law. *Family Law*, (UK).

Batty, D. (ed) (1989) *Working with Children (Practice Series 13)*. London: BAAF.

Bentovim, A. (1991) Significant Harm in Context. In M. Adcock, *et al. Significant Harm.* London: Significant Publications.

Black, D. (1984) Sundered families: the effect of the loss of a parent. UK, *Adoption and Fostering 8.2*, pp 38–43.

Boston, M. (1983) Technical problems in therapy. In M. Boston and R. Szur. *Psychotherapy with Severely Deprived Children*. London: RKP.

Bowlby, J. (1980) *Attachment and Loss 3*. London: Hogarth Press.

Bray, M. (1991) *Poppies on the Rubbish Heap – the Child's Voice. London: Canongate Press.*

Campbell, B. (1988) *Unofficial Secrets – Child Sexual Abuse*. London: Virago Press.

Channer, Y. and Parton, N. (1990) *Taking Child Abuse Seriously*. London: Unwin Hyman (Chapter on Racism, Cultural Relativism and Child Protection).

Coleman, J.C. and Hendry, L. (1980) *The Nature of Adolescence. London: Methuen.*

Cook, S. and Taylor, J. (1990) *Working with Sex Offenders*. London: Barnardos.

Cross, W.E. (1971) The Negro to Black Conversion Experience. In *Black World 2*, London, July.

Curnock, K. and Bayley, B. (1988) *The Welfare of Families in the Process of Divorce*. Leeds: RSD Probation.

Currer, C. (1984) Pathan Women in Bradford. *Transcultural Psychiatry 30*, 1–2.

Dale, P., Murray, D., Morrison, T. and Waters, J. (1986) *Dangerous Families* London: Tavistock Publications.

Dorfman, E. (1951) Chapter 6 In C.R. Rogers. *Client Centred Therapy*. London: Constable.

Fahlberg, V. (1981) *Attachment and Separation*. Practice Series 5 & 6. London: BAAF.

Fahlberg, V. (1988) *Fitting the Pieces Together*. London: BAAF.

Fahlberg, V. (1991) *A Child's Journey Through Placement*. USA: Perspective Press.

Firth, S. (1988) Hindu and Sikh approaches to death and bereavement. In A. Berger (ed) *Perspectives on Death and Dying*.

Fryer, P. (1984) *Staying Power: The History of Black People in Britain*. London: Pluto Press.

Gillet, S. and Morris, T. (1987) *Care and Discretion*. UK: Burnett Books.

Godek, S. (1990) Leaving Care. *Social Work Paper 2*, London: Barnardos.

Goldner, V. *et al.* (1990) Love and Violence. *Family Process 29*, pp 343–364.

Hazareesingh, S. (1979) Racism and cultural identity: an Indian perspective.

Hoggett, B. (1981) *Parents and Children*. London: Sweet and Maxwell.

Horne, (1986) When the social worker is a bridge. In (ed) P. Sawbridge. *Parents for Children*. London: BAAF.

Hoxter, S.(1983) Some feelings aroused in working with severely deprived children. In M. Boston, R. Szur, and B. Truckle *Psychotherapy with severely deprived children*. London: RKP.

Huby, G. and Salkind, A. (1990): In *Journal of Social Work Practice*. May, UK.

Jewett, C. (1984) *Helping Children Cope with Separation and Loss*. London: Batsford.

Kellmer Pringle, M. (1980) *The Needs of Children*. London: Hutchinson.

King, M. and Trowell, J. (1992) *Children's Welfare and the Law – the Limits of Legal Intervention*. UK: Sage Publications.

Kramer, E. (1978) *Art as Therapy with Children*. New York: Schocken.

Kroger, J. (1989) *Identity in Adolescence*. London: RKP.

Lawson, V. (1990) Culturally sensitive support for grieving parents. In *MC N (USA)*. March-April, pp 76–79.

Littlewood, R. and Lipsedge, M. (1989) *Aliens and Alienists*. London: Unwin Hyman.

Liverpool, V. (1989) Race Issues. In P. Sills (ed) *Child Abuse: Challenges For Policy and Practice*. London: Community Care.

Marsh, P. and Fisher, M. (1992) *Good Intentions: Developing Partnerships in Social Services*. York: Rowntree Foundation and Community Care.

Maximé, J.E. (1986) Some psychological models of the black self concept. In B. Ahmed, J. Cheetham, and J. Small. (eds) *Social Work with Black Children and Their Families*. Oxford: Blackwell.

Miller, A. (1987) The Drama of Being a Child. London: Virago.

Minuchin, S. (1974) *Families and Family Therapy*. London: Tavistock Publications.

Oaklander, V. (1979) *Windows to Our Children*. USA: Real People Press (2nd edition).

Parkinson, L. (1987) *Separation, Divorce and Families*. London: Macmillan (in association with BASW).

Parton, N. (1990) *The Politics of Child Abuse*. London: Macmillan.

Rack, P. (1982) *Race Culture and Mental Disorder*. London: Tavistock.

Ryan, T. and Walker, R. (1985) *Making Life Story Books*. London: BAAF.

Scott, P. D. (1973) Parents who kill their children. *Medicine Science and the Law* (UK) 13.2 pp 120–126.

Skellington, R. and Morris, P. (1992) *Race in Britain Today*. London: Sage Publications.

Sone, K. (1992) Unearthing Hidden Illness. *Community Care*, 27–2–92.

Stainton Rogers, W. (1989) *Child Abuse and Neglect*. London: Batsford (Chapter on Childrearing in a Multicultural Society).

Stein, M. and Carey, M. (1986) *Leaving Care*. Oxford: Blackwell; and (1989) *Leaving Care and the Children Act*. London: First Key Publications.

Triseliotis, J. (1988) (ed) *Group Work in Adoption and Fostering*. London: Batsford.

Truckle, B. (1983) Fieldwork: first visit to a foster family. In M. Boston, R. Szur and B. Truckle *Psychotherapy with severely deprived children*. London: RKP.

Wallerstein, J. and Kelly, J. (1980) *Surviving the Breakup*. London: Grant McIntyre.

Wikan, U. (1988) In *Social Science and Medicine*. UK. pp 451–460.

Winnicott, C. (1984) Face to face with children. In BAAF. *In Touch with Children*. London: BAAF.

Winnicott, D. W. (1978) *The Piggle*. London: Hogarth Press (in association with the Institute of Psycho-Analysis).

Wolf, S., Conte, J.R. and Engel-Meinig, M. (1989) Assessment and treatmemt of sex offenders in a community setting. In L. Walker. *A Handbook on Sexual Abuse of Children*.

Wolfendale, S. (1987) *All About Me*. London: National Children's Bureau.

Various papers related to Chapter Two are available from The Standing Committee on the Sexual Abuse of Children, NCH Action for Children, and Barnardo's.

Subject Index

Author Index